THE SECOND WORLD WAR AND IRISH WOMEN
AN ORAL HISTORY

This book is dedicated to Alan, for being who he is; to Fred Kelly, my father, wishing he was still alive to see where those Sunday afternoon conversations have led me; and to the wonderful women who shared their memories with me.

THE SECOND WORLD WAR AND IRISH WOMEN
An Oral History

MARY MULDOWNEY

Foreword by
DIARMAID FERRITER

IRISH ACADEMIC PRESS
DUBLIN • PORTLAND, OR

First published in 2007 by
IRISH ACADEMIC PRESS
44, Northumberland Road, Dublin 4, Ireland

and in the United States of America by
IRISH ACADEMIC PRESS
c/o ISBS, Suite 300, 920 NE 58th Avenue
Portland, Oregon 97213-3786

© 2007 Mary Muldowney

www.iap.ie

British Library Cataloguing in Publication Data
An entry can be found on request

ISBN 978 0 7165 2886 9 (cloth)
ISBN 978 0 7165 2887 6 (paper)

Library of Congress Cataloging-in-Publication Data
An entry can be found on request

All rights reserved. Without limiting the rights under copyright reserved alone, no part of this publication may be reproduced, stored in or introduced into a retrieval system, or transmitted, in any form or by any means (electronic, mechanical, photocopying, recording or otherwise), without the prior written permission of both the copyright owner and the above publisher of this book.

Typeset by Carrigboy Typesetting Services
Printed by Antony Rowe Ltd., Chippenham, Wiltshire

Contents

Foreword vi
Acknowledgements viii
List of illustrations ix
Introduction 1
1. Women's role – in Ireland and the West 7
2. States at war 20
3. Women at work 44
4. War work in Britain 70
5. Joining up 97
6. The home front 119
7. Health in wartime 146
8. Conclusion – Plus ça change, plus c'est la même chose? 167
Notes 176
Appendices 204
Select Bibliography 224
Index 232

Foreword

There comes a stage when it is simply too late to capture the stories, talk to the participants, record the memories and recreate the experiences. We owe a debt of gratitude to Mary Muldowney that this is not the case in relation to Irish women and the Second World War. This is an important book, not just because it is the first to be published on the impact of the war on Irish women, but because it places the participants centre stage. Official documents and accounts can tell us what happened, but the use of oral history – so expertly integrated into this book – can help us to understand what it felt like.

The result is an account of women during this period that is honest, multi-faceted and deeply absorbing, because of the combination of the women's voices and an exhaustively researched wider context that sheds light on many themes, including health, class, motherhood and the status of women in the workplace. It amounts to a wonderful social history of this period, with all the hardships and little triumphs that went with it.

This book challenges the idea that women during the war were just watching, waiting and weeping while the men fought. They intervened to help the most vulnerable; they often controlled the household income and some were given new employment opportunities. Many, like Olive, one of the women interviewed, chose to go to another country themselves, 'to sally off to the unknown over there'. They were difficult times, but people talked and connected and there was occasional defiance. Sectarian and class differences could often be forgotten because they were smaller differences than the enormity of the war effort that united them.

Ethel, another one of the women interviewed, recalls being proud of her service in a British uniform, and says of a later reunion with her former colleagues: 'I wasn't anybody's wife or anybody's daughter or sister, I was me and it was really marvellous. It's nice to be yourself once in a while'

Individual instances of liberation in the lives of women are set against a background of appalling housing conditions, a struggle with the cost of living, the adoption of strategies in the kitchen to make food last, infant and maternal mortality and a list of illnesses and infectious diseases that makes for sobering reading. Some women were giving birth to over 20 children, to be reared in tenements, while a belief persisted that bothering with birth control could make you neurotic. Women did what they could to help in the delicate areas of sexually transmitted diseases. Another interviewee, Susan, who worked in the Rotunda hospital, summed up her position: 'it's not my job to condemn. I'm here to help'.

Overall, this is not the story of a feminist revolution; there was a heavier workload for women during the war, and they continued in their domestic roles while called upon to make a public contribution to the war effort. But despite the absence of economic and legislative change, the war did make a difference, often in a positive way, in terms of improved opportunity for personal development, friendship, travel, the satisfaction of securing a job, and a sense of self-worth linked to the capacity to earn.

There is also an acknowledgement that one of the strongest elements of the wartime experience was a pride in survival and 'making do', and that most women still saw their domestic responsibilities as of paramount importance. Irish homes were full of strong mothers who shouldered responsibility for their families' welfare during the most difficult of times. Many of their daughters grasped whatever opportunities the war brought their way, helping to erode some of the social barriers that then existed.

By recording their perspectives, and integrating the stories of women in Ireland, north and south, Mary Muldowney has made a valuable contribution not just to women's history, but also to social and cultural history, and she has done it with empathy, skill and insightfulness.

Diarmaid Ferriter
IRCHSS Research Fellow
March 2007

Acknowledgements

So many people have helped me over the years, from the commencement of a PhD research project to the production of this book, that my thank you list threatens to turn into an Oscar awards marathon. My debt to the women who shared their stories and their time with me is incalculable, and I hope I have at least done justice to their strength, good humour and zest for life in my analysis of their interviews. I am grateful also to the various people who acted as go-betweens and gave me introductions to a number of women, even though not all of them decided to take part in the project. This book has been a long time in gestation, not least because my life and time, like those of the women who gave interviews, had many conflicting demands that had to be reconciled.

Professor David Fitzpatrick, as supervisor of my PhD dissertation, provided extensive knowledge and advice, and I learned much from Professor Eunan O'Halpin and Professor Mary Daly. Sandra McAvoy from the Women's Centre in UCC generously shared information about Moya Woodside, as did Paula Thompson from Sussex University. The staff members in Trinity College Library were always courteous and helpful, as were their fellow librarians and archivists in the National Library and the National Archives in Dublin; the Public Records Office of Northern Ireland in Belfast; the Irish Labour History Museum and the Guinness Archives in St James's Gate in Dublin; and the Contemporary Medical Archives Centre in the Wellcome Library in London. The staff members of the Mass-Observation archive in the University of Sussex were friendly and helpful.

Sheila and Paddy Condron and Michelle Thomas gave practical help and much-valued friendship. Special thanks to Paddy for introducing me to the wonders of Photoshop. Working in Room 3077 introduced me to three great history women: Cliona, Catriona and Eve. My mother and my two sisters have my admiration for their considerable abilities and my thanks for their support. Siân encouraged me and made me proud to be the mother of 'the one and only', while Oisin kept the faith and made me wish long-distance travel could be instantaneous. Alan patiently proofread, gave editorial advice and asked crucial questions. Most importantly, he makes me happy.

List of illustrations

1. Gala lipstick — 3
2. *Everywoman* cover, March 1943 — 8
3. Icilma vanishing cream — 17
4. North Strand after the bombing on 31 May 1941 — 21
5. Motorists' rush for petrol — 31
6. Carlow bombing deaths — 41
7. Announcement to women, 1941 — 45
8. *Everywoman* cover, April 1942 — 51
9. Advertisement for electrical gifts, Christmas 1940 — 59
10. *Jaeger Knitting Patterns* cover — 69
11. Frances in her nurse's uniform, Boston Hospital, Lincolnshire, 1945 — 71
12. Letter — 88
13. Tedworth House — 99
14. Memorandum from the Secretary of State for War, 1941 — 106
15. Clare on her confirmation day in 1939 — 120
16. Notice to ESB consumers — 127
17. Kathleen, Mary and Sheila in the garden of their Marino home — 142
18. Advertisements for tonics were a common feature of newspaper and magazine advertising during the war years. There were frequent references to women's 'nerves'. — 147
19. Advertisement for 'Sunlight' soap — 154
20. WAAF baby care classes — 170

Introduction

Like so many children, I was a fantasist when I was young. I pictured myself in a variety of heroic roles and I spent many daydreaming hours thinking about how I would save my family and friends from the perilous situations in which my fertile imagination had placed them. The majority of the scenarios reflected my avid reading of the Biggles books[1] and my brother's *Victor* comics.[2] The Biggles character was solidly upper-middle-class English while *The Victor* was notable for its attachment to working class heroes like Alf Tupper (the fish-and-chip-eating athlete) but these, and similar reading matter, shared a perception of the Second World War as a struggle against the forces of evil, in which men rose to heights of bravery and sacrifice to protect the good (the Allied forces). What they also shared was an almost complete absence of females and my youthful enthusiasm was tempered only by my frustration about the very tiny supporting roles that girls were permitted to play in these valiant battles against the Germans and the Japanese.[3] It was not until I studied history for the Leaving Certificate and later at undergraduate level that I began to understand that there were more multifarious forces involved.

As I grew up, I learned that gender is an inescapable element of every person's life, regardless of whether one is male or female and regardless, too, of economic or social position. Nevertheless, it does not necessarily define who we are and there are a range of influences, from class to sexual orientation to the kind of society we live in, that shapes how our gender impacts on the way we live. In this book, the word 'class' will refer to social class in terms of the social hierarchies that relate to people's access to the wealth of their society.[4] This is not to suggest that class is defined only by economic conditions and what people earn. Class consciousness is rooted in the real life experiences of flesh and blood people.[5] The term 'working class' is open to much discussion[6] but for the purposes of this book it will be used simply to include wage earners and their families and dependants. The 'middle class' will refer to salary earners, managers and professionals – the middle layer between the workers and the owners.

When I began to read the 'serious' history of the twentieth century I discovered that even though my childhood heroes had faded away, the presence of women in the events of the Second World War (and throughout the rest of history, of course) had been well and truly established. Thanks to a huge body of research (particularly from the 1970s onwards) women were no longer missing from the historical record.[7] There were lots of fascinating books about the role that women played in the war on the home front and in combat zones, but there was still an absence that was of concern to me. Where were the Irish women? Did the Second World War have the same kind of effect on Irish women's lives as it did on women in Britain, Europe and the United States? How did it impact on their domestic responsibilities and their paid employment? Were Irish women, in both Northern Ireland and Éire,[8] subject to institutional discrimination regarding employment, social welfare and equality of opportunity as were women in other Western countries in the years before the Second World War? To what extent was the war's impact on them differentiated by the fact that Northern Ireland was actively at war, while Éire remained neutral?

Research into various aspects of the lives of Irish women has been a growing area of scholarship in recent years and is producing a body of work that compares very favourably with similar research in other countries. However, no specific work has been published on the impact of the Second World War on Irish women.[9] Although Richard Doherty has written extensively about Irish involvement in the Allied forces during the war, using diaries, letters, memoirs and interviews as the basis of his analysis, there is only one chapter devoted to women in *Irish Men and Women in the Second World War*, despite the title.[10] Eerily echoing the masculine ethos of my childhood reading, the ambitiously titled *The Irish Experience during the Second World War*[11] includes only two women in the seventeen oral history interviews on which it is based. While the interviews are interesting, the main focus of the analysis is on the author's perception of the benefits to Éire of the policy of neutrality. A more useful source is Diarmaid Ferriter's survey of the history of Ireland in the twentieth century,[12] which sets out to reintegrate into Ireland's story many previously excluded and ignored sections of Irish society (including women). It is especially valuable for the attention it pays to women as a distinct element of Irish society, where other general surveys have tended to be written as if male and female experiences were synonymous.

Much recent research into the experiences of women in wartime has been based on the practice of oral history, which has opened up new avenues of historical exploration. Women's responses to major events or to social and economic changes may not necessarily be fairly represented by the predominantly masculine interpretations that have shaped the official reports and documentary sources on which most of the writing of history has been focussed. While this is also true of other marginalized groups, it is particularly problematic in the case of women, who comprise at least half the population but whose specific interests and concerns have not received a corresponding level of attention. The evidence of a female-centred approach to the history of the Second World War demonstrates the extent to which the traditional view of men as combatants and women as the symbols of the 'home front' – the protective focus for which the war was being fought – dominated the integration into the war effort of the social policies of the Allied governments. It should be questioned whether such a view of women (which was reflected in the domestic role assigned to Irish women in the inter-war years) was changed in any way by the impact of the Second World War on the two Irish states. By examining the experiences of a small group of women, in terms of the priorities identified by those women in their interviews, it is hoped to answer some general questions about the impact of that world war on the economic and social status of women in Irish society.

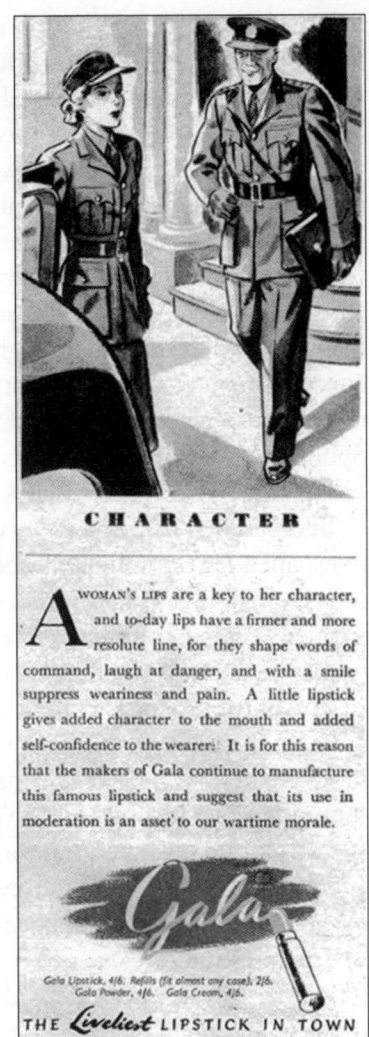

1. Gala lipstick. Many advertisements for quintessentially 'feminine' products connected them to the war effort in the graphic and the text.

One of the most important of these questions encompassed the difference between women who were full-time 'women of the house'[13] and those who were engaged in paid employment, because that difference is tied in so many ways to the economic and social status of women. International research suggested that wartime conditions in belligerent countries were very disruptive of women's domestic lives although this did not interfere with government efforts to recruit women into the public side of the war effort. The wartime situation in Ireland was complicated by the fact that Northern Ireland, as part of the United Kingdom, was a belligerent state whereas Éire remained neutral throughout the war years.

In this book the stories of a number of Irish women[14] who survived the war years will be compared with contemporary observations by government officials and other social commentators. For my purposes the most important of such contemporary commentators was Moya Woodside,[15] a Belfast woman who kept a diary for the Mass-Observation organization[16] in Britain between March 1940 and November 1941. Like the women whose memories will be quoted throughout the book, she had both private and public concerns about the war. Her diary was written from the viewpoint of a woman of the house who was affected by the wartime conditions, but she also had opinions on a range of subjects outside her domestic life that shed some fascinating light on other issues identified in the interviews.

International research clearly shows that there were women who wanted to escape the restrictions placed on their ambitions by the assumption that only marriage and motherhood were suitable destinies for them. While women were encouraged to seek a wider role during the war, it was also within constraints. Oral history interviews have been particularly valuable in illustrating the ambivalence that women felt, particularly if they were concerned that aspiring for a wider range of opportunities might damage their chances for domestic happiness, by making them somehow less feminine. The Second World War offered opportunities to Irish women to secure employment and training that was not available at home. There was encouragement for them to travel to Britain and beyond and many of them took advantage of such chances to broaden their horizons.

The question of class and its connection to social standing and attitudes to gender has not been considered in any detail even in countries where there is a longer history of research into women's involvement in the Second World War. The women whose stories are reproduced here were not asked explicitly if they thought that their class had as strong an impact on their wartime lives as their gender, but the thread of class consciousness ran consistently through their interviews, even if it was sometimes manifested as snobbery. Women's relationship to definitions of social class has been notoriously difficult to classify, even as late as the middle years of the twentieth century. Defining their place in the social hierarchy as dependent on their husbands' or fathers' status may be sociologically problematic, but it is clear from various studies of women's involvement in war work during both world wars that this assumed connection did define social class[17] and women's status was rarely decided by reference to their own employment.

The themes of the chapters in this book were decided by the interests of the women who took part in the interviews. When I started the research, my main interest was in the women's paid employment but it soon became apparent that this would not only be an inadequate measure of their work but that it would also fail to reflect the extent of their interests. For the most part, the women were unwilling to discuss sexuality and issues related to it, such as family planning, at least while the interview was being recorded. There are other questions relevant to the impact of the war that remained unasked because they were outside the experience of the women who were telling their stories.

The testimonies of most of the women who took part in this research subvert the conclusion that the absence of economic and legislative change during those years suggests that the Second World War made no difference to women in Ireland in either jurisdiction. Their stories show that the effect of the war on their individual lives was mainly positive, particularly for those women who grasped the improved opportunities for personal development, employment, friendship and travel that were offered by the wartime situation.

Inequalities of class and gender have been legitimized and institutionalized by the potent influence religion has exercised over society in Ireland. The insistence that women were 'naturally' suited only for domestic life was widely accepted in Britain, Europe and the United States of America in the 1930s. It was reinforced in the southern Irish state by the influence of Catholic social teaching on legislators and the public. This influence was strengthened by the introduction of several measures that had the effect of curtailing the public role of women.[18] The Constitution of 1937 established the family as the fundamental base of Irish society, although no mention was made of the right to payment for a woman's work in the home regardless of the importance that was assigned to it.[19] The classification of women as wives and mothers was potentially dangerous to women's citizenship, particularly as men were not defined as fathers and no mention was made in the Constitution of their role in the context of their families.

Article 41 (1–2) of Bunreacht na hÉireann
1. 1. The State recognises the Family as the natural primary and fundamental unit group of Society, and as a moral institution possessing inalienable and imprescriptible rights, antecedent and superior to all positive law.
    2. The State, therefore, guarantees to protect the Family in its constitution and authority, as the necessary basis of social order and as indispensable to the welfare of the Nation and the State.

2. 1. In particular, the State recognises that by her life within the home, woman gives to the State a support without which the common good cannot be achieved.
2. The State shall, therefore, endeavour to ensure that mothers shall not be obliged by economic necessity to engage in labour to the neglect of their duties in the home.

The doctoral dissertation on which this book is based compared the experience of women who were originally from Belfast and Dublin and who had lived and worked in either or both of those cities during the war years. I have conducted additional interviews since that research was undertaken, some of which are included and some not. When I was identifying women who would be willing to be interviewed my practice was to ask people whom I knew to suggest to likely participants that they might volunteer. If agreement in principle was given, I followed up with an explanation of what I was doing and made arrangements for the interviews, which took place in the women's homes in nearly every case. Some women changed their minds about taking part in the project while others decided not to give me permission to use their interviews after they had read the transcripts and considered that the material was too personal for publication. The women are identified only by first names but all of them are recognizable by their willingness to take advantage of whatever opportunities came their way, including those created by the Second World War.

Remembering the past is crucial for our sense of identity. Self-continuity depends wholly on memory and recalling past experiences links us with our earlier selves, however different we may since have become. The testimonies reproduced in this book provide evidence of the potential of oral history to extend our knowledge of the way our society has been shaped, not just by 'significant' individuals and events but also by the relationship of so-called 'ordinary' people to that society. Since the oral history interview is a social process, what emerges is the result of the interaction between the interests of the interviewer and those of the subject. In the course of the research for this book I have been constantly reminded of the discrepancy between my enquiries into the impact of the Second World War on women's daily lives and the concerns and experiences that shaped the narratives that emerged in the interviews. This divergence proved to be a source of additional value for the women and for me. It opened new perspectives for them at the same time as reminding me that an exercise in patterning human behaviour, no matter how scrupulously conducted it might be, must always be subordinate to the feelings that the tellers have for the details of their own stories.

1

Women's role – in Ireland and the West

The men here leave that sort of thing to the women. For example, they would not be seen wheeling a baby or washing the dishes or anything like that. That is considered a woman's job. In fact, if you saw a man doing things like that, you would consider him a traitor.[1]

Nineteenth-century political economists generally held the notion that men's wages had to be sufficient for the support of a family, in order to allow a woman's 'necessary attendance on the children'.[2] The children were essential to the reproduction of the workforce so this was essentially a pragmatic view of a sexual division of labour. It is one that combined easily in the twentieth century with the Roman Catholic ethos that informed the 1937 Constitution of Ireland[3] and did not challenge the determination to maintain the Union that motivated much of the social policy of the Northern Ireland government.

Social welfare services developed slowly during the first half of the twentieth century, in both parts of Ireland. In the Irish Free State and Éire, innovations included the introduction of unemployment assistance in 1933, a widows' and orphans' pension scheme in 1935 and a universal scheme of children's allowances in 1944. Social thinking in Éire in regard to income support could be summarized by the directive principles of social policy contained in Article 45 of the 1937 Constitution. These principles were entirely in line with papal encyclicals[4] that stressed the independence of the family unit from the State and emphasized the separate gender roles to be played within the home. Education policy was also influenced by Catholic social teaching as girls were prepared for domestic responsibilities and boys for paid employment.

The provision in Article 41(1) of Bunreacht na hÉireann reflected Fianna Fáil policy during the 1930s and 1940s, which was to discourage married women from working outside the home while school attendance and employment legislation limited the possibility of children working.[5] The establishment of children's allowances during the Emergency is

2. *Everywoman* cover, March 1943. In addition to making do and mending, a 'good mother' passed on her skills to her daughter.

therefore not as remarkable as it might seem in a period of economic privation as it did provide a way of supporting poor families who had been particularly hard hit by wartime inflation. It was also a measure that was very popular with Fianna Fáil's target voters – small farmers and the working class.[6] The payment of a children's allowance supplemented rather than superseded the family wage and was thus in accordance with Catholic social thinking. Significantly, the payment was made to the father of the family.

Although social welfare provision in Northern Ireland generally mirrored that in Britain, the social context in which the legislation operated was significantly different. The desire for parity with Britain was part of the general unionist aim of maintaining integration with the mainland but it was administered locally and parity in the sense of equality was not achieved until after the changes recommended by the Beveridge Report in 1942 were implemented.[7] Family allowances were not introduced until 1945 and although they were paid to the mother, they did not commence until there was a second child and they did not include wives' benefits.[8] Allowances paid to the wives of servicemen lasted strictly for the period of service and rates of payment frequently left women in debt. The Stormont government seems to have been particularly concerned about the disproportionate benefit of family allowances on the Catholic minority, because of their higher birth rate.[9]

While the status of women as citizens in both Northern Ireland and Éire was technically equal to that of men, in practical terms they occupied an inferior position because of a legal system that institutionalized inequality in both the public and private spheres of their lives. Women's representative groups in the South did campaign throughout the 1930s and 1940s for equal citizenship.[10] Although there is no evidence of similar groups at work in the North, this is probably because there was no specific legal definition of a woman's place like that in Bunreacht na hÉireann, and campaigning tended to be focused on improving the quality of daily lives rather than on more abstract concepts like equality. Some efforts were made to foment debate about women's role in society but it is not surprising that this tended to be a minority pursuit, given the difficulties caused by the wartime conditions. It should also be noted that the majority of women in both states did not challenge the identification of themselves as homemakers and mothers.

Much of the international research into women's lives in the inter-war years focused on women's role within the family and the changes in that role which derived from the evolution in both individual and social expectations of the family unit.[11] From the first decades of the twentieth century, married women, in particular, spent less time in wage-earning activities because their domestic responsibilities became more time-consuming, with the important exception of the First World War years. Those women who sought paid employment did so to improve the standard of living of their families rather than for personal fulfilment. Opportunities for work were restricted, as many employers claimed that because women were expected to choose marriage and child-bearing as their long-term commitment, they did not merit investment in education or training, and could be consigned to part-time, often low paid and low status jobs.[12] It is difficult to judge if women's own choices were the prime motivator or whether it was their consignment to poor conditions simply because they were not male that made paid employment unattractive. The two processes seem to have been happening simultaneously in the inter-war period but there is little evidence of how women themselves felt about it at the time.[13]

The identification of women with the domestic sphere and the impact that this had on women's employment outside the home had to be reconciled by the governments of the Allied forces with the need to recruit women into the mainstream labour force during the Second World War.

The governments of Britain and other belligerent nations desperately needed women to do war work but were hampered by a reluctance to force women (particularly married women) to leave their 'traditional' place in the home. These competing political priorities inspired some very complex manoeuvring to overcome the potential conflict between the urgent need for female labour and the recognition that after the war it would probably be desirable to persuade women to relinquish their place in the workforce. Given that women had quietly acquiesced in their removal from the jobs they had undertaken in the First World War, however, it is not likely that any great difficulty was expected and, in the event, there were no widespread protests.[14]

The twentieth century was a time of progress for women, commencing with the liberation supposedly brought about by women's involvement in war work during the First World War, and continuing with the extension of the franchise to women in most western countries through to a similar opening up of formerly male-only employment during the Second World War. For some time in the second half of the twentieth century it was believed that the total wars of the first half of the twentieth century were agents of social change, particularly for women.[15] Recent research in a number of countries has challenged this view and shown that such changes as were instituted were temporary and disappeared when the war ended. This does not mean that the absence of permanent legislative and structural shifts in women's economic, political and social position at the end of the war was the whole story. A concrete link has not been established but it is likely that the altered perspective on women's status that came about because of their participation in the war effort contributed to the significant changes that had been brought about by the end of the century.[16]

Increased prosperity in working-class households in the twentieth century was partly due to improved housekeeping techniques made possible by the extra time that women spent at home. Mothers could raise living standards, not by bringing in additional money, but by producing the goods and services that were increasingly considered necessary to the well being of the family. This was reflected in the popularity of domestic education classes in the 1920s and 1930s where the emphasis of the lessons was on the ideal of 'hearth and home' for women.[17] The appeal of the classes was largely due to the manner in which they maximized the social contribution of women who had chosen domesticity as a way of life. Nevertheless, the recognition that women had and would continue to have a place in the industrial workforce (however low paid or low status it might be) was evident in the widespread attention paid to protective legislation for women workers which was an item on the agenda of most international women's congresses in the 1920s and early 1930s.[18] The International Labour Organisation gave gender-specific legislation a prominent place in its programme of demands as early as its inaugural conference in 1920. It provided an influential platform for debating the economic role of women, with members in fifty-five states, including both the victorious and the defeated belligerents of the First World War. The debate about protective legislation that was carried on into the early 1930s was heavily influenced by the assumption that women's domestic role was of primary importance to society.[19]

Many women did not seek self-fulfilment in taking work outside the home because they saw little distinction between their own good and that of their families.[20] This identification of women with their families could act to their detriment in that they had to deal with increased expectations of their domestic role while the male 'breadwinners' may not have been earning enough to allow their wives to give up paid work altogether.[21] The women of the poorest families suffered most from the combination of increased domestic responsibilities with decreased employment opportunities. These women had little control over where and how they worked. They needed to be close to home and were not in a position to bargain for better wages. Married women who had to get paid work generally sought jobs as casual labourers and devised their own short-term employment strategies, often by taking on badly paid factory outwork which they could do in their own homes. A survey of the health and home life of working class wives in Britain, conducted in the 1930s, found overwhelming evidence that the conditions of life of the 1,250 working-class mothers questioned were such as to make it impossible to maintain their pre-marriage standard of health and well-being unless their family incomes were significantly increased.[22] While individual responses to this situation would have varied, it seems that the majority of women believed that their destiny was to get married and they continued to believe that their primary commitment should be to home and family.

Traditionally, young European women in working-class families worked to supplement the family income until they had families of their own. However, there is much evidence that in the early decades of the twentieth century these young women experienced a growing autonomy, being allowed to keep and control a significant portion of their wages. They spent more of their money on clothes and entertainment, in contrast to their mothers, whose earnings, if any, were used for the benefit of the family.[23] When these young women married, they usually returned to financial dependence [on their husbands] but also assumed authority in their role as household managers. Young couples often settled near their families and became active participants in family networks, particularly in the relationship between mothers and daughters. Extended family relationships assumed greater importance when children were born, regardless of whether the young mother was working outside the home or not.[24]

The belief that childbirth should take place within marriage remained strong during the first half of the twentieth century. If a woman wished to remain childless, or even wanted to limit the number of births she wanted to experience, her decision making could conflict with the public perception of a woman's supposedly maternal nature.[25] The social stigma associated with pregnancy outside marriage was evident in the British Poor Law system of relief in the nineteenth century (which also included Ireland). Social welfare payments for dependents and the allocation of public housing reflecting the preference for 'respectable' families had been well established by the second and third decades of the twentieth century.[26] Although women had a great deal to gain by using birth control, the means to do so were not readily available, despite the fact that in the inter-war years the risks of maternal mortality rose with every birth, even with the increased preference for the assistance of medical professionals such as midwives, rather than local 'handywomen'.[27]

Traditional areas of women's employment contracted during this period. There was a lower demand for domestic servants, partly because of the higher wages expected for this work after the First World War and partly because the changing nature of housework no longer necessitated the full-time, live-in service which had previously given employment to so many women. The middle-class ideal of the two-parent family with gender-specific roles was also reflected in official policies, and women certainly subscribed widely to their confinement in the private realm of the home. This did not mean that they saw themselves as playing a subservient role. Women could earn respect in their role as household managers and arbiters of family and neighbourhood standards, from which they were excluded in the public world of work.[28] Government intervention in terms of subsidizing families was minimal, aiming only to help the very poor to survive (such as widows and orphans who could not subsist as a man's dependants), so a woman who made the most of the family income was valued for her management skills.

The emphasis on women's domestic role suggested that women's paid work was problematic, a subversion of their 'natural' function. Not the least difficulty with this viewpoint is that it assumed that all women were married, with family responsibilities, and that their paid employment would be temporary. It ignored the existence of single or widowed women who had no male earner to depend on or of women who chose to take paid employment outside the home for their personal fulfilment. Home and workplace were seen as separate spheres, and the best means of keeping women in their appropriate categories was to ensure that the workplace was less attractive to them than the home. This could be achieved in several ways, not least by maintaining gender-specific wage rates that discriminated against women workers, and by the insistence in social policy on the pre-eminence of the family unit over the rights of the individual woman.

Most of the recent documentary and oral histories of women's experiences during the two world wars of the twentieth century contradict the widely propagated association of women with peace, as the non-combatant focus of the warrior male's protective impetus. It is obvious that in the conduct of wars by the western Allied governments,[29] while this image was useful as a propaganda weapon, the same governments worked hard to achieve a balance between maintaining the image and at the same time enlisting the 'weaker sex' in both the armed forces and in war work. As Penny Summerfield described it, recruitment of women 'upset the wartime gender contract, in which women watched, waited and wept while men fought'.[30] The distinction between combatant and non-combatant roles became fluid, because the position of the front line was not fixed due to air attacks and the threat of invasion. Nevertheless, women who aspired to don uniform, as the outer symbol of their more active role, met resistance in many forms, not least from public figures who argued against provision of military clothing for women in the auxiliary forces because it would be perceived to undermine their 'femininity'.

Many families objected to their daughters joining the services because they feared that the women would be labelled 'immoral' and some women in the services were discriminated against because their commanders shared this fear.[31] However, it was the determination of governments to maintain the *status quo* in relation to gender roles that had the greatest influence on policy concerning the standing of women who joined the armed forces. Despite this, the war created opportunities for women to travel and experience the sharper side of life that would have been unthinkable in peacetime, given the strength of social conventions. For the majority of women, however, the changes in the employment of women represented continuity with pre-war trends. In Britain, for example, neither the Women's Consultative Committee nor the Ministry of Labour to which they were advisers seemed very concerned that women would abandon their families for war work. They assumed that everyone shared their basic respect for the conventional role of women in the home. This coloured their attitude to the provision of childcare, one of the most essential services necessary to ensure full participation of women in the workforce.[32]

The belief that war can be liberating for women appeared during the First World War and similar claims were made quite early in the second. It was used as an incentive in national recruitment campaigns to encourage women to join the armed forces or to volunteer for civilian war work. It was also an argument used by feminists anxious to see women's potential as war workers being properly utilized and, even more importantly to them, being properly credited.[33] However, another viewpoint is that while women were enabled to escape from gender-defined roles, they were also forced back into the home as soon as the war ended and their contribution was no longer required by the state. Dorothy Sheridan points to the fact that the debate has tended to ignore the extent to which women themselves made deliberate and informed choices about how they contributed to the war effort and that their experiences were far from homogenous. The women who joined the armed forces, in particular, knew that they were very different to the helpless figures in need of defence by male soldiers that were the basis of many propaganda images. For the governments that were trying to exploit women's capabilities, there was always a tension between that need and the deeply held beliefs that a woman's destiny was to be a wife and mother.

Sonya Rose's recent work on national identity and citizenship[34] suggests that the symbolic equation of home and family with stability and order suggests why there was so much attention paid to the roles of women during the war. Women on the 'home front' were identified as the 'second line' of defence and it was argued that women's obligation to their families was also an obligation to the nation.[35] The national community was portrayed as a family, with a gendered structure of authority and a sexual division of labour. In the later years of the war, prescriptive articles in women's magazines and the national press urged women to think about preparing themselves for the return of their husbands. Not the least of this preparation would lie in curbing their new-found sense of independence in order to reassure husbands that they were still the authority figures in the family, regardless of how well their wives had coped with their absence.

Part-time and shift working was introduced on a wide scale in Britain and the United States in order to mobilize women while not interfering with their continued domestic responsibilities. The fact that part-time work was offered to women alone reinforced the stereotypical view of women as casual workers who merely supplemented the family income. Part-time and shift work had the additional advantage for employers that it reduced their wage bills while increasing productivity. Appeals were made to the patriotic sense of women in the belligerent nations in enlisting them for war work while the war effort in these countries was also assisted significantly by the willingness of women to cooperate with government policies on rationing and price and wage controls which often made their lives more difficult.

Women workers frequently faced resistance from their male co-workers, who were concerned that the influx of women to war industries represented a dilution of their skills,[36] particularly in engineering works and other areas from which women had traditionally been excluded.[37] Women were perceived as a 'cheap' replacement for skilled male labour so that the potentially transformative effect of a broader range of employment opportunities was diminished by the fact that women workers did not receive equal pay to the men they were replacing and by the constant emphasis on the temporary nature of their involvement in the workforce. Concerns about the wartime assault on gender roles were shared by some women, who recounted how they had used the war as an opportunity to assert their 'conventional femininity' by stressing their maintenance of the 'home front' as their contribution to the war effort.[38]

Despite women's proven ability to work as hard as men, to organize themselves and their families in difficult and dangerous conditions and generally to cope with the hardships of war at least as well as men, the enduring image of women's role during the Second World War was as the inspiration for warriors, the keepers of the 'flame of humanity'.[39] In Britain, both Mass-Observation and the Wartime Social Survey collected evidence showing that large groups of women wanted to go on with their wartime jobs and that many other women resented the fact that their decisions were dependent on the conditions of work in the post-war world. Regardless of these views, however, both surveys reported that an overwhelming majority of women saw marriage and family as their post-war destination. The belief that marriage, home and dependency were the appropriate conditions for women survived the challenge of the war, but it was also a major determinant of wartime policy towards women.[40]

Surveys of popular opinion in countries other than Britain also showed negative images of women war workers, whose patriotism was held up to question because of the perceived gains that individual women could make from the collective struggle. In the United States, women benefited from the economic boom created by the war, following the widespread unemployment and particular discrimination against women that had been a feature of the Depression in the 1930s. This was particularly intense in white-collar jobs where women had traditionally found employment, such as primary school teaching and clerical work in banks and insurance companies.[41] In 1937, a survey conducted by the Department of Labour found that women generally worked in occupations and industries that were predominantly female and they earned substantially lower wages than men. In 1940, of the 27 per cent of all women over 14 who were in the labour force, about one-fifth were unemployed.[42] During the war, the female labour force grew by almost half, to a total of twenty million women.[43] While the percentage of women in the total labour force was proportionately less than that in Britain, in the war years both countries saw an increase in the numbers of women employed outside the home. In the United States, the wartime recruitment of women, which occurred between March 1940 and July 1944, was over six million, nearly 31 per cent of the total female workforce aged between 14 and 65. This compared to an additional two and a half million women recruited in Britain between June 1939 and June 1944, just under 32 per cent of the total female workforce of the same ages, of whom one and three quarter million were employed in industry, agriculture, commerce and the public service.[44]

During the war, the context for public discussion of women's work was the assumption that major social change must be limited. It was emphasized that women would only be replacing male workers for the duration of the war and that they would do so in addition to their domestic responsibilities. They would continue to care for their families but new methods of doing so might be necessary because of the extraordinary circumstances. Women were therefore not abandoning their femininity but were in fact operating within traditional boundaries. Wartime recruitment posters underlined this by showing glamorous women at work in factories, impeccably groomed with cheerful smiles on their faces.

In both Britain and the United States, the typical working week for women was forty-eight hours, with one day off. Petrol rationing meant that public transport was crowded as private cars became impossible to service and this meant that more time was spent getting to and from work. Scarcities of food and other commodities meant that shopping was more difficult and almost impossible for women who could not get to stores until late in the evenings, when they were either closed or had sold out of produce. The sexual division of household labour was not disturbed by the war and the fact that many men were away from home meant that the majority of mothers were left with sole responsibility for childcare. Many women worked because they needed the money,[45] despite the difficulty of combining paid employment with domestic duties. Between April 1940 and March 1944, the number of married women gainfully employed in the United States increased by two million, so that they represented 72 per cent of the total increase of women in the workforce.[46]

In 1942, the US National War Labour Board established that the same pay rates should be paid to women workers when the work they did was the same or substantially the same as work done by men. However, union contracts containing inequitable pay rates were allowed to remain in force and pay scales for jobs traditionally performed by women were not changed. Unequal pay was also allowed in some cases where men's jobs were classified as 'heavy' and women's jobs as 'light'. However, the disparity between the average earnings of men and women workers did narrow during the war years, primarily because of the increased demand for women workers and the wider occupational distribution created by the recruitment of men to the armed forces.[47]

Government propaganda offices working closely with established media outlets fostered the image of women as homemakers and mothers who were prepared to leave their homes because of the national emergency, however reluctantly. In the United States, the Office of War Information worked in tandem with newspaper and magazine editors to weave the specific demands of the labour market into stories and advertising.[48] The connection between civilian labour and soldier welfare could be underscored by portraying romances between hardworking women and admiring men in uniform, while support for the various fundraising and welfare drives was also mobilized by this means. Film stars and other well known figures were also used extensively to promote the war effort. Advertising reinforced the image of women war workers as the tough and resilient guardians of the home front. This meant that women could be enlisted in the war effort by appealing to their commitment to their families as the inducement for their active role in the war effort. War work would be their contribution to the protection of those families

3. *Icilma vanishing cream* The less than subtle message of this advertisement and many others was that a woman could not be fulfilled without a man's love.

without mounting too strong a challenge to the image of women as the object of male military defences.

In Britain, the Ministry of Information had a similar influence on the contents of newspaper columns and magazines that were aimed at women readers, and advertisers combined exhortations to duty with conventional blandishments to buy their products. Typical advertisements assumed that women would be playing an active role in the war effort, whether in the forces or on the home front, and referred to that role in approving terms while linking the women's patriotic impulses to the advertiser's product, as in the following example:

> Yet it is your duty these days to be beautiful because beauty inspires happiness and cheerfulness in yourself and others ... With Icilma you go on the job looking as charming and radiant in uniform as you do in your best party frock.[49]

A similar idea formed the basis for a special supplement to the *Daily Mail*, on 'Woman and Beauty', which was issued in December 1939. The message on the front page of the supplement was unambiguous:

> You're doing a man-size job, BUT men still love femininity ... and above all the world still wants BEAUTY.[50]

In conscripting women for war work, Britain went further than any of the other Allied nations although it has been suggested that the employment of women represented a development of peacetime trends rather than an overturning of social mores and gender relations.[51] Certainly, some of the lighter industries, like the textile mills in northern England, had long relied on women for half or more of their labour force. By mid-1943, however, the proportion of the nation's women aged between 15 and 60 who were in the forces, munitions work, or essential war industries was about double that in 1918 at the corresponding stage of the previous war. Nearly three million married women and widows were employed, as compared with a million and a quarter before the war. It was calculated that, among those aged between 18 and 40, nine single women out of ten were in the forces or in industry while eight married women out of ten were similarly occupied. Many other women were in part-time employment, many of them in improvised offices and workshops that took the work to those who could not leave their own homes for long, because of childcare or other family responsibilities.

In the United States, the government did not intervene in the provision of childcare or day nurseries for the mothers who worked outside the home, mainly because of a reluctance to suggest that the requirement for women workers was anything other than temporary.[52] Although initially equally reluctant, the British government began a programme of expansion in the provision of day nurseries from 1941 onwards and by 1943 there were some 1,450 such nurseries available through local authorities, with places for 65,000 children.[53] In 1942, the Standing Joint Committee of Working Women's Organisations held a conference on wartime nurseries at which a resolution was passed declaring that the care and supervision of children of employed mothers was a national responsibility. They protested against the Ministry of Health circular, circulated to local authorities in December 1941, which recommended that most of the children must be cared for by means of private arrangements made by the mothers, suggesting that the government was trying to evade previous promises that the children of mothers volunteering for war work would be properly looked after.[54]

It would seem that both men and women who were called upon to fulfil a role as responsible citizens in the war effort of the belligerent nations were expected to do so within existing constructions of gender roles and social expectations. Wartime was one of the key periods in which separate gender roles were clearly delineated, and in the Second World War women were still firmly associated with nurturing and supporting the military role of men, but were definitely not expected to cross the gender boundaries by engaging in combat. The recruitment of women into traditionally male areas of work, especially in industries directly connected to combat such as munitions and heavy engineering, was often perceived as transgressing society's boundaries. Although membership of the armed forces, work in industry and work on the land gave many women a relative social freedom and higher earning power compared with the pre-war years, they did not cause fundamental changes in social policy as regards the general position of women in the Allied nations in the immediate post-war years.

2

States at war

Didn't feel so bad about my inward panic when the siren went last week, as I have since heard of people who (a) fainted (b) had hysterics (lots of these) (c) spent the entire night and not merely the duration of the 'alert' under the stairs. Also of a woman who put on a new frock not previously worn and dressing gown over it, and her fur coat over that again. As for the cups of tea made, they must have been in thousands.[1]

One of the most notable aspects of the impact of war on any state is the extent to which the community must be reorganized around the demands of the war effort. This was particularly true for women, whose domestic role tended to be severly disrupted by wartime conditions. That it was also the case for many Irish women, in Éire and Northern Ireland, will be demonstrated in this and subsequent chapters. Just as the impact of war is not confined to combatants, disturbance of the *status quo ante* is not restricted to belligerent states and the government of Éire was forced to impose measures on the civilian population that mirrored the response of the Westminster and Stormont governments. The impact of modern warfare on urban populations is of a different nature than its impact on rural communities, where economic activity is most likely to be based on the continuity of agricultural production, in which the means tend to remain the same, regardless of peace or war. Civil defence in urban areas is much more complex than in rural areas, and the latter are also more likely to have access to local substitutes for rationed food and consumer goods. In the years between the First World War and the second, European theorists of air war and defence became preoccupied by an important change they saw taking place in the way wars would affect civilian populations.[2] The development of aerial bombing, in its infancy in 1918, meant that cities would now be much more vulnerable to attack than had been the case when warfare was largely concentrated on the ground or at sea. In broad terms, this recognition had a particular influence in the 1930s on the planning of major European cities, especially where urban regeneration

4. North Strand after the bombing on 31st May 1941. Courtesy of Dublin City Council.

projects were ongoing. Schools of architecture, particularly where the theories of Le Corbusier[3] were prominent, advocated the development of tall buildings, separated by wide boulevards and public spaces where the damage from bombing raids could be limited. Advances in the technology of war did not just influence the physical design of cities. Aircraft and tanks, submarines and ships and heavy armaments are all dependent for their manufacture on methods of mass production, which are normally accessible only in the most highly industrialized countries. The huge demand for war material required the productive efforts of skilled, urban populations, who became essential elements of the war effort in a way that in previous centuries had been relevant only to the armed forces. The disadvantage of having such skilled populations available for war production is that the cities and urban areas in which they are situated consequently become the objectives of military attack and this blurs the division between civilian and military forces in war.[4]

Another difficulty associated with mass production of war material was concern about storage of ammunition and ordinance so that they would be readily available when required but not allowed to pose additional danger to the population of areas in which they were kept. In Britain, construction work on underground depots commenced almost immediately after the ending of the First World War, driven by the army council's belief that the next war would be won predominantly by airpower.[5] These projects included the building of gigantic underground storage depots as well as aircraft engine factories that were situated countrywide. One benefit of this construction programme was the improvements in employment, housing, roads, railways and water supply in cities and towns where they were situated, while rural electrification was accelerated by at least a generation.[6]

Pre-war discussion of civil defence in Britain was based on the expectation of very heavy casualties (based on the experience of the First World War), which in the event proved to be an over-estimate, but as early as September 1935 the Westminster government issued its first circular on air raid precautions to all the local authorities, including those in Northern Ireland, inviting them to start thinking about the problem and to take responsibility for the protection of the citizens. Two main methods were proposed for local authorities to plan around: the first was evacuation of the civilian population (or at least sections of it, such as children) and the second was the construction of air-raid shelters in densely populated areas. The first was intended to be administered nationally, while the latter would be a local concern. The response was mixed, with some local authorities doing little or nothing about defence, even after compulsion was introduced in 1937.[7] Belfast Corporation was one such local authority, with few steps taken for civil defence, even as late as 1939.[8]

In May 1938 the Westminster parliament set up the 'Committee on Evacuation', with instructions to examine various evacuation schemes and to consider the experience of other countries.[9] The committee identified two main problems: firstly, what to do with the evacuees once they were out of the cities and, secondly, how to encourage people to leave voluntarily. A significant proportion of the responsibility for organizing the evacuation of city people to the countryside was given to the Women's Voluntary Service (WVS), which had been formed in June 1938, primarily for recruiting women for civil defence activities.

In addition to bombing, one of the fears connected to danger from above was the possibility of gas attacks. This resulted from the use of gas in the trenches during the First World War. Many victims of those attacks were still around, with their poor health offering tangible evidence of the destructiveness of poison gas. In August 1938, thirty-eight million gas masks were issued throughout Britain, for men, women and children (although there were none for babies) and barrage balloons appeared in the sky over London.[10] Gas masks were uncomfortable to wear, and beards or elaborate hairstyles could interfere with their effectiveness. In October 1939, the Ministry of Home Security issued the following warning to women:

> The attention of women is drawn to the fact that the temperature conditions inside the face-piece of the mask causes eye-black to run, leading to smarting of the eyes, profuse tears and spasms of the eyelids. This produces an urgent desire to remove the mask, with dangerous results if gas is present.[11]

In France, the government decided on a programme of large-scale evacuation of the civilian population from the major cities and industrial areas, commencing in 1939 with the removal of civilians from areas along each side of the Franco-German border.[12] While this was done in an orderly fashion, when the German army swept into France in the spring of 1940, huge waves of refugees rushed before them, leaving whole communities vacated in some instances, displacing at least seven million people, albeit only briefly.[13] Although the German government initially resisted making plans for evacuation from the cities, when bombing raids began in autumn 1940 it was agreed that children, mothers and mothers-to-be should be evacuated to the countryside. As was the case in Britain, problems with differences between urban and rural dwellers came to the fore when they were forced into proximity.

As part of the United Kingdom, Northern Ireland assumed belligerent status as soon as war was declared on 3 September 1939 and Belfast was especially vulnerable: as the seat of government, as a centre for industrial production and as the base for the production of much needed aircraft and shipping. Although Dublin was the capital city of a neutral state, the government was aware that the threats to urban areas outlined above could also be a possibility for that city, not least because of its position on the eastern seaboard, and many of their responses to wartime conditions reflected the plans and actions of belligerent states.

The formation of a civilian defence force in the United Kingdom was announced in May 1940; initially it was called the Local Defence Volunteers, and later in the year renamed the Home Guard. Training was set up on a freelance basis organized by veteran commanders, but from August 1940 Home Guard units were affiliated to county regiments of the army and given khaki overalls as standard issue. Their main duties were to keep vigil over coastline, airfields and factories. From October 1942, the Home Guard was used as a training ground for boys of 17 and 18, prior to call-up for compulsory military service. In June 1943 (the highest point of recruitment) there were more than 1,700,000 men involved in Home Guard activities but throughout the war it was the only auxiliary organization that refused to recruit women.[14]

The Stormont parliament was empowered to recruit local volunteers for the Home Guard but when the scheme was announced on 28 May 1940 it was significantly different from its implementation elsewhere in the United Kingdom. It was decided that the B Specials[15] would form the nucleus of the new force because Prime Minister James Craig believed that a policy of open enrolment would facilitate republican infiltration. The force was placed under the authority of the Royal Ulster Constabulary Inspector-General and not under military command, as it was in England, Scotland and Wales. Although this arrangement was bound to exclude Catholic volunteers, it was agreed after some discussion with the London government that the status quo should be maintained, since Catholics were unlikely to join a predominantly Protestant force, regardless of who controlled it.[16] Moya Woodside was not convinced by the argument:

> On the subject of L.D.V. (Local Defence Volunteers) in Ulster, my friend, who is a member of the University unit, says there are no Catholics in this particular unit and that Catholics everywhere are 'discouraged' from joining ... Craigavon and Co. however, prefer to play the party game and continue to cold-shoulder Catholics (many of whom are anxious and willing to undertake National Service) while at the same time reproaching them with lack of interest and non-cooperation.[17]

An Air Raid Wardens' Service was created in April 1937, and by the middle of 1938 this had more than 200,000 recruits. Although their chief duty in the first year of the war was to enforce the blackout regulations, by the time bombing raids were becoming regular in late 1940 their duties were extended to assisting the emergency services in dealing with the casualties, overlapping with medical personnel and the members of the WVS. Even when the heavy bombing raids ceased, the civil defence services were maintained at the ready and there were still hundreds of thousands of volunteers in June 1944, with women joining in increasing numbers.[18] All of the United Kingdom's civil defence organizations had branches in Northern Ireland.

In the United States, civil defence was not seen as an important issue, even after the bombing of Pearl Harbour in December 1941, mainly because geographical isolation from the major theatres of war provided a sense of security. There was little likelihood of bombing raids being perpetrated on the urban industrial centres and security concerns tended to be focussed on the 'enemy within' and the danger of sabotage. Following the declaration of war on Japan on 8 December 1941, Japanese nationals living on the west coast of the United States were rounded up and interned in camps in remote areas. They were confined in very bleak conditions until the war ended in 1945.

Civilian defence squads were organized in all the major cities and by mid 1941, even though the United States had not formally declared war at that point, plans had been drawn up for the evacuation of New York, Washington and Boston by the newly created Office of Civilian Defence.[19] With a staff of only one thousand federal employees, the Office of Civilian Defence played its most important role in coordinating activities with existing federal, state and local agencies. It provided millions of gas masks for the protection of urban dwellers that were never used but were manufactured following desperate demands by various city authorities throughout the country.

Another legacy of the development of the technology of war in the First World War was the use of the submarine, which both sides had deployed with great effect to attack shipping convoys, thereby disrupting lines of supply. This tactic was used again during the Second World War and its impact was felt in neutral countries as much as in belligerent states. The British government had learned the lessons of the First World War and merchant shipping was mobilized as part of the total war effort, thereby denying its use to Éire, which was dependent on it for vital imports. The British government reacted to the government's refusal to make the so-called 'Treaty ports' available to the British navy by denying access to British-registered vessels to Irish exporters. In order to maintain his government's position on neutrality, de Valera decided that Éire would have to manage for a time without ready access to sea transport for imported supplies although this situation was remedied in the course of the Emergency.[20] The number of persons on the live register[21] (residing in cities and urban districts) was 7.9 per cent higher in the first six months of 1939 than it had been in the same period in 1938, while the numbers continued to increase steadily in the first six months after the declaration of the Emergency in September 1939. The reduction in employment was attributed to the scarcity of raw materials for industrial production.[22]

The decision to keep Éire neutral in the war was widely supported in the state, not least because many people still saw Britain as the enemy that had needed to be forced from Irish shores. Although the southern state's neutrality was inclined to an unofficial friendliness to the Allied side in the course of the war, making preparations to protect the country from potential invasion by British or German forces involved practical measures to secure the government and the populace that were similar to those adopted by the Northern Irish government.

In the spring of 1939, the likelihood of impending war and the IRA bombing campaign in Britain that had commenced in January of that year gave rise to the enactment of a piece of legislation called the Treason Act 1939, which was passed by the Dáil on 30 May, and which declared treason to be a capital offence. It also provided for the imprisonment of anyone convicted of assisting treasonable acts. The Treason Act was followed shortly afterwards by the Offences against the State Act 1939, which was passed on 14 June. This Act provided for the detection and punishment of any actions or conduct calculated to undermine public order and the authority of the state. On 2 September, Article 28 of the Constitution was amended by the First Amendment of the Constitution Act 1939 to include a state of emergency in the provisions for wartime governance. Having allowed for the concept of an Emergency, which would have a similar impact on the state in many ways as if Éire were not neutral, on 3 September the Oireachtas passed the Emergency Powers Act 1939, to 'make provision for securing the public safety and the preservation of the State in time of war and, in particular, to make provision for the maintenance of public order and for the provision and control of supplies and services essential to the life of the community'.[23] This was the most wide-ranging of the wartime laws, in that it was used as the basis for the control of virtually every aspect of civilian life during the Emergency period, from food rationing to transport regulation to wage rises.

The provisions of the Government of Ireland Act 1920[24] concerning the demarcation between the powers of the Stormont parliament and its counterpart in Westminster were overcome by the establishment of local offices in Northern Ireland where representatives from the relevant ministries carried on business.[25] Since the Westminster government retained control of the armed forces, military training and the defence of the realm in general, the issue of military conscription in Northern Ireland was decided in London. However the Westminster parliament also passed emergency laws that affected Northern Ireland, touching areas that would usually fall within the jurisdiction of the Stormont parliament. When this happened, the Northern Irish parliament passed emergency provisions to legislate for such matters as social services, the control of employment, the war service of local government staff and reparation for war damage to property.[26]

Although pre-war thinking about defence in Northern Ireland had been dominated by the assumption that the area was unlikely to experience hostile air action, nevertheless the legislative groundwork for the protection of the province in the event of air attack was laid on 24 November 1938, with the enactment of the Air-Raid Precautions (Northern Ireland) Act 1938. No further measures were undertaken until the Emergency Powers (Defence) Act 1939 was passed in Westminster on the following 24 August. Its terms were similar to those of the Emergency Powers legislation passed in Éire. Section 1(6) of the Act allowed for the extension of all the emergency powers enabled by it to be applied in Northern Ireland. On 25 August, the Defence (General) Regulations empowered the Home Secretary in Westminster to delegate officers or departments of the Government of Northern Ireland to carry out many war functions.[27] On 7 September, the Stormont parliament passed the Civil Defence Act (Northern Ireland) 1939. It made further provision for civil defence, particularly the designation of premises as public shelters, although the implementation of this measure in Belfast left something to be desired, according to Moya Woodside:

> When in one of the poorest districts of the city this morning I notice that the air-raid shelters have mostly been built at the edge of narrow pavements (in some streets barely 3 ft. wide) thus blocking out light and air from the houses opposite. The effect, in an already narrow street, is oppressive and to judge from the smell, they are being used as a public convenience![28]

The Civil Defence Act also dealt with measures to be taken if it should be deemed necessary to evacuate the civilian population.[29] Although evacuation plans were drawn up early in the war, there were special difficulties in relation to Belfast that complicated efforts to protect the lives of citizens, particularly women and children. Belfast was the only large city in Northern Ireland, with a population comprising roughly one third of the state's total numbers, and the primary area requiring evacuation also housed the densest concentration of that population. Therefore, it would have been necessary to identify additional accommodation for evacuees, when billets were already at a premium for the allied forces arriving in the province. There was the further complication of the necessity to house evacuated children in the homes of co-religionists. Maureen's father made his own arrangements for his family and after the blitz on Belfast she and her mother and siblings moved from the Falls Road to Cushendun:[30]

> At Easter, Easter Tuesday I think it was, or Easter Monday, there was a very bad bombing in Belfast and my dad went out and had a look

round and came back and said, get packed, you are going to the country. But Mum and Dad had already arranged with people we always went on holiday to, in Cushendun, that if necessary we could go to them, so Dad packed us all off to the country ... I did know people who, every night, went off up into the mountains and slept in tents and things and then came back into the city in the morning. But we went to Cushendun and we stayed there for over a year ... We went to school and all there ... Well, my mother came with us and she stayed with us. We had a house there ... the government paid the people who owned the house so that we could stay there.

In the South, the issues of state security and public order were the subject of Emergency Powers (No.5) and (No.6) Orders 1939. The former (passed on 13 September) enabled the government to prohibit the importation of 'extern newspaper' (that is, newspapers published outside Éire) in the interests of public safety. Under Section 6 of Order No.5, the Chief Press Censor was empowered to censor publication of any 'specified matter' and every newspaper proprietor in the state was ordered to send a copy of the newspaper to the Press Censorship Office 'as soon as may be after the publication of each issue'. The press became self-censoring to a great extent, in that they avoided what might upset the Censor and therefore did not have to withdraw their publications.

Article 52 of the Emergency Powers Order 1939 extended the censor's power to reject a film if it was likely to expose the Irish public to the propaganda of any of the belligerent nations, thereby causing a breach of neutrality. Order No.6 (passed on 26 September) empowered the official censor to refuse a viewing certificate to any film 'which would be prejudicial to the maintenance of law and order or to the preservation of the State or would be likely to lead to a breach of the peace or to cause offence to the people of a friendly foreign nation'.[31] The practical impact of this policy is evident in the following diary entry from Moya Woodside:

'The Great Dictator' is showing here at 2 houses this week. I notice great lamentations in the local press about Eire's attitude to cinema managers and railway and bus companies. Neutrality has gone so far as to even forbid papers published in Eire to accept advertisements of the film, together with times of special excursion trains which it was proposed to run (as was done for 'Cavalcade', and the Coronation film). Of course, the Ulster papers circulate freely in Eire, everyone knows about it, and the whole thing becomes a laughing stock.[32]

Specific powers for a postal and telegraph censorship were contained in Part 4 of the Emergency Powers Act 1939, Articles 17 to 27 inclusive. These authorized control over posts, private and public telegrams, telephone communications and other forms of communications, including the use of carrier pigeons. On 12 July, censorship of the mail was extended by Emergency Powers (No.36) Order 1940, which enabled the censor to suppress any document seen as 'prejudicial to the public safety or the preservation of the State or the maintenance of public order'. Although the government had the legal power to impose complete censorship on all communications, they chose not to do this because it would have meant devoting scarce resources to the scrutiny of all mail and maintenance of tight border controls. In practical terms, Éire's censorship measures were more useful in securing information about black marketeering activities, which was given to the Departments of Finance and Supplies, than they were in combating potential espionage.[33]

The government used some of the information revealed by the postal censorship to further the suppression of homegrown dissidents and political activists and groups opposed to the *status quo* in the state. Uinseann MacEoin, who was interned in the Curragh during the Emergency for his membership of the IRA, explained how the publicity department of the IRA produced and distributed a newsletter called *War News*, despite the censorship regime:[34]

> About 20,000 a week were published. I don't know what effect it had on the general public. It was published and distributed widespread. It was a marvel to get it published and distributed and so on because of the dangers of the war and the emergency building up. Much of it was actually posted, amazingly enough, by the general post office. A package posted here and a package posted there, and they all went out pretty safely.[35]

Although the authorities in Britain were concerned about security, particularly in light of the open border with Éire, censorship of civilian mail to Northern Ireland was only implemented from Liverpool in early 1940. In July 1940, the Ministry of Information opened a Belfast office for the permit branch of the censorship division and officers were authorized to work in conjunction with the customs, confiscating unsealed packets, parcels, goods and commodities passing between Northern Ireland and Britain or from Northern Ireland and Éire. The Belfast Censor Office was opened on 1 October 1940, using the legal powers afforded by the Emergency Powers (Defence) Act 1939. Moya Woodside's observations about some possible drawbacks of having a local depot also tell us something about popular assessment of the operation of the food offices:

> Yesterday we learnt that a censorship office to deal with incoming mails is to be set up in Belfast, and a staff of 300 will shortly be recruited under a distinguished military gentleman ... This innovation seems to be very unpopular. It is one thing to have one's correspondence, however innocuous, pass before the eyes of remote and unknown censors in Liverpool and quite another to have it read by individuals living *in the same town*, who may know one either personally or by repute. No doubt employees are sworn to secrecy, but if recruitment for the staff proceeds on the same principles of nepotism which prevail in the local Food Office, one cannot have much confidence.[36]

The British government had the power to compel cooperation with censorship and to suppress dissent, if required. The total control over the information that reached the press ensured that nothing would be published which the authorities did not wish to be published although the power was rarely used. The decision not to censor opinion 'was made from the relative safety of knowing that all news released on which the media could form their opinions had already been censored at source while giving the impression of a voluntary system which provided an effective cover for official propaganda and a clearer conscience for a liberal democracy at war'.[37] Another note about censorship from Moya Woodside's observations, made later in the year, draws attention to the potential for misuse of the emergency powers:

> Notice in the paper this morning banning [under the Special Powers Act] about eight different publications in 1941. Mostly they are papers which would give the extreme Nationalist point of view (so I imagine from the titles) but 2 of them are mildly Communist or simply anti-Ulster Government, which of course in this embryo fascist state is enough to warrant their suppression. With the censorship *and* the Special Powers Act in force, the left-wing groups over here are completely isolated.[38]

The state's security was also maintained by the extension of the Official Secrets Act 1939 to include Northern Ireland.[39] This Act was passed in Westminster in order to amend Section 6 of the Official Secrets Act 1920 by giving powers to police to arrest anyone suspected of an offence under the Official Secrets Acts of 1911 and 1920.[40] Section 7(2) of the Treachery Act 1940, enacted on 23 May, provided for the trial and punishment of anyone convicted of treachery, up to and including death. The possibility of the invasion and occupation of Northern Ireland was recognized in the Defence (War Zone Courts) (Northern Ireland) (Regulations) 1941, passed on 1 July. This law permitted for the trial and punishment of offenders in a military court in Northern Ireland if the 'military situation is such that criminal justice cannot be administered by the courts with sufficient expedition'. In order for these regulations to be operable, the Ministry of Public Security in Westminster had to order the declaration of a war zone.

The first of the Emergency Powers (Control of Prices) Orders was passed in Éire on 7 September 1939, setting the maximum price for a range of goods at the level that was current during the week ended 26 August of that year.[41] Nearly two hundred such orders were issued in the course of the Emergency; some of them setting price controls on scarce goods, while others removed controls as various items became more readily available. Allied to the Control of Prices Orders, such measures as the Emergency Powers (Motor Spirit Rationing) (No.1) (Order) 1939 (which was passed on 13 September) gave the government power to ration petrol by means of coupons and licences that were issued only to authorized dealers.

Until 1941, Éire had no food rationing system and the rising prices meant that poverty and malnutrition were widespread, with children suffering most. A group of women in Dublin[42] decided to mount a petition to the government for the introduction of a system to ensure the fair

5. Motorists' rush for petrol. *Irish Press*, 3 January 1941, p. 7. Courtesy of *Irish Press* archive.

distribution of food and measures to control prices. They also campaigned for better public transport, for school meals and for milk for pregnant and nursing women to be supplied at a special price. In the course of their campaign, they lobbied doctors, TDs and members of Dublin Corporation, although they did not always secure unanimous agreement with their proposals:

> When putting our case to the Schools Committee of the Corporation one reverend gentleman said that we would be breaking up the sanctity of the home if children were fed at school.[43]

Following intense lobbying by such groups as the Irish Women Workers' Union, the Irish Housewives Association and various senior clerical and political figures, the Department of Supplies was set up in mid-1941 and, immediately, sugar, tea and fuel were rationed. In 1942, bread and clothing were added to the list of rationed goods. A little later, gas and electricity were also rationed. There was no domestic coal available at all, and less than a quarter of the normal requirement of textiles was obtainable. Women were likely to be disproportionately affectd by rationing of food and clothing because of the presumption that provision of such household requirements was their responsibility.

Arrangements for the control of food and travel between Northern Ireland and Britain were among the first elements of the Emergency Powers to affect the population. Food Control Committees were set up throughout the United Kingdom on 1 September 1939 and an officer of the Northern Ireland Ministry of Commerce was appointed to act on behalf of the Minister of Food in Westminster.[44] This officer became the Divisional Food Officer for Northern Ireland and was given a wide range of powers. Under Section 3(1) of the Food Control Committees (Constitution) Order 1939, the Northern Ireland committees were allowed to be composed of nine members, compared to the usual fifteen members in the rest of the United Kingdom. There were three trade members, to be a retail grocer, a provision merchant or a retail butcher. In an effort to make the committees as representative as possible of the areas they were servicing, Section 3(3) had the following provision:

> The remaining six persons ... of whom at least one shall be a woman, shall be persons who in the opinion of the appointing authority or authorities, as the case may be, are representative of all classes of persons within the area or areas, as the case may be.

Food rationing in Britain was organized by using the information collected after the National Registration Act 1939 was passed on 5 September. Personal details of all citizens were required to be registered, comprising names, sex, age, occupation, profession, trade or employment, residence, conditions of marriage, membership of naval, military or air force reserves or auxiliary forces or of civil defence services or reserves. In Northern Ireland, at the end of September, application forms for ration books were sent directly to each household. The householder was required to furnish details of every person normally resident in the house, including those temporarily absent (apart from those in the armed forces), and to return the completed form to the local food officers, who then issued ration books to the 'head of household'. Although it was usually the women of the house who administered the rations, returned census forms indicate that the 'head of the house' was generally male, unless a woman was widowed or living alone.

The Prices of Goods Act 1939, passed in Westminster on 16 November, empowered the Ministry of Food to set price controls on a range of essential foods while the Board of Trade was authorized to make a determination on the basic price of a range of goods. Section 3(1) of the Act defined basic price as 'the price at which, in the ordinary course of the business in which those goods were sold, agreed to be sold or offered for sale, goods of that description similar to those goods were being offered for sale' on the 21 August 1939.[45] The various statutory orders that were made on foot of the Act were very detailed in the descriptions of food items and the prices set. Specific orders relating to the maximum price of eggs, sugar, milk, condensed milk, meat, apples and bread were regularly amended in the course of the war as these foods became more or less available. Moya Woodside sent a note to the Mass-Observation about the rise in prices of essential goods that had occurred in the first fifteen months of the war in Belfast, comparing them to what she had paid before the war started:

> Since 1937 I have kept detailed accounts of the total expenditure on food, fuel, wages, replacements etc. and up to 1939 they came out remarkably similar, in some cases even to a matter of shillings (this of course for the same numbers of people and same way of living). As I expected, however, 1940 totals reveal some interesting changes.
> *Baker and groceries*: always the largest item in any year, shows a 23% increase on the 1937–1939 averages.

> *Fuel*: (includes coal, coke, blocks, etc. but not gas or electric) is up 59%! This staggering rise is due to higher costs and (less obviously) to a wet and cold Ulster summer and to the fact that we are at home in the evenings so much more than formerly.
> *Fruit and veg*: shows a fall of 14% simple because there has been nothing to buy.
> *Fish and poultry*: is also down 10% and this in spite of rising prices. I attribute the decrease to economy and to the fact that we have practically stopped entertaining.
> *Butchers*: shows a small increase of 33%.
> *Dairy* only 5% decrease, so rationing is offset by higher prices.
> All other non-food items are down, some considerably. I suppose some sort of important conclusions can be drawn from these figures? The two most obvious ones are (1) general, that the cost of living index lags far behind actual conditions; (2) personal, that I am still trying to maintain a high food standard which so far has been balanced by economies elsewhere.[46]

As in Éire, it was primarily the intervention of women's representative groups that drew attention to the special needs of the most vulnerable members of the population. Moya Woodside was an active participant in a number of campaigning groups in Belfast and in late 1940 she was bemoaning the apathetic attitude of women to political organization:

> Attended meeting of Women's Labour Advisory Council. Very small attendances and everyone very depressed about the hopelessness of organising women in Ulster when everything is split from top to bottom by the sectarian issue. Suggested that Labour women should concentrate this winter on some domestic and non-political object such as family allowances or free milk for tubercular children. They seemed to think this might be a good idea.[47]

Although there is no direct evidence of the outcome of Woodside's suggestion in Northern Ireland, in Britain there was significant lobbying by women's organizations such as the Women's Institute to ensure that the special health requirements of children under five, pregnant women and nursing mothers were recognized in the rationing system, which made them an allowance of one pint of milk daily and twice the normal ration of eggs. They were to be given first choice of any available fruit, as well as cod liver oil, fruit juice and vitamin supplements and, of course, these provisions also applied to Northern Ireland.[48]

Rationing was extended to virtually every commodity essential to the daily lives of the citizens of Northern Ireland. Coupons for basic necessities like cosmetics, clothing and household textiles were issued to households on the same basis as ration books for food. Consumer rationing orders detailed the numbers of coupons required for specific items and these had to be given to retailers in exchange for goods, in addition to the money price.[49] Various strategies were adopted for making better use of existing goods, as more and more items disappeared from the shelves. Newspapers and magazines were full of helpful hints for economies, many of them carrying columns headed 'For Women'[50] or a similar title, which made it clear who was considered to have the responsibility for ensuring the nation's well-being, despite the shortages. The language of many advertisements recognized the extra workload created for women by the war shortages, as in advertisements for tonics and indigestion remedies, which made frequent reference to 'times of extra work and strain'.

One aspect of the rationing system that frequently marred the efforts of the authorities to ensure an equitable distribution of the available goods was the difficulty inherent in adapting to the seasonal shortages that arose at different times throughout the war, and of course, to the special needs of particular groups, such as the mothers of young children. The difficulty was exacerbated by the failure of the authorities to consult a wide range of interest groups about the problems that might possibly arise. While it made administrative sense to appoint the divisional distribution officers from the ranks of the Civil Service, they generally worked in isolation from the community they served and were not always aware of potential obstacles to the fairest distribution of available resources until they turned into causes for dispute. Again, Moya Woodside's reports to the Mass-Observation point to issues that were clearly the cause of some concern for many women:

> Friend who has studied the Clothes Rations order with care (which I haven't) says she thinks it is unfair in many ways and full of flaws. Those who make their own clothes, she points out (we both do) are being actually penalised for their ingenuity, as it will often take *more* coupons to purchase material for a garment than to buy it readymade. 'What about expectant mothers?' she asks. They've *got* to have maternity clothes and obviously can't go on wearing them after the baby is born. Again on the subject of made-up versus home made clothes, she remarked that it was all very well to say that clothing for children under four was exempt, but what use was this when you could not buy wool or material for them to make their clothes

yourself? And what about unborn babies? Have people to give up their own coupons to get wool and flannel for them? These points hadn't occurred to me, but E. who is the mother of one, and expecting another in September, can speak with some sense on the subject.[51]

While rationing arrangements were publicized through local and national newspapers and recommended prices were also widely notified, this did not prevent some of the resentment about the scarcity of goods manifesting itself in suspicion of shopkeepers, who were considered, rightly or wrongly, to be benefiting from the situation.

As raw materials became restricted and workers were laid off, the southern government said it would protect remaining employment by imposing a Wages Standstill Order. This was Emergency Powers Order (No.83) 1941 (which became operative on 28 May) and it prohibited increases in wages and prevented workers from striking for higher pay by removing the legal protection of the Trade Disputes Act from such strikes. Following strong campaigning from the trade unions, in April 1942 workers were permitted to obtain increases in wages by way of bonus orders, but these rises had to be related to increases in the cost of living. The passing of the Trade Union Act 1941 was mainly a result of the government's determination to curtail any possibility of industrial action in response to the wages standstills and the increasing cost of living that resulted from wartime conditions. Despite many demonstrations against the terms of the new law, particularly in Dublin, it was passed by the Dáil, and provided for the licensing of bodies empowered to carry on negotiations over wages and conditions. It also enabled the setting up of a tribunal, with members appointed by the Minister for Labour, which would have the power to restrict the rights of organization of trade unions.

In Britain the household registration information was also used for conscription to the armed forces and for work in war industries. The Conditions of Employment Act 1939, passed on 21 September, vested the power to control employment in the Minister for Labour and National Service. However, even at this early stage of the war, the extension of conscription to Northern Ireland was recognized as likely to pose political difficulties, and Section 9 of the Act made it clear that the Northern Ireland parliament would have jurisdiction over all matters of employment, notwithstanding anything in the Government of Ireland Act 1920. Similarly, the Administration of Justice (Emergency Provisions) (Northern Ireland) Act 1939, passed on the same day, gave full control of the justice system in the province to the Lord Chief Justice of Northern Ireland for the duration of the war, without any need for recourse to London.

A series of strikes in 1942 raised concerns about the Northern Ireland government's capacity to deal effectively with industrial unrest, as the proposals to introduce labour conscription, as in the rest of the United Kingdom, were rejected for the same reason that conscription to the armed forces was not implemented; that any moves in that regard were likely to be met with determined resistance by nationalists, and possibly even an armed response by the IRA. There was also concern that if workers from Northern Ireland were conscripted into the Allied forces, that the employment vacancies arising in their absence would be filled by people from Éire.[52] Not all of the disputes related to wages, particularly in Belfast, where some were focussed on the lack of protection for industrial workers whose workplaces were likely targets of bombing raids. Even though strikes were illegal in Northern Ireland from 1942 onwards, there were 270 of them in the course of the war.[53] During the first few months of the war there were over 900 strikes in Britain, almost all of them very short but illegal nonetheless. Order 1305 of the Emergency Powers Act 1939 banned strikes, but there were very few prosecutions until 1941 because the Ministry of Labour was anxious to avoid labour unrest.[54] The number of strikes increased each year until 1944 when the draconian Defence Regulation 1AA was introduced, making even incitement to strike unlawful. The strikes were divided almost equally between support for increased wages and protests about the deterioration in working conditions.

As early as March 1939, an advisory committee of the Passport and Permit Office in London had decided that traffic between Northern Ireland and Britain should be routed through approved ports only.[55] Air passenger traffic was temporarily suspended. A Travel Permit Office was set up in Belfast and was run by the former chief inspector of public service vehicles, whose staff and premises were now used for the issuing of travel documents.[56] Éire's neutral status was viewed with suspicion and regulations governing travel over the border between the two states were designed to prevent anyone using the southern state as a 'back door' into Britain. A valid permit or passport issued by the British authorities had to be in the possession of any person attempting to land in Britain from Éire. On 21 November 1940, a new order came into force and Irish (northern and southern) residents in Britain were allowed to make a temporary visit to Ireland to see their families, although not more frequently than once in six months. British residents in Ireland were allowed to travel on the same terms. Except in exceptional circumstances, the concession was confined to parents visiting their children, or vice versa, or to husbands and wives visiting each other.[57] Travel restrictions from Éire were focussed on Irish citizens who wished to take up war work in Britain and limitations were based on occupational status. Permits were not granted to anyone who voluntarily left a job in Ireland, nor to anyone in particular jobs, such as turf cutters or agricultural workers. Concerns about unaccompanied young women travelling to Britain will be discussed in later chapters.

There was virtually no restriction on the movement of individuals between Northern Ireland and Éire, but concern about the possibility of spies coming from the southern state led to a tightening of border inspections and the possibility of sending people back into Éire if the authorities were not satisfied about their *bona fides*. A further reason for concern from unionist politicians was the danger that large numbers of people coming from the South in search of work would settle in Northern Ireland and cause changes to the demographic balance of the province, possibly threatening thereby to alter the electoral balance as well.

One of the drawbacks of the security concerns was the problem that was created for arranging musical or other forms of entertainment that involved visiting performers. Moya Woodside was active in a local musical society whose programmes were completely disrupted by the wartime conditions:

> Attended Committee meeting of Annual Musical Festival to be held next week. Running this under wartime conditions is truly a labour of love and a measure of our enthusiasm for the cause of music-making. The secretary told us of some of the snags which are occurring. 1. In spite of repeated requests, wires, pressure on authorities, we don't yet know if any of our 3 adjudicators from England have been granted travel permits. 2. One of the Halls, booked since last summer, is being used as a Canteen, and there is some doubt if the people running it will clear out for the week of the Festival. 3. Entries from Dublin have dropped to about 1/3 of the peacetime average. Reason: rations, blackout, fear of bombs. 4. Rationing makes private hospitality for the adjudicators out of the question, so they have to be put up at a hotel, costing the finances so much more. 5. No extra tea has been allowed to the Committee for the serving of refreshments at the mid-morning and mid-afternoon break. Of course, I suppose between us we shall manage to scrape up a few ozs, enough for our hard-worked judges and stewards; but all these difficulties do mount up and dishearten people.[58]

In a diary entry more than a year later, she noted the difference between Belfast and Dublin in terms of the quality of available entertainment:

> The Royal Dublin Society (whose winter programme I have just seen) has a splendid series of chamber concerts arranged with artists from

London (including such well-known performers as Mersewitch, Thelma Reiss, the Guillen Quartet, etc.) while here in Belfast we face a completely concert-less winter. Dublin too has lectures given by such people as T.S. Eliot. Here all we ever seem to have are pep-talks by M.O.I. propagandists, or concert parties by or for the troops.[59]

In terms of the serious necessity to protect the population of Northern Ireland from attack, the Stormont government's responsibility to provide shelters for householders and the general public proved to be inadequate in practice. The failure of the Northern Irish government to give any more than rudimentary attention to civil defence meant that even after the fall of France, which underlined the necessity to protect vital air and sea installations that might be vulnerable to attack by aircraft based on the coast of France, a revised scale of defensive measures could not be implemented quickly because of shortages of equipment. When the bombing of Belfast started in April 1941, there was only shelter protection available for approximately one quarter of the population of the city. When the blitz in Belfast ended, it did not bring immediate relief for the people of the city because they had been so traumatized by the events of April and May 1941. One of Moya Woodside's diary entries, made two weeks after the April 1941 raid, suggests some practical reasons for the lasting impact of the bombing:

A woman in the slums told me this morning that before she left Birmingham 'one o' them insanitary bombs' had fallen on her house. Visited another bombed-out family, also back from Birmingham, who are now living (5 people) in 2 minute and dilapidated rooms for which they pay 8/- rent. They are awaiting £50 compensation for their mined house; and in the meantime, have literally only what they stand up in. No bedclothes whatever, some makeshift furniture and a borrowed saucepan. The man's job has gone too, from earning £4.15 a week they are now reduced to Unemployment Benefit. *And nobody cares*. War affects everyone but as usual the very poor are the worst sufferers.[60]

Despite the concentration of industry in Belfast's docklands, for example, a large number of ordinary residents in the area had virtually no protection.[61] The shoddy quality of the housing in working-class areas was reflected in the relatively high number of people killed outright in the poorer areas. Moya Woodside went in to one of these areas two weeks after the major bombing raid on the night of 14/15 April 1941:

> Out on Welfare case work in the blitzed area. Bitterly cold and a wind which swirled dust, plaster and ashes about the ruins so that one could scarcely see. I had 5 families to visit and found one burnt out and departed, whereabouts unknown; 3 others also gone from houses uninhabitable though still standing and the 5th 'evacuated' from an undamaged house. It was a scene of desolation: whole streets of roofless and windowless houses, with an occasional notice chalked on the door 'Gone to Ballymena' or some other country address. Not a soul about, except demolition workers. Enormous gaps, or mounds of bricks, where formerly some familiar building had stood. More than a fortnight now since the raid yet it still looks raw and obscene.[62]

A week later, even before the next major bombing raid in May, there were scenes of devastation in the city centre and Woodside drew attention to the implications for the future:

> Went to town on bicycle to do some shopping. Belfast will certainly never look the same again. I should say that 1/3 of the centre of town has gone. Streets littered with glass, water, charred beams and debris. Many roped off and firemen still working on smoking buildings. Crowds standing about, many appearing to be employees and owners of shops and offices which don't exist any more ... My fish shop was some way down the roped-off main street, but the assistants were there and walked up and down to the barriers taking orders and carrying bits of fish for inspection. This would have been very amusing if the scenes round about weren't so awful ... Less people were killed than in the previous blitz, as this was mainly directed on city centre and shipyards – but now we have an unemployment problem of staggering proportions. *Thousands* and *thousands* are walking the streets, with only the faintest hope of being employed again till *after* the war. What is going to happen to all those people, many of them homeless and bereaved (as they will be) as well as without work? At present this side of things has scarcely been realised, but material repair or reconstruction is of small importance beside this human problem.[63]

More than one thousand people died and over 100,000 people were made homeless by the bombing raids on Belfast. The psychological impact was worsened by the lack of preliminary warning before the first attack on the night of 7/8 April 1941 and by the inability of the emergency services to cope with the subsequent devastation.[64] James Doherty was an air raid

6. Carlow bombing deaths. *Irish Press*, 3 January 1941, p. 1. Courtesy of *Irish Press* archive.

warden in Belfast and in his memoir of the Belfast blitz[65] he described the effect on the local community of the obliteration of the York Street Flax Spinning Company on the night of 4/5 May 1941, which resulted in the deaths of thirty-five people and the demolition of more than sixty homes:

> The York Street spinning factory was the largest of its kind in the world and its destruction led to many economic problems in an already deprived and run down area. The war as yet had not brought full employment to Northern Ireland and the mill was one of the few factories which was working at full capacity ... With its passing went the familiar early morning scene of dozens of girls and women, some of them wearing men's boots, moving along through the narrow streets with arms linked and singing at the tops of their voices the well known mill songs or parodies based on the popular songs of the day.[66]

Belfast had insufficient facilities to deal with the aftermath of the blitz, with one of the biggest difficulties facing the authorities being the absence of sufficient mortuary space to deal with the large number of dead.

In the course of 1940 gas masks were issued to 370,000 people throughout the twenty-six counties but despite being the capital city, Dublin had virtually no active defences and had bomb shelter accommodation for fewer than 30,000 people. Those measures that were adopted were almost a carbon copy of those in place in Britain and were administrative in nature, primarily concerned with the maintenance of law and order.[67] The most widespread precaution against bombing raids was the imposition of a blackout during the hours of darkness, as Minnie recalled:

> You had to have black blinds, or black curtains, that would keep out the light. And I remember all the lamp posts, they had kind of hoods on them to shine the light down onto the road, kind of in a straight line down on the road, and everything had hoods on them, even motor cars. There weren't many motor cars, but everything had to have little hoods to shine the light down on the road, but you daren't have a light. There'd be someone at the door saying you can see a sliver of light at the window and you'd have to make sure the curtain was folded not to see it. And even like, some of the lamps like, if there was a lamp in our keyhole it wouldn't be lit because they were trying to save electricity. And the only lamp would be on the main road. It was pretty dark, you know, if you went out at night.

The blackout was regulated by the Emergency Powers (Control of Lights) Order 1939, which was passed by the Dáil on 16 October.

There were incidents of German bombs dropping on the South, most of which have been dismissed as pilot error, although various rumours at the time suggested there might have been more sinister motives, none of which were ever substantiated. On 26 August 1940 three women lost their lives when a bomb struck Campile creamery in Co. Wexford. The German government subsequently apologized and offered £9,000 in compensation to their families. Three members of a family at Knockroe, Co. Carlow were killed when a bomb struck their farmhouse. There were also incidents in counties Laois, Louth, Kildare, Wexford, and Wicklow but no lives were lost. The worst case was on the night of 30/31 May 1941, when thirty-four people were killed and at least ninety injured when four bombs fell on Dublin. The bomb that hit the North Strand was estimated to be at least 500 lb and caused most of the death and destruction in the city. The North Strand incident made a deep impression on everyone in Dublin who witnessed it, particularly because many of them thought they would now be subjected to a sustained campaign. Josie remembered the night very clearly:

> I was on the landing when I heard Mammy. Well, when I looked out, I pulled back the blind and looked out, and all you could see was lights, you know, big lights. ... We were all stood on that little

landing in Cabra and I'll always remember, she put her arms around us and she said, now, said she, if we're going, we'll all go together.

The southern state was as ill prepared to defend itself in 1939 in terms of manpower as it was in physical defences. In 1938 the strength of the regular army, at 5,915, was less than 65 per cent of establishment. This state of affairs was remedied by a massive recruitment campaign, despite obstruction by the Department of Finance, but the army remained ill equipped throughout the Emergency years. Although modern warfare was as likely to be waged from the skies as from sea or land, air defences were virtually non-existent and the focus of the armed forces was almost entirely on the defence of the national territory from invasion by one or another of the belligerent powers.[68] The impact of the recruitment campaign on Irish women was confined to any benefit they might have acquired as the spouses or relatives of the many men who exchanged unemployment for an army uniform, since women were not considered for enrolment in the Irish army in any capacity, including auxiliaries like the Local Defence Forces.

The impact of the wartime laws passed by their respective governments on the lives of Irish women in Éire and Northern Ireland was manifested in the effect that the various Emergency Powers orders had on their domestic responsibilities and their opportunities for employment. In their domestic lives, particularly for women with families to look after, the war led to a significant rise in the cost of food and fuel and this had an immediate impact on their capacity to make their incomes cover all of the basic necessities. Apart from the unequal pay rates that women workers endured, the Wages Standstill Act enabled the Éire government to suppress any attempt by workers, whether male or female, to press for wage demands in line with the rising cost of living. The rationing systems introduced by both Irish governments enabled a fairer distribution of scarce goods and this benefited lower paid women, but the queuing for rations and the 'making do and mend' policies promulgated by those governments also entailed an increased domestic workload which was mainly borne by women.

3

Women at work

> Every worker is entitled to:
> Adequate Leisure, A Just Wage, Respect for Personal Dignity
> We call upon the Government and all members of the Oireachtas to assist us to secure these rights.[1]

Although the claim that the two world wars were liberating for women has been undermined by recent research, it has been shown that in belligerent nations like Britain, Canada and the United States greater employment opportunities were opened up for women during the war years. In Ireland, the position was more ambiguous. Éire was neutral and although Northern Ireland was at war, this did not have an immediate impact on the availability of work. Unemployment rose every month from the declaration of war until February 1940 and as late as May 1940 more people were still unemployed than in the last full month of peace. Moya Woodside noted some of the consequences of the government's policy of encouraging unemployed workers to take up jobs in Britain:

> Unemployment figures still reach the 46,766 mark (March 17th), and nothing is done. Some two thousands of men work overtime and Sundays in the shipyards but the rest derive no benefit from the supposed boom ... Men who have been on U.A. or P. assistance have no resources, yet their families are expected to tide over anything between 10 days to 3 weeks till the husband's money comes through from England. If he falls sick, is on short time through bad weather or bombing, or – iniquitous practice – works 2 weeks before receiving one week's pay, well, it's just too bad for his wife and family.[2]

Although there was no conscription, workers were subject to a certain level of coercion to take up work in Britain as the Unemployment Insurance (Emergency Powers) Order 1940 enabled the authorities to deny unemployment benefit to anyone who refused to take up a job in Britain without 'good reason'. At a cabinet meeting in September 1941 approval was given to a proposal by the Ministry of Labour that single women over 21 years of age who had been unemployed for five months or more should be offered employment in Britain and that an examination should be made of the 'title to unemployment benefit of any woman claimant who refused such work'. The scheme involved a four month training period at a basic rate of 38/- per week for work in engineering and munitions.³ Once placed, wages were at a minimum 38/- per week plus a cost of living bonus, and in large firms after a month this would rise to £3 with a maximum of £4/7 including cost of living bonus. Food and lodgings were to cost 22/6 a week. Some workers were also transferred for textile and NAAFI work (canteens for the troops).⁴

The Ministry of Commerce questioned the policy of encouraging women to leave home for training in Britain for fear they would not return to Northern Ireland and the new industries developing there would be left short of workers. They were particularly concerned about the munitions factory and the fuselage factory being opened in Belfast by Mackies and Bairds Engineering, respectively.⁵ Generally, employers seem to have preferred to train workers in the factories and some employers came to favour young women workers in preference to older men:

7. Announcement to women, 1941. In 1941 the UK government introduced conscription for all single women aged between 20 and 30. This announcement was intended to persuade British women to enlist voluntarily for war work or the armed services before they were called up. Courtesy of the National Archives, ref. CAB66/15

> We would appreciate the training of girls in the Government Training Centres and would be prepared to engage them, but so far, our experience of trained men of other trades has been bad. It is quite obvious that a young girl, round about the twenties, is very much

> more adaptable than an elderly man of the fifties or sixties, who has perhaps been doing bricklayers' or painters' work for a number of years. We find that almost invariably a girl, after three weeks training in the Works, can knock spots off this type of elderly man. Therefore, I would say that we would be prepared to take a considerable number of young girls who have had a course of training.[6]

In late December 1941, the Ministry of Labour set up a course for women to train in machine operation at Lurgan technical school. A four week course was set up at Belfast Technical College in May 1942 and one at Bangor College in June 1942. At this stage, government announced its plans to train unemployed women and girls, as part of a recruitment drive for war work. They were looking particularly for 'suitable women' aged 18–35 years. By December 1942, the Ministry of Labour records state that 696 women had been sent for training under this scheme and of those 558 were working in the war industries while 72 were still in training.[7]

A voluntary registration scheme for women workers was set up in November 1943 but the majority of the 3,000 registered unemployed women workers were living in Belfast and were unable to move to other areas of Northern Ireland to work. In response to the appeal for women workers, unions and other campaigning groups made various comments and suggestions, such as the need for nurseries, school meals, shopping and laundry facilities, if married women were to join the paid workforce in large numbers. The Women's War Effort Association, an *ad hoc* group of women, campaigned to promote opportunities and facilities for married women to work so they could contribute to the war effort, arguing that:

> the government must take into account that the vast majority of the women to whom the appeal will be made are women with family and domestic responsibilities. It is, therefore, absolutely necessary for the government to provide such facilities as will enable women to fulfil their home duties and at the same time participate in the war effort.[8]

The low number of respondents to an advertising campaign to recruit women for work in new industries was such that it was decided not to advertise for new industries in Northern Ireland because of the uncertain labour supply outside Belfast. The range of employment opportunities for women widened considerably in the course of the war, though not to as great an extent as in Britain.[9] In 1935, 46.5 per cent of the industrial labour force in Britain was female, compared to 26.4 per cent in Northern Ireland.[10] While the total number of insured women workers in the state did not increase dramatically, from 111,900 in 1939 to a wartime peak of 118,600 in 1943 (a rise of only 6 per cent), the sort of work open to them did alter quite considerably. Appendix 3 compares the breakdown of employment figures by occupation as recorded in the 1926 and the 1951 census reports. At the start of the war, British unions with branches in Northern Ireland had reached agreement under the Relaxation of Existing Customs Agreement, which meant that for the duration of the war, if need be, some jobs could be broken down into components so that semi-skilled, unskilled and women workers could do them, but that at the end of the war there would be a return to 'normal' work practices.

Another avenue of employment opened up to women was entry to the women's auxiliary arms of the services, such as the Auxiliary Territorial Service (ATS). This kind of work, more than any other, opened to question traditional perspectives on women's place in society. It was also better paid than other forms of work open to women:

> A woman doctor I know rang up to see if I could get her a refugee for domestic work. She said they had been without anyone, except for 2 short and unsatisfactory spells, since last June, and that the registry offices are worse than useless. Her opinion is that all the available labour *which is any good* has either been absorbed in the ATS or NAAFI or been snapped up by English evacuees or officers [sic] wives who are accustomed to pay much higher wages than those prevailing locally.[11]

Advertisements for maids and other domestics in Belfast daily newspapers offered between £35 and £52 per annum during the war years. Women who worked in clerical jobs before the war also found that pay and conditions improved when the government employed them.

In Éire urban industrial unemployment figures began to rise in 1938, after the expansion in employment of the previous seven years. While the agricultural sector was recovering from the hardships of the Economic War, it could not provide an alternative for workers laid off from manufacturing concerns. The number of persons on the live register (residing in cities and urban districts) was 7.9 per cent higher in the first six months of 1939 than it had been in the same period of 1938, while the numbers continued to increase steadily in the first six months after the declaration of the Emergency in September 1939. The reduction in employment was attributed to the scarcity of raw materials for industrial production.[12] Production and employment in the industrial sector of Éire were already slowing down in 1939 when the outbreak of war in Europe added further major difficulties to those already being experienced by manufacturers faced with a contracting market.

Finding a job in Éire in the early 1940s was difficult, but especially so for women, whose employment opportunities had already been curtailed by the terms of the Conditions of Employment Act passed in 1936. The Civil Service was outside the scope of the Act and it employed one of the largest groups of women workers in Éire. There was a significant increase in the number of male and female employees recorded in the Census of 1936 and that of 1946 and this may well have been due to the additional demands made by the Emergency situation on government services. The security of an established post in the Civil Service is underlined by the numbers described as 'out of work' in Dublin County Borough in both 1936 and 1946 – only three out of 2,179 at work in Public Administration in 1936 (0.14 per cent) and eleven out of 3,556 in 1946 (0.31 per cent). Female civil and public servants also had to retire on marriage while a man, whether married or not, had a job for life if that was what he wanted.[13] Some grades were confined exclusively to women because they were considered to be better suited to the work requirements and these were generally at the lower end of the pay scales. While some of the objections to women workers seem to have been based on the perception of lesser physical capacity, others were social, as in the belief that it was not appropriate for women to work at night.

Even apart from the restrictions imposed by the Conditions of Employment Act and the scarcity of jobs, women who had to provide for their children alone were particularly vulnerable. Catherine's husband worked as a cooper in Guinness's until he died of a duodenal ulcer when he was only 40, leaving her with six children to care for on the very low income that she could earn from working in the brewery as a cleaner. The need to look after her children prevented her from taking up the relatively skilled printing work she had done in Dollard's before her marriage, which would have paid her much more than the cleaning work. The early shift in Guinness's suited her family commitments. Although she received a pension for herself and the children under the Widows' and Orphans' Pensions Act 1935, the amount payable was not raised between 1935 and 1942 when Catherine's husband died, and the most she would have received was 10/- per week for herself and 5s per week for the eldest child, with a further 3/- per week each for the other five children, and she needed the supplement of the Guinness income.

Colette made many employment applications through her secretarial college, but her first job was secured through the intervention of a family friend, after she had completed her secretarial course. Although the job became available as a result of another woman leaving to get married, a marriage bar was not official policy for all women working in the private sector, although some companies did operate their own policy in this regard. In the public sector, a marriage bar was operative in the clerical and administrative grades of the Civil Service, as well as in the teaching and nursing professions. In Guinness's brewery, where Colette spent most of her working life, she would have been required to resign if she had got married, although occasionally the company allowed a woman to stay on for a limited period after marriage, if it was to the company's advantage and she was an exceptionally good worker.

Colette was dismissed from her first job after an illness had made her absent from work for some time. She was horrified by the experience of going to the employment exchange, where one of the women behind the counter had been to tutorial college with her and she felt humiliated to be in the position of looking for social welfare payments. Colette shared the belief with most of the other women that people at that time were reluctant to claim social welfare, because of the perceived social stigma attached to being unemployed. She applied for work in a range of companies and she was called for an interview in Guinness's:

> I was terrified, but my father said to me to buy myself a new hat, we wore hats and gloves in those days; we were always very formally turned out, even when you were riding a bicycle. There was no such thing as slacks; that was quite unheard of. Well, it wasn't quite unheard of but it was certainly unusual. Well, I had my interview ... but they hadn't taken any lady clerks in for a few years and I think they suddenly discovered that they needed them so they held an examination. There were quite a big number of lady clerks who attended for the examination; it was quite formal, like the Leaving Certificate or something like that, and out of that so many were picked.

Lady clerks were first employed by Guinness in the late nineteenth century and the first special female clerks department was set up in 1905, where the women were graded as bookkeepers, typists and shorthand writers. The entrance procedures for lady clerks had three stages. Firstly, there was a preliminary interview with the lady superintendent 'in order to eliminate the socially undesirable candidates'.[14] This was followed by an interview with the managing director and the chief accountant, for which marks were assigned to the candidates. Finally, there was a written examination, which was to be one 'which could not be crammed for at the various commercial classes which are attended by a large majority of the candidates'.[15]

Women workers were not paid at the same rate as men. The Northern Ireland government took its lead on the question of equal pay for women in government service from the Ministry of Finance in Westminster. The policy in respect of pay for women workers was to adhere to the practice observed by non-governmental employment:

> In the industrial sphere, in those cases where men and women are paid alike in industry, they would normally be paid alike in Government service. In the non-industrial sphere, however, the position is that equal pay has not been adopted for clerical and similar work. Two Royal Commissions have considered whether a departure should be made in the Government service. Neither has been able to recommend adoption of this proposal. The Government does not see its way to alter the existing position.[16]

Alice's first job was in Thompson's[17] where she enjoyed the work, but she was glad to move to a job in the Ormeau Bakery when the opportunity arose. Although she was set to work in the chocolate and confectionery department of the bakery, she was employed as a female baker, and this meant that she got higher wages than she would have done working under the Sugar Confectionery Trade Board regulations, although that might have seemed more appropriate:

> I immediately had, it wasn't a lot of money now but in those days to get ten shillings a week more than where you were leaving was a lot of money, especially during the war years.

A female baker was defined by the Trade Board as a worker over 21 years of age, who had served a learnership of not less than five years, or who, in the case of home bakeries, had not less than five years' experience in the trade of baking, employing any or all of a variety of processes[18] in the making of bread, pastry or flour confectionery.[19] Workers in the baking trade had a 48 hour week, for which the male bakers' rate was set at 80/- per week in November 1940, while female bakers were paid 47/-, a difference of 41 per cent.[20] By August 1944, the male rate had been increased to 87/-, compared to a female rate of 50/6, with the difference between them at 42 per cent. In correspondence dated August 1940, between the Ministry of Labour and T.F. Hall, the Secretary of the Office of the Trade Boards, Mr Hall noted that the baking trade schedule of wages was 'considerably in advance of the rates fixed by other Trade Boards in Northern Ireland for comparable types of workers'.[21] Male workers in the

8. *Everywoman* cover, April 1942. By early 1942 conscription in Britain had been extended to women aged 19. Women's magazines like this one (available in Ireland) portrayed attractive young women happily doing their patriotic duty.

sugar confectionery and food preserving trade also worked a 48 hour week, for which they were paid 49/- per week in 1941, while female workers were paid 30/- for the same working hours, a differential of 39 per cent. By 1944, the male rate had increased to 64/- compared to 41/- for the female workers, decreasing the differential to 36 per cent. Minutes of trade board meetings suggest that the increases were intended to keep up with the rising cost of living engendered by wartime conditions and there is no mention in the deliberations of any need to balance male and female earnings.

Appendix 4 shows the weekly rates set by the Northern Ireland trade boards for all the industries regulated by them in which both male and female workers were doing generally similar work. There was often considerable disparity in the wages they were paid as, for example, in the aerated waters trade where the male workers were paid 63 per cent more than their female colleagues who were doing exactly the same work in the same conditions, or the general waste materials trade where there was a 72 per cent differential, again for exactly the same work. The situation was slightly different in some other trades, like the baking and the shirt-making trades, where there was respectively a 70 per cent and 78 per cent differential. In these trades, male and female workers were not doing exactly the same work because certain aspects of the trades were gender specific and only men were hired for some work while only women were hired for others, although the skills demanded were comparable if not identical. Women were never employed as cutters in shirt-making factories while men never did the sewing, although both aspects of the trade required similar levels of skill and training.[22]

In Éire, women whose jobs came under the auspices of trade boards benefited much more than men from the restricted wage increases permitted under the Wages Standstill Act of 1941 because they were starting at a lower level – see Appendix 5. Many of the jobs that were taken up mainly by women, such as personal service and work in the trading and finance areas, were not subject to trade board or Joint Labour Commission regulation. Wage levels in the industries regulated by the trade boards were based on acceptance of the notion that women should be paid less than men, even in situations where they were performing similar work. All of the weekly rates were based on a 48-hour week for adult male and female workers. The age at which workers were classified as 'adults' varied in different trades from 18 years and over to 22 years and over.[23] Women workers were often vulnerable to replacement by lower-paid juniors or apprentices at times of slackness but efforts to regulate the number of apprentices permissible in individual enterprises were resisted by the employers, particularly in small firms, who were reluctant to surrender their autonomy in relation to hiring practices.

All of the married women who were interviewed believed that their primary responsibility was to their families and their paid work was supplementary. Because of this, their relationship with their employers assumed a secondary status in terms of their priorities. This attitude was reflected in their acceptance of the inequality between male and female pay rates, although none of the unmarried women questioned the difference either. Employers and male trade union representatives supported its continued presence, despite the often-repeated concern that cheaper women workers would be more attractive to employers. Even Maureen, who became an active trade unionist, was uninterested in the fact that men got paid considerably more than women for doing the same work. In Ireland, North and South, in the 1940s, there was no agitation for widespread reform of pay structures for women workers and claims for increased rates were confined to specific employments and were made in the context of acceptance of the fact that male workers would automatically be paid more than female. Most women's public representatives worked within this framework, even such prominent figures as Louie Bennett, General Secretary of the Irish Women Workers' Union. Her report to the 1939 annual convention of the union regarding her work on the Commission on Vocational Organisation was probably written as much for wider public consumption as for her members and therefore exaggerated her position, but the main point she makes about woman's primary role is consistent with other statements made by her and other influential figures at the time:[24]

> We are often told that woman's place is the home. We agree that it is her special sphere. But war and social injustice are both enemies of the home. Women and children are their victims as well as men. It is in order to defend the home and the family that women must now take a larger part in public life and politics. Because the woman as mother has a deep-seated conviction that family life can only be soundly based on religious and moral principles, she realises very clearly that the life of the community as represented in Government and Public Bodies must also be based on such principles.[25]

The *Times Pictorial Weekly* magazine[26] had a column called 'Four Corner Survey' in which current affairs and social events from all around Ireland were discussed each week. In May 1943 the column referred to the annual conference of the Irish National Teachers' Organisation (INTO) which had been held in Dublin in the previous week. While the tone is flippant, the report raises several important points, not least being the fact that women teachers were still protesting about the marriage bar in their profession, some years after its imposition:

> I got around to the Teachers' Conference in Dublin to hear a few robust female delegates thundering against the regulation which insists that women teachers shall resign their posts some suitable time before they walk to the altar with a man, usually a teacher. I never could make up my mind whether marriage improves the intellect of female teachers, but many unmarried female teachers appear to have very definite views on the subject. I am one of those old-fashioned people who, steeped in the words of the Constitution, believe that a married woman's place is in the home.[27]

The columnist went on to suggest that a woman's acceptance of a marriage proposal was both a Christian and a patriotic act. He[28] went on to question whether a husband could be 'supremely happy' knowing that his wife was 'belting on her bicycle to the local school' to look after other people's children while her own were left at home in the care of a maid. The report concluded with a quotation from Dr T.J. O'Connell, General Secretary of the INTO, claiming that a married woman was the 'most proper person' to teach young children. The 'Four Corner' surveyor was not convinced:

> If that last statement does not result in a wholesale rush of unmarried teachers to change their status, the INTO Conference will almost have been held in vain. If all women teachers were permitted to continue in the class-rooms after their marriage, where, one may ask, would the vacancies arise for the young women who seem to be falling over themselves to become JAMs?[29] If these young women cannot have jobs, after some years of training at a fair cost to the State, then there will be more bag-packing and tear-dropping, and more talk about our departing youth – and more hypocrisy.

There were some occasions during the war when Irish women fought inequality and won. In February 1940, the women members of the Amalgamated Transport and General Workers Union who were employed by Ewart and Company, the biggest linen manufacturing enterprise in Northern Ireland, went on strike over the issue of union recognition in the company. The origin of the dispute was a technicality and the core of the matter was the very low wages being paid to the women workers, even after protracted negotiations with the company had finally secured a minimum wage for the men employed outside the craft section:

> The case of the Women Workers demands special consideration. Their whole existence is a fight against a small wage-packet at the end of the week. Every defect in the Management, every flaw in the Departmental Organisation, every hold-up, every break-down, is reflected in the wage packet of the woman worker – especially the Weaver and the Winder. A large proportion of every forty-eight hours spent in the Factory is wasted in waiting. It is not an uncommon thing to see a Woman Worker, after standing about half the week, leave the Factory with HARDLY ANY WAGE AT ALL ... Many women are receiving more on STRIKE PAY than they receive in WAGES. THIS IS THE BACKGROUND TO THE STRIKE.[30]

Concern over the possible effect the strike might have on the war effort led to an intervention by the Ministry of War and the employer's representatives were forced to abandon their refusal to meet the workers' representatives and to attend talks in London at which a resolution to the dispute was worked out and the women workers secured a significant pay rise and improvement in their conditions.

Trade union membership in Northern Ireland increased during the war years. According to the Northern Ireland Registrar of Friendly Societies, responsible for the registration of trade unions, the membership of trade unions increased by 16.9 per cent between 1938 and 1942 and increased by 22.4 per cent between 1942 and 1946. The membership included trade unions registered in Northern Ireland, in Britain and in Éire although the largest number of workers (male and female) belonged to the British-registered unions, accounting for 90.3 per cent of the total in 1938, 92.1 per cent in 1942, and 90.5 per cent in 1946.[31] The increase in trade union membership was consistent with the experience in Britain, where tightly controlled labour markets and the British Labour movement's alliance with the government contributed to rapid growth in the course of the Second World War.[32]

Of all the women who were involved in this research only Maureen was ever a trade union activist and that was later in her life. Alice, Nora and Flora were members of trade unions during the war years but none of them played an active role, and most of the others had no recollection of trade union activity in their workplaces because they had not been members. Daisy and Ivy remembered that the management of the linen mill where they worked was very hostile to trade union activity:

> There was one woman, she was a Union woman and she was taking money for the girls ... she was sacked. She went somewhere else. Her forewoman was against it.

As late as 1940, only a small number of textile workers belonged to unions in Northern Ireland. The Textile Operatives' Society of Ireland was the only women's trades union in the linen industry until the female mill-workers' branch of the Irish Transport and General Union was founded in Belfast in 1911.[33]

During the Second World War trade union membership among women workers in Britain increased significantly. Between 1939 and 1943, approximately 900,000 women entered trade unions, bringing the proportion of women in trade unions to over 23 per cent of the total membership in 1943, compared to 11 per cent before the war started.[34] Similarly, in Northern Ireland the numbers of women who were members of trade unions grew from 12,007 in 1939 to 21,590 in 1945, an increase of over 44 per cent.[35] In 1939, female members of trade unions in Northern Ireland comprised 14 per cent of the total membership, whereas by 1945 this proportion had only risen to 15 per cent, suggesting that while there were more women in paid employment, they were not significantly more active in workplace organization than they had been at the beginning of the war. In Éire, where women's traditional areas of employment were reduced by the wartime conditions, trade union membership seems to have remained consistent with pre-war levels.[36]

Alice took her position in the Ormeau Bakery very seriously and was available for extra work if the company needed her. When asked if she had been paid overtime rates for this work, she explained that she volunteered because she was needed but the management had appreciated her commitment:

> Well, you volunteered, you know, because it would be after hours and maybe in the summer time, you know it was a very warm job, type of thing. But I remember when I got my pay one Friday and I remember I said I'm overpaid and I went back to the accounts and I said look, it was ten shillings or something which in those days was a lot of money. I said there's an error in my pay packet, there's extra money in it and they said oh well, I was given that instruction, you'd better talk to Miss Grahame. Which I did, and she said that I had more than earned it. You know, you got it that way … Oh no, it wasn't formal overtime, it was because of the work you had done. They showed their appreciation of it.

Miss Grahame made a strong impression on Alice because she set high standards of behaviour and 'manners'. Miss Grahame joined the Ormeau Bakery in 1929 and started the homemade cake department. The booklet issued by the bakery for their centenary celebrations in 1975 refers to the owners' claim to have the highest standards of quality and hygiene of any bakery operating in Northern Ireland and credits Miss Grahame with their implementation.

Alice looked on her years in the Ormeau Bakery as part of her education, especially because of the training she was given by Miss Grahame, and apart from recalling that she was paid more there than in her previous employment, she responded to questions about pay with a reiteration of how good the Ormeau Bakery was as an employer:

> Discipline was very strong and manners were everything. I mean when we met our lady superintendent in any department, if I had have

said 'Good morning' she'd have turned to me and said: my name is Miss Grahame. You see, we had to say: Good morning, Miss Grahame and this for me, anyway, I thought was a wonderful way to grow up ... Yes, they called me Alice, they didn't say Miss S., but they were absolutely, they treated the staff wonderfully, so they did ... You know, I was a girl guide all my life and I always say that the Guides and the Ormeau Bakery made me what I am.

It seems that the most important aspect to Alice of her position in the Ormeau Bakery was that the quality of her work was recognized both on a daily basis and in the long term, when she was promoted to a supervisory position that had previously been held only by men.

Colette did not remember being paid overtime in Guinness's brewery but she believed that the company compensated staff very well for any extra work that might be required.[37] The practice with regard to overtime was to pay employees (weekly paid workers) of the brewery for agreed overtime worked, while staff (salaried workers) were given time off in lieu unless there was a notably large number of hours that had been agreed in advance to deal with a particular situation. The department manager of the area seeking the overtime had to give a full explanation to the board to get clearance, like the situation outlined in a memorandum from the manager of the Registry (Personnel) Department to the Managing Director, which also gives an insight into some of the benefits in kind enjoyed by Guinness employees:

> There is a considerable increase in the work of this Department in connection with British, Northern Ireland and Eire Income Tax work. It is now necessary to state on the Income Tax Forms the amount paid to each employee for cash allowance in lieu of Beer, Annual leave, cash allowance etc. and Brewery Savings Bank Interest. There is also a certain amount of incidental work, which has to be performed during each month in connection with the payment of British and Northern Ireland Income Tax.[38]

When Colette joined the company, she would have been recruited to Class D, which was a probationary grade for lady clerks. The pay scale rose from £2 per week on entry to £2/10 after four increments. The grade carried an annual leave allowance of eighteen working days. After a probationary period of one year, it was possible to be promoted to the C grade, which was paid on a scale moving from the minimum of £2/10 per week to the maximum of £4, again after four increments. The B and A grades were for posts of significant responsibility and were paid at the maximum rate of £5 per week for the B grade with twenty-four days annual holidays and a maximum of £6 for the A grade, with a twenty-six day holiday entitlement:[39]

> When I went in it was £2 a week, which was double what I was getting. But you were paid by the month so that you didn't always get £2 a week, you know. If you had a five-week month it was different but it was good, well I thought it was great. I wasn't complaining but I was living at home, of course.

The point about living at home with her parents was that Colette did not have to pay rent, although she contributed to the family income by giving housekeeping money to her mother.

All of the women who lived at home when they started work had handed their pay to their mothers, who then returned a small sum for pocket money:

> We got so much back, you know, but there was no stress about it or difficulty. We were glad we had got to the stage where we were working and of course, in those days, you could buy material and somebody could make you something to wear.

Alice's reference to dress-making skills was one that was repeated in other interviews, where women suggested that they had been very skilled money managers because their resources were so limited. Moya Woodside drew attention to a different aspect of the home dress-making habit:

> Called at the shop to enquire why a Butterlea pattern ordered September 25th has never arrived. The assistant tells me it is held up in the *censorship*! All paper patterns, it seems are censored.[40]

Mothers kept control of the housekeeping and most of the women remembered their fathers and brothers also handing over unopened pay packets to them and the mothers deciding how the family income would be spent. In certain circumstances, another woman could take control of the family budget, but none of the women remembered anyone but women having this responsibility. Daisy and Ivy's mother died when they were young and their aunt effectively took her place, including taking over the spending of the family income when the women went out to work themselves:

HAPPY THOUGHTS — ELECTRIC GIFTS

1940

THEY SOLVE EVERYDAY PROBLEMS

It's Christmas and you want to help people—that's the Christmas spirit. Look through our list of Electric Gift suggestions, and you'll find that every one of them, besides being a good Christmas gift, will give years of helpful service to your friends in their everyday life.

Electric Fire	From 11s. 8d.	Electric Kettle (copper)	From 31s. 6d.
Electric Immersion Heater	From 12/-	Electric Kettle (nickel-plated)	Price 34/-
Bowl Fittings complete with mounts	From 14/-	Electric Clock	From 35/-
		Study Lamp	From 38s. 6d.
Electric Iron	From 15/-	Quick Service Cooker	Price £4 2s. 6d.
Electric Heating Pad	Price 21s. 6d	Electric Warming Plate	Price £4 8s. 0d
Electric Toaster	Price 23/-	Electric Vacuum Cleaner Price	
Electric Hair Dryer	Price 28/-		£12 17s. 6d.
Electric Coffee Percolator	Price 30/-	"Dustette" Model at £3 10s. 0d.	

GOOD WISHES COME BEST WITH ELECTRIC GIFTS BECAUSE ELECTRIC GIFTS MAKE GOOD WISHES COME TRUE

ELECTRICITY SALES SHOWROOMS
35 ST. STEPHEN'S GREEN, DUBLIN .. AND BRANCHES

PRESENT PLEASURE — LASTING SERVICE

9. Advertisement for electrical gifts, Christmas 1940. Electrical goods such as those advertised here were beyond the reach of women on low incomes. Such advertisements had virtually disappeared by 1942 when electricity rationing was introduced in Éire.

> You handed up your money. Oh aye, you got maybe a half a crown, you were lucky if you got a half a crown[41] ... My mother died Christmas Eve and my aunt Maureen took us over. You got your pay and you'd give your money in. You didn't open it; you'd have been afeared to open it ... Now don't get me wrong, she was the best, my aunt was the best and my mother, but I mean it wasn't that they were strict but you knew not to do them things ... The week before you were married you gave your mother your money. She'd give you back a wee bit of it.

When Flora started work in Woolworths as a counter girl she also handed her pay packet to her mother. She was very satisfied with her wages from Woolworths, even though she did not get to spend very much of it on herself:

Woolworths was reckoned as one of the best paid firms and when I was 21, I got 27/6 per week, which was big money in those days.[42] That would be about 1939 and as I say, 27/6 was a terrific wage because things were very cheap in those days.

Taking responsibility for their own spending was almost a rite of passage for young women at the time, often coinciding with leaving the family home or marriage. It was an important recognition of their maturity, although in some families it happened later than others. Betty handed up her pay to her mother for her first few years of work, but she then started to pay for her share of the housekeeping and kept the pay packet for herself:

Well, when I started work, my wages was 14 bob a week, for the whole week I got 14 bob.[43] Well, it was around that, because I went to work in 1944. I was fifteen ... We all did that and then the money would be given back to us if we needed anything. But after a few years, I started keeping the money and gave Mammy housekeeping.

An amount was decided upon that was fair for board and lodging and that would help maintain the rest of the family, but acknowledgement of the younger woman's development was made when earnings in excess of that amount were retained and independent decisions were made about how it would be spent. The daughters rather than the mothers seem to have decided on the appropriate time to change the arrangement. Handing over cash to their mothers, directly from their pay packets, underlined the nature of the family chain of command.

Nora's job as an Executive Officer in the Civil Service was 'regarded as a plum job, it was better than teaching'[44] but the status she enjoyed at work did not follow her home and her mother did not treat her any differently to other members of her family:

You were brought down to size when I went from this very important job and I came back home again. It was very good but I was expected to toe the line and do domestic work ... Well, none of the sons were working. One of them was a clerical student, both of them were students, we were keeping them more or less, with fees.

Most of the women remembered that they had to do housework in addition to handing up their wages, while their brothers were not expected to help. However, men often had specific chores such as fetching coal or doing repairs around the house that reflected the gendered division of work in the home.

As a student nurse, Olive had to live in the nurse's home attached to the hospital where she did her training. Her parents had to pay for her training but she did get paid a small monthly wage in addition to her food and lodging. The students were permanently hungry because the food was not very good and Olive was glad to have her pay supplemented by her mother and especially by her older sister, who was working and who sent her 10/- every month:

> We got paid once a month, on the last Tuesday of the month there would be a board meeting, so on the first Wednesday after the last Tuesday of every month, we would be paid. And we'd all go down to the medical office – there was a great gulf between office staff in hospitals and nurses, and we'd all meet at this office to collect our pay and the people would say here they are again, they think of nothing but money and the ones that smoked borrowed from the ones that didn't, and as soon as they got paid the people they owed money to were turning round, saying you owe me this, you owe me that.

While some of the women continued in the work they had gone into after school, getting promotion and achieving better conditions through seniority, others moved into different areas. They were not always motivated by increased pay or better conditions. Susan started her working life as a music teacher but after a couple of years she decided to train as a medical social worker because she wanted a greater challenge. She trained as a medical social worker (almoner) at London University and at the Institute of Almoners in London. She was offered a job at the Rotunda hospital[45] where she stayed between 1939 and 1943 and then she moved to the Royal Victoria hospital in Belfast in 1944.[46] Her position at the Royal Victoria was a groundbreaking one, in that she was the first person to hold such a job, and she encountered some initial difficulty in convincing the medical staff that her attitude to patients would be as professional as theirs. She overcame these obstacles very successfully but she maintained that her subsequent long career was enhanced by the fact that she did not marry, although there was no formal marriage bar in her profession.

Nora shared Susan's assessment of the benefits of remaining single for an ambitious woman. She felt that if she had married she would never have reached the senior position to which she was eventually promoted because the marriage bar in the Civil Service would have excluded her during the important years when she was building her career. Around the turn of the twentieth century it was established that 30 per cent of Irish men and 25 per cent of Irish women had never married.[47] According to the 1946 census, the marriage rate in Éire in the ten calendar years 1936 to 1946 was 5.4 per 1,000 of population; that is 159,425 marriages in a population of 2,955,107. The rate in Dublin County Borough, where Nora was living, was higher, at 7.4 marriages per 1,000 or 36,919 in a population of 506,051.[48] This rate reflected an increase in the marriage rate from the earlier census period, which was 4.6 marriages per 1,000 between 1926 and 1936. Research in other countries has shown that marriage rates generally increased in wartime[49] and the neutrality of the southern state might explain why the pattern there was different. It must be noted, however, that in the early twentieth century Ireland was a demographic anomaly in western Europe because of the combination of its low rates of marriage and high rate of births per marriage.[50] The long gap between the Northern Irish census of 1937 and that of 1951 means the generalized figures in the latter are of little use in drawing conclusions about the marriage trend there.

While pay rates were low, additional benefits were rare and few women enjoyed membership of an occupational pension scheme. Alice was involved in a savings scheme in the Ormeau Bakery, to which staff contributed instead of a pension scheme.[51] When she migrated to Canada at the end of the war, she withdrew the lump sum she had saved and gave it to her mother; in lieu of the money she would normally have given her from her wages:

> Say I allowed two shillings to be deducted from my pay every week, the firm put two shillings to it, and we got, when you would retire, a lump sum. When I left, like, after fifteen years, my lump sum was £50, you know. Well, under the circumstances in our house, I had to put that on a book for my mother to keep her until I would get work in Canada, so that's where that went. Then we got jobs and then once I got earning, I was able to send my mother money.

Nora's decision to abandon a teaching career and take up a position in the Civil Service was largely motivated by the salary and the fact that the job was pensionable. She was admitted to the Civil Service pension scheme when she joined the Department of Supplies, at the age of 19. Apart from the higher salary pertaining to the Civil Service position, the pension scheme was better, as women teachers at the time had to retire at 60. Female Civil Servants had the option of retiring at 60, but it was not compulsory.[52]

Most of the women remembered being expected to work on Saturdays, generally for half a day to lunchtime. Alice had an early start, having to be ready for work in the Ormeau Bakery at eight o'clock in the morning:

> In the Ormeau Bakery you couldn't start work any day without first having a shower and woe betide you if you didn't and you were told on, you know. You were as good as gone ... I started work at eight and I had to be in and be showered and punch the clock so that I was ready. And if you didn't punch for maybe a couple of minutes after eight there'd be a red mark on your card and if it went to five past, there'd be another one and if it went any further than that, you were called in.

Alice thought it was perfectly acceptable for the management to insist on the showers being taken before work started, even though it meant that people had to be in the bakery earlier than the time for which they were being paid.

As cleaners, both Mary and Catherine had to be in Guinness's brewery very early in the morning to get the bulk of their work done before standard working hours commenced at 8.30 a.m. Catherine found it very hard to leave her children, but she was also very nervous going out on dark winter mornings and usually one or two of the older children accompanied her for part of the way. Neither she nor Betty gave any indication that they considered it less than desirable for young children to have to walk home again in the dark on their own, which would have been the case:

> I'd be in at six. I'd leave here at half five and I'd have to walk down the Canal, walk into James's Street and round by the harbour ... I might get two flights of stairs to scrub, and all the usual, kitchens, washing and cleaning all the time, you know, whatever was there. I got home by about half nine, to see that the children got out to school, you know ... I'd have a load of work to do, maybe for them too. They might say to me, will you bring home the towels and do them, because we're short of towels ... I used to wash sheets, pillow slips and all, because there was a night-staff of number one clerks, and they used to stay, they'd be the night clerks and some of them would be sleeping there and of course, they'd beds in James's Street there.[53]

Catherine had a good relationship with her supervisor in the brewery and she explained her difficulty about the early mornings. It was decided that she could work at home, which suited her better for looking after the children, but actually involved her doing longer hours:

That's why they said to me, if there was too much for me, to go home and not have the worry of the children. That's why they gave me the chance of the washing, they said they'd put me on and you could take home the washing and do it for us. And I'd be here until three in the morning, I needn't tell you, especially when you only got such a short time to have them ready.

Although Betty remembered helping her mother with the washing, Catherine said she got no assistance from Guinness's with bringing the heavy loads to and from the brewery.[54] She had to wash the linen by hand, although she had a mangle to wring out the heaviest wetness and she had to dry the washing in front of the fire overnight. She did not get a washing machine until the 1950s, when several of her children were working and were in a position to buy one for her.

A much wider introduction of part-time working was a feature of war production in Britain and the United States, mainly because it allowed women who had families to care for to combine their domestic duties with work in the war industries. It had the advantage for employers of allowing them to operate factories and other enterprises on the basis of much longer hours, without having to pay overtime, provide childcare or otherwise increase their costs. In order to employ women on a system of shifts and overtime, the Northern Irish government had to bring in certain regulations to alter the Factory Act (Northern Ireland) 1936. To do this, they utilised Section 156 of the Factories Act (Northern Ireland) 1939 and Regulation 59 of the Defence (General) Regulations 1939 in order to exempt certain premises from the provisions of the Factory Act. In December 1942 the Ministry of Labour made the Factories (Hours of Employment of Women and Young Persons) Northern Ireland Order 1942 which applied to every factory within the meaning of section 157 of the Factories Act (Northern Ireland). This allowed for women and young people to work more than forty-eight but not more than fifty-five hours per week (maximum eleven hours per day) and there had to be a certain number of breaks in the day. Women and children were not to be employed on Sundays.

During the 1930s awareness of the poor conditions of many shop workers in the United Kingdom prompted an investigation. The Committee on the Shops Acts reported in 1938, making a range of recommendations with which to improve the working conditions of shop assistants, including the provision of seats, better heat, light and ventilation, a reduction in working hours and the introduction of paid holidays.[55] The report was shelved until 1943 when the recommendations were incorporated in a Shops Bill. In the meantime, war had brought some changes. Shop opening hours were restricted because of the blackout.[56] Women working in other areas found the new hours very difficult to fit into their other responsibilities while women who wished to open shops themselves were now constrained by increased red tape. People who were employed in shops, rather than owning them, also suffered, as Moya Woodside pointed out:

> The debacle begins! A neighbourhood fruit shop, which previously did a thriving trade, is closed down this morning. That means at least four assistants thrown out of work. Commenting on this when paying a bill in the dairy, I heard that two more fruit shops nearby were rumoured to be closing. In one still open, they had nothing to sell but two sorts of apples and vegetables. It seems a pity that this should be happening just when people of all classes were realising the importance of fruit in their daily diet. Couldn't we have more fruit imported and less tobacco? (I make this suggestion as a non-smoker.)[57]

Woodside belonged to the employing class and her references to work throughout her Mass-Observation diary were written from the point of view of an observer and analyst, rather than someone directly affected by the impact of war on women's employment. On occasion this caused her to be somewhat insensitive to the plight of people adversely affected by wartime conditions, as evidenced by her concentration on the shortage of fruit in terms of the impact on diet rather than the much more fundamental issue of jobs being lost.

The interviewees generally agreed that conditions had improved for workers, not just because pay and conditions were better but also because technological developments in the workplace made most people's work easier to do. The extent to which office work had changed, for example, is illustrated by Nora's recollection of the area where she worked in the Department of Supplies:

> From Higher Executive down we were all in the one big space. The Assistant Principal had his own room but there was no distinction that way, you were just sitting at a table and the other staff were sitting there too ... In fact, a lot of the letters that were sent out were handwritten ... I mean, the phone was hardly used at that point, very few members of the public, in fact no members of the public would have telephones and the first time most of the members of staff would have used a telephone would be actually at work. I remember one poor man he was so terrified – he was an Executive Officer too – he was so terrified of using the phone that he used to walk out when the phone

would ring so that someone else would answer it. He'd go red in the face at the thought of it.

Although the work done by most of the women was low paid and consequently tended to be of low status, they got considerable satisfaction from the skills they acquired and pride when they were promoted, as Alice remembered:

> I speak with love of the Ormeau Bakery and I never cried leaving home because we figured well, if we don't like Canada we can come back. But I cried leaving the Ormeau Bakery. I just thought what am I doing, you know? I could have gone back into it ... but I probably would have been subordinate to some of the people I had trained and that didn't appeal to me at all.

Alice continued to be in employment for another thirty years until she retired in the 1970s, but she says herself that she never enjoyed any other job as much as her work in the bakery. It is clear that the promotion she achieved and the fact that the management seemed to value her more than other workers contributed significantly to her nostalgia for the company:

> You can see I'm sitting beside a silver tea service that I got for a wedding present when I left, and you always got a gift from the works, you know they always gave. Which I did, I got a canteen of cutlery but no one up to that stage had ever got from the management, which I did, so that was really something, you know.

Alice is very conscious of the fact that she could have gone on to secondary education and maybe further if her family income had been sufficient, and the Ormeau Bakery's recognition of her talents compensated for that disappointment to some extent.

Few of the women remembered exactly what they had been paid; although they all agreed that, while their wages were low, they said the cost of living was much lower then and money had a greater value. This point came up frequently in the interviews but in fact it was not the case for the majority of the women who took part in the research, who were low paid and for whom basic necessities would have constituted a significant proportion of their weekly wages. The trade boards in Éire answered to the Minister for Industry and Commerce and changes in wage rates were only permitted under an Emergency Powers Order or a Bonus Order in extreme circumstances. The Wages Standstill Order of 1941 imposed a complete embargo on increases in some areas, despite the rise in the cost of living that resulted from shortages. There was a steady rise in the cost of living index from the pre-war level of 176 in 1938 (1914 = 100) up to 298 in 1945, as outlined in Appendix 6.[58] The index of weekly industrial earnings (based on money earnings per worker in manufacturing industries and transportable goods) rose slightly, but was very much out of line with the rise in the cost of living.[59] When the Emergency Powers Orders (under which pay had been controlled during the Emergency) were repealed in September 1946, there was a steep rise in wages and salaries and by the end of 1948 the earnings index almost exactly equalled the cost of living index.[60]

In some larger employments, social clubs were set up to allow workers to get together for shared activities outside the workplace, sometimes with the assistance of the employer. The St James's Gate Fanciers and Industrial Association[61] in the Guinness brewery was one such organization, run by members of the staff and given an annual grant by the board of directors.[62] Colette remembered it very well and usually got involved herself:

> The Fanciers was an association which was set up, and the lady staff was usually hounded by the senior ladies to come and produce things for it. It happened in July every year and the Fanciers were originally pigeon fanciers, pigeons and then dogs and they had a show and then the Fanciers and Industrial Association, that's right. The Industrial Association was for home crafts, they made jams and cakes and bread and handicrafts, sewing and knitting and embroidery, and there was a flower show, flowers and vegetables. Tremendous excitement – we all went and did our bit. They'd have very senior ladies from the Department of Education and Cathal Brugha Street[63] who would come to judge the exhibits and the Horticultural Society would judge.

The Annual Reports of the Fanciers Association suggests that the Emergency had little impact on the activities of the association, especially in regard to the annual show. The membership increased each year in the course of the war and in 1944, there was a record number of exhibits, which the report said 'considering the difficult times, was most gratifying'.[64]

Unlike Guinness's, the Ormeau Bakery did not have a sports club, but there was a table tennis table in the canteen that staff could use during their lunchtime break, as Alice recalled:

> There wasn't a sports club but we had a table tennis table in the canteen, which I was on every minute I could get, you know. And

even Mr Wilson[65] he used to watch us in his lunch hour, you know, on the table tennis table. We did have a choir, of which I was a part also, and we did enjoy that a lot and every year what they called the Trust[66] meeting, you know business was discussed and all that and the choir would perform, you know, after tea. It was a lot of fun, you know, but work came first in the Ormeau Bakery, it came first.

The table tennis table also became the centre of other activities that brought the staff together, particularly during the war years. The company management encouraged the workers to get involved in contributing to the 'war effort', even to the extent of supplying wool, which the women workers knit up into items to be sent to the troops:

> a part that was very good too because the wool used to come in, you know all this dark green wool and so many of us, you know we'd take lots of it home or we'd knit around the table tennis table. You know the table tennis had to stop because you had tea, and you know, you were eating and you were knitting because they wanted a dozen pairs of socks and so many pullovers and balaclava helmets, you know, all that and we used to bring it home too. My mother used to knit and my sister and all. I remember one weekend they needed, we were one pullover short and I brought the wool home and my sister knit the back and my mother knit the front with the vee-neck and I knit the two sleeves, in a weekend. We got it all together to get the parcel ready for the troops, so we did. There was lots of things like that.[67] There was a lot of fun during the war, as well as a lot of sorrow, because there was so many nice young fellows in the Bakery went into the services and some of them didn't come back.

Alice also thought that because it was mainly during the war that she worked in the Ormeau Bakery that this contributed to her enjoyment of her job, as a result of the extra excitement generated by the extraordinary conditions. The Ormeau Bakery supplied food for the troops and she gained a sense of importance from involvement in this work.

It seems from the limited evidence available about women workers in Northern Ireland that their entry to a narrow range of occupations was not as dramatically altered by the war as was the case in the United Kingdom, although some women did find employment in previously all-male preserves, such as engineering. Women workers in Northern Ireland were subject to the same institutionalized pay inequality as women in Éire and the war did not change this situation. Even when women did secure pay

10. Jaeger Knitting Patterns cover

rises so did men, so the gap between their respective scales remained equidistant from before the war until well after it ended. What someone remembers can be a good indicator of what has been most important to that person over time. The women whose interviews have been quoted in this chapter, regardless of social or economic background, recalled their experience of workplaces during the Second World War period much more clearly if their work was the primary criteria by which they defined themselves. Women who thought of their lives mainly in terms of their experience outside the workplace, usually as wives and mothers in the home, were much more vague about their working terms and conditions and were much less likely to have considered responses to questions about their own or society's attitude to women as workers.

4

War work in Britain

> Nobody wants a war but there were some happy days and happy times and you met lovely people and you made a lot of friends. (Alice)

One of the recurring themes of women's recollections of the Second World War in Britain and other Allied states is their recognition that they were necessary to the war effort. This was combined with the belief that the exigencies of the situation would create new opportunities for them to break out of the strictures of the domestic role usually assigned to them.[1] The suggestion that the social and economic conditions created by the war could change the status of women in society echoed similar claims made during the First World War. Despite the fact that in the inter-war years women had largely been discouraged by legal and social barriers from involvement in work outside the home, the linking of war work and liberation was used as an incentive in national recruitment campaigns in Britain to encourage women to volunteer for the armed forces or for civilian war work. It became possible for young women whose working lives had been strictly controlled by their parents or family circumstances to find new roles for themselves, with the justification of their country's necessity to support them. However, it is also essential 'to acknowledge the ranges of experience which result from differences of class, age or even temperament in order to avoid characterising women's experience as if it were homogenous'.[2]

Emigrants from Ireland seem to have moved primarily to better themselves economically, both before and during the war years, with the majority heading for employment in Britain's industrial areas.[3] The women whom I interviewed about their wartime emigrant experiences indicated that family influence was a significant element in how they usually made decisions about their lives, but in regard to their decision to leave Ireland, with one exception, they had chosen to go to England themselves. During the period 1921 to 1939, the successive governments of the Irish Free State and Éire had paid little attention to emigration,[4] but during the Second World War, both the Irish and the British governments introduced regulatory

11. Frances in her nurse's uniform, Boston Hospital, Lincolnshire, 1945

controls, which were then abandoned when the war ended. As a means of monitoring emigration, passengers to Britain from Éire were required to obtain travel permits and these were not issued to anyone who already had a job in Ireland or who had left their employment voluntarily. Restrictions were placed on persons with skills considered essential for the Irish state.

Intending emigrants had to apply for travel identity cards through the Garda Síochána. They had to supply a certificate from the Department of Social Welfare, which stated that they were exempt from emigration restrictions and their application had to be accompanied by a written offer of employment in Britain.[5] A number of regulations were introduced in the course of the summer and autumn of 1941 specifically to control the flow of emigration from Éire to Britain, including the requirement that anyone applying for a travel permit had to be over 22 years of age. The role of recruitment agents for British employers was curtailed because their overt activities had caused some public outcry and the censor was instructed to ensure that no advertisements that offered employment outside the country appeared in the national press.[6]

From 1940 to 1945, Irish workers going to Britain were classified as 'conditionally landed'.[7] This term implied that Irish workers were excluded from conscription if they returned home after two years. When the British National Service Acts were passed in June 1939, men living in Britain for longer than two years were treated as 'permanent' residents and consequently liable for conscription. Irish citizens who could prove that their residence in Britain was of a 'temporary' nature were specifically excluded from military service. In practice, Irish emigrants to Britain throughout the course of the war were regarded as 'temporary' and therefore not subject to conscription. Presumably, persons who were resident in Britain for longer than two years prior to the outbreak of the war and who did not return were willing to take their chances as regards conscription. However, any Irish citizen living in Britain who was called up for service could return home, and in 1941 an assurance was given by the British authorities that this would remain the case. Female emigration from Éire was strictly controlled and limited throughout the war years, according to the Department of External Affairs.[8]

The Westminster government maintained records relating to wartime travel to and from Northern Ireland and they did not differentiate between Northern Irish passengers and those from the southern state. It is therefore not possible to ascertain exact figures for Northern Irish women who emigrated during the war, although John Blake maintained that more than 7,500 Northern Irish women transferred to war work in mainland Britain, basing his estimates on figures obtained from the Ministry of Labour.[9] According to the briefings prepared for Blake when he was writing his history of the war, the peak year for transfer of women appears to have been 1942, when there were 2,536 work placements in Britain.[10]

As employment opportunities decreased in the South, mainly due to the rationing of raw materials for industry, greater numbers of workers, both male and female, went to Northern Ireland and Britain to take advantage of the need for personnel to service the war industries. Appendix 7 classifies the numbers of passengers migrating from Éire to Britain by sex, showing the very high proportion of residents from Dublin in the total number of travellers. Dublin County Borough had the second-highest rate of emigration (72 per 1,000) in the years 1940–43, surpassed only by Co. Mayo.[11] The large number of travellers from Dublin may have been because of easier access to transport but is also likely to have been due to the greater impact on industrial employment caused by wartime shortages of raw materials. Letty had worked in a sewing factory in Dublin since leaving school at 14 and she was one of the casualties of the shortage of raw materials:

> We were laid off, yes, there was no material coming in, you see, there was nothing coming in. Everything was stopped. You see, the people that didn't live through it, they don't know how bad it was.

She applied for unemployment benefit but the weekly payment rate was so low that she felt unable to manage on it. The labour exchange in Dublin offered her an alternative:

> I went with a couple of other girls I was working with. I think a whole lot of us, like we were only in our twenties when we went. And we said there's no sign of this war being over so we had better go and do something, you know? There was no work and you only had about 12/- a week coming off the Labour – that was the money at the time. And my goodness, sure you'd give that up to your mother so you'd no money left, like, you know? And so I decided to sign up and some others, you know the way the word goes round, and they took our names and so we were signed on.

One of the most unpleasant aspects of the emigration experience was the delousing procedure that was performed in Dublin, introduced because of unease in Britain about the spread of infectious diseases. A health embarkation scheme was reluctantly set up by the government at the Iveagh Baths in Dublin, where prospective emigrants were examined and certified before leaving for Britain.[12]

Letty and several of her friends were sent to a munitions factory in Reading.[13] They were accommodated in a hostel, which she described as being extremely comfortable, with every convenience. She was happy enough with the job she was given, even though it was quite dangerous, involving packing explosive into shells. Letty did not remember any of her fellow workers complaining, in contrast to the experience of an assistant welfare officer who was responsible for helping Irish women settle in to a factory in Aston, near Birmingham, which was the subject of a Mass-Observation investigation in July 1942:[14]

> So much of my work is smoothing the girls down when they first come. They're not told that it's heavy dirty work when they're in Ireland – it's left to me to deal with smoothing that down at this end.[15]

In *Across the Water, Irish Women's Lives in Britain*[16] there is an account by a Cork woman, Noreen Hill, of how she left her home city in 1945 because she could not get work. She was recruited for British war work in Leicester through the local labour exchange and she recalled the regulations governing her work permit:

> We were able to move freely, but when you changed your address you had to report to the police. You were alien, because our country was

> neutral and we were under suspicion actually, we were aliens in a country that was at war with Germany. In the police station there was two sides – Alien Visitors, Residents. So we had to go in the Alien door. And if you changed your job or changed your address you had to report to the police straight away.[17]

Frances moved several times in the course of the war but she had almost forgotten about the registration requirements until she was asked about them:

> I think it was every six weeks, with my identity card, and if you moved out of the area you had to go and tell them. I forgot that part ... I think she must have taken me over to the British embassy, I think it was in Merrion Square, she took me over there but there was no passport. I have my birth certificate somewhere and on the back it has an oval stamp, 1 September 1941 and that was the entry thing to cover me.

Frances was in England because her mother had decided that her daughter was very badly behaved and needed discipline:

> and the reason that I went so meek and mildly was that you did what you were told by parents in those days and in a way, because my mother and I, we didn't really get on, because as I say, I was a bit cheeky growing up, mouthy, in a way I was glad to get away from her.

Frances' mother answered an advertisement in one of the Catholic newspapers[18] looking for domestic help and she arranged to send Frances to Birmingham to work in a convent school, despite her young age. She had not expected to be staying in school but had never thought of leaving Dublin until her mother sent her away:

> I was 15 on the 1st August and I came to England on the 1st September and I didn't even have to have a passport, because I wasn't 16. My birth certificate was stamped at the emigration entry at Holyhead.

In an extract from a Department of External Affairs memorandum written in 1944, it was noted that there was 'deep public uneasiness at the number of young girls in the late teens and early twenties who are being allowed to leave the country'.[19] The same memorandum noted that the rate of emigration was heavier in women aged less than 22 years of age than over it:

> We have had cases of Irish girls being sent back to this country by the British police on the ground that they were too young and immature to be away from home! The taking of employment in Britain by young girls of 18 and 19 may be justifiable on other grounds, but it is certainly not good for the girls themselves and, in many cases, it is very humiliating for the country.[20]

The only money Frances had with her was five shillings that her father had given her and which he told her much later in life he had obtained by breaking open the gas meter in the family home. Sending young girls off by themselves was not an unusual practice and was not confined to girls from Éire, according to the account of an Independent Unionist member of the Stormont parliament:

> If I would tell you some of the heart-rending tales I have of the plight of these girls in Liverpool and Manchester it would make even cabinet ministers blush with shame, and that is no mean feat because Stormont cabinet ministers have skins as tough as alligators. Once you get them on board the Liverpool boat you don't care what happens to them ... from all parts of Belfast. Some of them had to be befriended by Belfast men working in Liverpool. They were sent across the water without a farthing in their pockets, no different from cattle.[21]

Frances' mother had arranged for a cousin to meet her at the train station in Birmingham and bring her to the convent but the plan went awry:

> I hadn't seen him for years and we missed each other. I was stood there for the longest time and eventually came out. It was wartime, there was a blackout and I asked people how to get to St Bernard's Road and I had to get a bus to Acocks Green[22] in the dark, with my gas mask and the big case and a Ministry of Works label on my coat. I eventually got to St Bernard's Road and I walked up this long, dark road and I came to a police station. I went into the police station and asked them where the convent was. There was a policeman behind the desk and there was another gentleman outside the desk. I don't know to this day if he was a policeman but he said I'm going that way, I'll give her a lift. I was delighted to get rid of the load of the case. He was a decent man. He took me up to the convent gate which

was about five minutes away and he said don't ring the bell until I'm gone and I did ring the bell. This was half past ten at night and I'd left Dublin that morning at half six.

Frances' mother's failure to ensure that her young daughter would be safe in another country, especially one in a state of war, was consistent with the attitude of the Irish government to the welfare of female emigrants. Despite the repeatedly expressed alarm concerning the moral dangers for female emigrants, the Catholic Social Welfare Bureau was given no state aid or municipal grant by the Irish government to support their work in Britain.[23]

Kathleen was living in Portstewart[24] when she first met her husband. He was in the British army and was based in a camp near the town. They met in a WVS[25] canteen and were married at the end of January 1941. Her sister also met her husband at the same canteen. Kathleen and her husband could only have a weekend for their honeymoon because he could not get a longer pass. Shortly afterwards, he was told he was being posted back to England to train for going to Europe, and he asked Kathleen to move over there and to stay with his family in Berkshire. She went to live in the village of Cookham[26] with her parents-in-law and her sister-in-law. Kathleen's father-in-law had recently retired from the police force. When the war started, he had become a night watchman at a nearby factory where secret war work was going on:

> He was on nights, which was a great strain for my mother-in-law because of the dog barking and the least little thing that woke him up during the day. So we all had to, we were all under a bit of a strain trying to keep quiet. At weekends, he used to go in so we were able to let go a bit at the weekend. We used to do the housework when he went. He was a lovely man but he just had to sleep.

Kathleen and her mother-in-law shared the household chores. They got most of their vegetables from their vegetable garden, which was cultivated by her father-in-law. He supplemented their meat allowance with rabbits that he hunted and caught himself.

When Kathleen registered for work with the Ministry of Labour she was given the choice of working as a bus conductor or going into a factory, neither of which appealed to her very much. Both Mass-Observation and the Wartime Social Survey showed that potential recruits from 'respectable' backgrounds were often put off working in factories because of the conviction that factory girls were low class, rough, dirty and immoral.[27] Kathleen felt fortunate that her father-in-law knew somebody in Maidenhead[28] where a small light industry had been set up and she was given a job there:

> It was attached to a very, sort of high-class jewellers. Queen Mary used to come down and shop there, the old Queen Mary. So they set up a small light industry. It was doing meters for aircraft ... They were very nice there. What they did, they did it to keep their staff, more or less, because they had very skilled people. It was mainly I think to keep the staff, the men, so that the men who were older didn't have to go to war.

During the First World War, the British government had exerted draconian control over the labour force, leading to considerable resentment and unrest. In the Second World War, the Labour Party in Britain joined the National Coalition government led by Winston Churchill in May 1940. The Minister for Labour and National Service was Ernest Bevin, leader of the Transport and General Workers' Union, the largest union in Britain. He established a joint consultative committee of seven employers' representatives and seven trade unionists to advise the government on the conduct of the war effort on the home front. Strikes and lockouts were banned under the Emergency Powers Act 1939 and the 1941 Essential Work (General Provisions) Order allowed for the dilution of labour and the deployment of skilled workers to wherever they were most needed.[29] Despite the powers available to the government to prosecute strikers, industrial action increased steadily throughout the war years. The situation was different to that of the First World War, not least because the government made much greater efforts to spread the burden of sacrifice than had been the case between 1914 and 1918 and several measures of social reform were delivered. However, there was resentment of the impact of conscripted workers on skilled trades, including the deployment of women.[30] The women were known as 'dilutees', just as they had been in the First World War, and this reinforced their secondary status, not least in the matter of their low pay relative to their male fellow workers.[31]

Kathleen's job was to check the setting of altimeters at the end of the manufacturing process. She inspected them and made sure that they were balanced correctly. It was quite a responsible job because the next stage was installation of the altimeter in the aircraft. The planes were outfitted at a small airfield close to Maidenhead, which she remembered as the Ferries Field. Amy Johnson[32] had flown from the airfield while serving in the Air Transport Auxiliary. In the early days of the war, female pilots were allowed only to ferry planes from the factory to airstrips and there was even hostility to this 'concession', regardless of the women's experience. However, as the war continued more women were permitted to fly further because male pilots were needed for combat duties. It was while she was flying such a delivery run that Amy Johnson was forced to bail out over the Thames estuary, where she was drowned.

Nursing was a much more acceptable profession for women to enter, combining as it did the traditionally 'female' skills of caring and nurturing. Entry to nursing training in Ireland had to be paid for by the applicants or their families, and this forced many women from both parts of Ireland to go to Britain for training. There was a shortage of trainee nurses in Britain from the late 1930s onwards and young Irish women were welcomed.[33] Nancy's parents had sent her to a secretarial college when she finished her secondary education, but she did not want to pursue a career in administration:

> Well, my mother was absolutely appalled when I went home and said that I wasn't going back, nobody had ever said anything like that in our house before, and she said well I'll have to speak to your father. You'd think my father was somewhere else, the way she said it, but she came good; she came back when she had had the discussion with my father. She came back and she said he said you can go and do the nursing and you can go to England, if you want, which I thought was very good of her ... My mother didn't say I couldn't do it but she was so flabbergasted that I think her way out for the time being was to say, well I'll have to talk to your father.

Nancy's mother wanted her to train in a Catholic hospital and so she applied to several in London. After waiting some weeks, the only response she had received was a suggestion that she wait until the war was over. The head of her secretarial college suggested that Nancy should apply to the Selly Oak hospital in Birmingham, and in the summer of 1943 she was accepted there as a student nurse and she took the mail boat to Holyhead:

> We had to wear our life jackets all the way over because of the possibility of being bombed from underneath,[34] and then by train.

Meta was already in England when the war started. She had travelled to Liverpool in 1937 to help her older sister, who had recently given birth. While visiting her sister in hospital, she met some student nurses and became interested in their work. She was quite frank about her reasons:

> I said to her you know I think I might do nursing. I said at least I will have my food and lodgings and I will be looked after that way and I will be working with a nice sort of person. You see, we were conscious of the sort of people we mixed with.

Meta's concern about the social background of her colleagues was not exceptional, either among the interviewees or in general. 'Niceness' was a desirable quality, frequently alluded to in women's magazines, and seems to have had little to do with income or class and was frequently linked with 'respectability'.

By the time Meta qualified as a nurse the war had started, but she decided to remain in England and took her training in midwifery, which would enable her to do more specialized nursing and increase her employment prospects. She was planning to get married and she found that restricted the range of opportunities that would be open to her:

> Then I went to stay with my sister at Parbold[35] and applied for all sorts of jobs, but because I was going to get married I wanted a staff nurse's post. No one would employ a nurse getting married, and marrying a soldier. They thought, you see, that you'd always be wanting leave and I think in those times, I think when soldiers were given leave they were expected to let the wife have that time off. And someone suggested to me to try the Civil Nursing Reserve and that's what I did. I applied to the Civil Nursing Reserve with Lancashire County Council and their headquarters were in Preston.

Following an interview with the chief medical officer[36] Meta was given a choice of two posts: running a first aid post in Manchester or a sick bay for evacuated children in Blackpool. She chose the latter because the thought of working in Manchester 'with the bombs falling around you' was not very appealing.

When Olive completed her nursing training in Dublin, she got engaged to be married, but because of the couple's financial position, they could not afford to buy a home and they decided to wait for a year or two before the wedding. If she had got married straight away, because of the marriage bar on public hospital nurses at the time, the only work available to her would have been to go in to private nursing,[37] which did not appeal to her. She decided to go to England where she could get further specialist training:

> I went off to England to an RAF hospital to do plastic surgery, down in Sussex, and I had a great time there for a year and a half. They had

all these RAF pilots who'd been terribly badly burned and wonderful plastic surgery.[38] At that time, there was no plastic surgery in Ireland ... it was a very exciting place after the parochialism of the Irish hospital ... But I was terrified going there. I went on my own. I was supposed to go with a friend and she discovered she couldn't leave her boyfriend so I had to sally off to the unknown over there.

Olive remembered that the *Nursing Times* then was 'thick with jobs vacant' and Irish nurses had a wide choice of opportunities because of the wartime pressure on the British hospital services.[39] She was nervous going away but soon discovered that the training she had been given in the Irish hospital was more than adequate for the demands of her new job and this boosted her self confidence.

The hospital had originally been a cottage hospital before the war but after the Battle of Britain there was so much need for a specialist burns unit that it was expanded on a very large scale. A New Zealander, Sir Archibold McIndoe, ran the hospital[40] but the American and the Canadian governments had also contributed new wards and this further emphasized the cosmopolitan nature of the operation. Olive was chastened by the numbers of men who were still in need of the major surgical treatment that was being developed in the hospital, even as late as 1946 and 1947:

> Most of them had twenty or thirty operations by the time they got there, because they were in the Battle of Britain, which was 1940, I suppose, and they were still coming back and you know, a lot of them, their faces were burnt and they had remade their faces and they were coming back to get grafts over years and years. I still look at the Cenotaph every year and I see the Guinea Pigs[41] marching by, and these were the men who were not much older than me and were in this place and were being treated and needed plastic surgery.

The Ministry of Labour advertised for women to move to Britain during the war to take up the many job opportunities. Despite Éire's neutrality, there seems to have been widespread facilitation of the recruitment drive. Posters were put up in the local labour exchanges advertising work in England but also urging Irish women to enlist in the British forces.[42] Being Irish does not seem to have been a problem and none of the women remembered any resentment of Éire's neutrality. Nancy remembered that some Irish women in the hospital where she worked felt discriminated against but she thought they were being unreasonable:

> Well, you see, people could make trouble for themselves by trying to be Irish, in a sense. For instance, we couldn't go to Mass every Sunday so that what happened was Sunday morning you got to go to Mass once in three weeks, when you were junior, every three weeks because one Sunday morning off, one Sunday afternoon off and one Sunday evening off. We had to take it in turns because somebody had to be in the hospital. But they felt that they should go to Mass every Sunday. They'd go to the Matron ... they would make trouble for themselves by feeling that they were against the Irish, which was not true.

The employment situation in Britain was certainly better than that in Éire or even Northern Ireland, largely due to the extra opportunities created by the demands of the war. Pay and conditions depended very much on the job that was being done although even so-called 'traditional' women's jobs, like domestic service, were generally better paid in England, so much so that the emigration rate during the war resulted in a shortage of domestic workers in Ireland.[43] Appendix 8 gives a general comparison between the wage rates and cost of living in Ireland and Britain between 1939 and 1945. The figures from the Westminster Ministry of Labour included the wage rates and cost of living index for Northern Ireland.[44]

By any standards, the job in domestic service that Frances was sent to do in the convent boarding school was very tough and the accommodation provided by the nuns who ran the school was primitive, although she believed that the food was much better than she had been getting at home and that this compensated for the other conditions:

> We worked very hard at the school, there were no dishwashers then and everything was done by hand but again, I was a bit cheeky and I used to fall out with the nuns ... I'd be put down in the laundry to stand up on a stool with these big massive tubs with these big paddles to stir the clothes. There were long corridors to scrub – no wonder I've arthritis in my knees. Mass every morning and polish the church and one thing and another. They had a Montessori school there and that had to be polished and when the girls went on holidays we used to clean all the paintwork and the curtains in the dormitories. But the food was very good and there was no shortage because the nuns cooked all their own food ... So we were quite safe there. There were three of us girls who lived in the convent. We were up in the attic. There was no electricity and we had candles for light.

One of the girls with whom Frances shared the attic was 16, a year older than Frances, and they spent their weekly one half day off together. On one such day they went to the cinema at Acocks Green, which was near the school, and got into trouble with the nuns when they returned at six o'clock because one of the teachers had seen them at the cinema and the nuns were angry with them, although they had not been forbidden to go. Apparently the problem was that the cinema was full of 'soldiers and sailors and foreign people'. During the war, there was a considerable increase in public comment and denunciation of the romantic escapades of women and girls, intensifying both official and unofficial scrutiny of their behaviour.[45] The growing presence of American soldiers on British soil clearly stimulated the commentary.

Frances and her friends were not allowed to go to the cinema again, even though there was very little else for them to do when they were not working:

> You knitted or sewed and there was no radio, no television, nothing. You didn't read or anything, just talked to each other. You could read *The Universe* and just talk to each other. Things like that. Then we went to bed at eight and we were up at half past six in the morning.

She was often locked in the air raid shelter for the night as punishment for what was perceived by the nuns as misbehaviour, including talking too loudly at night and being reported by the nun who occupied the bedroom beside them.

Frances was paid ten shillings a week, from which her mother had stipulated that she wanted five shillings. Frances did not think she was badly paid because her father was only earning three pounds ten shillings a week in Dublin, working as a barman. It never occurred to her not to send the money to her mother. She did not resent having been sent to a strange city at a time of war, even though the nuns were very strict:

> And then when I used to come home on holiday, I came home on holiday the first time and I was just inside the door when I got a slap on the side of my face from her. How dare you misbehave in front of the nun and have her write to complain to me? I made a show of her. And she didn't even know them, really, this kind of thing. I also was wearing a pair of trousers, slacks, and my father said: get those trousers off. He said only low, bad women wore trousers, but it was from an economical point of view because we'd clothing rationing and clothing coupons and sweet coupons and that.

Frances' father's attitude to women wearing trousers was not peculiar to Éire, as a story from the *Belfast Telegraph* in March 1942 illustrates:

> Belfast Girl in 'Slacks' fined. Question to Sailor.
>
> Josephine Lavery, Amelia St., a young woman wearing blue 'slacks' was at Belfast Custody Court today, fined 20s and bound over for 12 months imprisonment, for disorderly conduct last night in York St.
>
> Special-Constable Ferguson said he overheard the woman asking her sailor companion about a new type of engine, and thought the sailor might be giving away information. He asked the woman for her identity card, and she became abusive and alleged she had half-killed a policeman before.
>
> Mr. W.F. McCoy, K.C., R.M., said the police had more to do than be troubled by women like the accused.[46]

While the reporter's disapproval of the young woman is obvious, it is not clear how much it was a reaction to her wearing trousers to court or to the disorderly behaviour that brought her there in the first place. There was a strain of concern about the moral welfare of young Irish women in England that was the focus of many newspaper articles during the 1930s in particular that was carried on for some decades. Louise Ryan suggests that this was because of the 'extraordinarily high incidence of young women emigrants'[47] and she supported her argument with an in-depth study of Irish newspapers, particularly the *Irish Independent*, where there were regular contributions about the dangers posed by a non-Catholic environment to naive young emigrants: 'Their freed sexuality represented a threat not just to their own health and well-being (pregnancy, disease, poverty) but also to their souls (loss of religion) and to their national identity (de-nationalisation).'[48]

With the increase in emigration during the 1930s, pastoral and newspaper interest in the 'moral welfare' of emigrants, particularly young women, had begun to exercise the interest of the Catholic Church, in Ireland and Britain. The crux of the matter was where the ultimate responsibility lay for the welfare of young Irish female emigrants in Britain. So far as the state was concerned, this was a matter for the Irish and British clergy. In any event, the outbreak of war in 1939 and the introduction of travel restrictions ensured that the Irish authorities could regulate the flow and therefore these problems seemed less urgent. The broader significance of the representations made by Catholic clergy on both sides of the Irish Sea is that the Irish state was forced to formulate a policy on the welfare of Irish citizens in Britain which resulted in the Irish state abrogating all responsibility for the problems that Irish citizens faced and relying on the voluntary efforts of Catholic clerics.[49] The Church of Ireland and other Protestant denominations do not seem to have had the same concerns about the moral welfare of emigrating female parishioners as that exhibited by Catholic clerics, although Protestant welfare organizations in Britain raised concerns about the numbers of unmarried and pregnant Irish women who were coming to them for help.[50]

After a year at the convent school, Frances was sent away by the nuns. Locking her in the air raid shelter in the basement and writing to her mother had not stopped her getting into trouble and they found a 'suitable' job for her:

> They got me another job at Grantham[51] with a Catholic family ... I was house parlour maid there and the cook was Irish. They were evacuated from London – they were quite posh people, they had butlers and cooks and maids and all in London. They lived in Onslow Square in London and they were evacuated to Grantham during the war ... The nurse came and lived in for a couple of months, I think and then the nanny came and lived in. Quite a big household they had.

The family's lifestyle does not seem to have been affected by the war. They had found Irish replacements for their absent domestic staff because they would not be subject to conscription. The house was large and Frances' accommodation was very pleasant. She was also being paid twice the amount she had earned in the convent. Because the house had large grounds, the family's gardener was able to keep them almost self-sufficient for food. The housekeeper, who administered the coupons, kept the staff's ration books. This system, which operated in institutions as well as large households, seemed to work better than getting individual or family rations, particularly when it was possible to supplement them with fresh garden produce.

Although Olive had gone to England straight from her nurse's training in Dublin, where she thought the hospital had fed the students very badly, she found the situation in England to be even worse. She was not very impressed by some of the measures taken to feed the staff:

> The rationing was frightful and I remember the first week I was there, we had one egg a week and my egg was bad. Oh, they said, hard luck and the next week my egg was bad again and I realised that everybody's egg tasted like that, they were so stale, and after a while I was eating the bad eggs ... We used to eat whale meat, which was

dreadful. Another thing was rook pie, which was a bag of black bones in a sort of gravy, and I suppose they were out shooting pigeons.

Letty was very impressed by the meals that she and her co-workers were given in the munitions factory hostel which were simple but better than the food she had eaten at home, in her opinion. She was convinced that the rationing in Dublin was much more severe than that in England. Letty's family were not poor by contemporary standards, but their finances were sufficiently precarious to be badly affected when she lost her job. It is likely that they were not eating as well as they had done before the war, as a result of restricted income rather than rationing, since the food rations in England were much smaller than they were in Éire at any time during the war years. Letty also thought that munitions workers might have been given better food than anyone else because their work was so vital but I have found no evidence to support this suggestion.

The assistant welfare officer referred to in the Mass-Observation investigation[52] believed that very few of the Irish women who came to England did so because they wanted to assist in the war effort, although she did not hold it against them. She thought they were good workers and she was constantly frustrated by the failure of the Ministry of Labour to spell out the conditions that the women would be working in before they left Ireland. She was also bothered by the refusal of the wages department in the factory where she was based to explain exactly how each woman's wage was arrived at and spent a lot of time dealing with grumbles from the women because their pay varied from week to week, because they were paid by piece rates. In the factory, women made up 25 per cent of the workforce, compared to 15 per cent before the war. The single largest group of women came from Ireland:

> I'm afraid very few of them (Irish girls) are here to do 'war work'. It's the money that brings them over – they're eager to earn as much as they can. That's why most of the Irish girls work pretty well on the whole. There's very little evidence of their having the right spirit towards the work.[53]

Letty was particularly pleased that the wage she was earning was sufficient for her to have a good time in England and still have enough to send money home to her mother every week. The factory where she had been working in Dublin got a big contract for army uniforms, some months after she had left for England, and she could have gone home but she was happier staying where she was at that point.

Queuing for goods in the shops seemed to be an integral part of the rationing system, and for women who were working outside the home it could make significant inroads into their spare time. Kathleen described the way news of a scarce or prized product would be circulated:

> Of course, we had to queue up for everything, for different things, you know. In your lunch hour, if you heard somebody had some bananas or something you just gave up your lunch hour and queued to get the few bananas, or nylons, or whatever. If you wanted makeup and you heard Boots[54] had something in, you just had to queue up to get it ... Someone would say they saw something and they would say it to somebody else and so on that something was going.

This occasionally led to the development of an informal barter system whereby a family that did not use much sugar might swap their ration for something else. Kathleen's mother used to send food parcels to her because a wider range was available in Northern Ireland. Other women also remembered their mothers doing this while Letty reversed the process, especially when she could get hold of tea for her mother, who found the ration available in Dublin too small for her needs. Letty's mother sent more than just tea and on one occasion she got in trouble because of it. She had sent Letty a small parcel containing elastic, which was very scarce in England. The parcel fell foul of the customs officers who wrote to her requesting her presence at their offices:

> They wouldn't open the parcel and she had to come down and open it and whatever. They knew what was in it but she had to open it and declare it. In front of all the men and she had to tell them what it was for – the girl's knickers had no elastic. There was no elastic over there and they could get it here, you know ... The letters would be opened, and parcels, like that. I'll always remember the elastic, the way she was sent for and she was saying, what do they want me for, you know?

All of the women who were interviewed believed that they had been better paid by going to England than they would have been if they had stayed in Ireland, even if pay was not their primary reason for going. Kathleen got an allowance from the army while her husband was away and she saved that and lived on her own pay. The factory where she worked provided a subsidized canteen for the employees so that she had a very good meal there during the day and if the staff had to work late, the canteen stayed open for them. Towards the end of the war, there was no call for the aircraft equipment being made in the factory where Kathleen worked and the contract ended:

> The contract was finished then but I was still eligible to go to work and they were going to put me on the buses as a conductor, but anyway, I said no to that and then they put me up to Slough[55] which was the nearest town, it's a very industrial area. So that was working with – I presume it was things to do with aircraft but they never really said.

Kathleen did not have children so she had not been particularly interested in childcare arrangements but so far as she could remember there had not been a crèche in the Slough factory or the factory in Maidenhead. She thought that women with children had left them with family members or had worked part-time shifts that coincided with the children's school hours. At a conference of the Standing Joint Committee of Working Women's Organisations on the provision of nurseries in wartime, held on 14 February 1942, a resolution was passed declaring that the care and supervision of the children of employed mothers was a national responsibility and protesting against a Ministry of Health circular that had been sent to local authorities in the previous December, suggesting that most of the children must be cared for by means of private arrangements made by the mothers. The conference described the suggestion as an 'attempt to evade promises previously made by the Government that the children of mothers volunteering for war work would be properly looked after'.[56]

Nancy was paid from the beginning of her nursing training, as well as getting full board and lodging:

> Well, it would be more or less pocket money because you see, we had three meals a day, we had full board and lodging. You know bedding, the whole lot, plus our education, plus everything else. I think it was about £3 something a month that I got, when I first started, which would have been a lot, especially in comparison that I didn't have anything to buy. Clothes or stockings, whatever you went over with, would have lasted you at least a year before you would be replacing things so that really your stockings and your pens and your pencils and your books – you did have to buy your books, textbooks and things.

Nancy thought her conditions were particularly good because the City of Birmingham funded the hospital at Sellyoak where she was doing her

COUNTY OF HOLLAND JOINT HOSPITAL BOARD.

E. J. CASE
CLERK

TEL: 2561   A/B.

Municipal Buildings,
Boston,
Lincs.

10th May 1947.

Dear Nurse Flynn,

At a recent meeting of the Board reference was made to the difficult period through which the hospital had passed due to the shortage of nursing and domestic staff.

The members realise that this placed additional responsibilities and demands upon certain of the small staff remaining at the hospital. To mark their appreciation of the extra services you rendered during the year ended 31st March last, I am directed to send you the enclosed cheque for £5.

Yours faithfully,

E. J. Case

Clerk.

Miss C. Flynn,
Isolation Hospital,
Boston.

12. This letter was not sent until 1947, when Frances had been dealing with her 'additional responsibilities' for nearly two years.

training and nurses who were training in voluntary hospitals would not have been as well off:

> But when the Rushcliffe rate of salaries came in, because some of the nurses were getting very little, they brought it up to, actually not quite what we were getting at that time, but because we were all getting the higher rate, we continued on it. Whereas those coming in after me, in fact about three months later, they were getting according to the Rushcliffe scale.

The Rushcliffe Committee on the Pay of Nurses (for England and Wales) undertook a major review of salaries and conditions in 1940 and 1941, following representations from a variety of organizations concerned about the huge discrepancies in pay rates for nursing staff in different areas of the health service, particularly between public and private institutions. It was chaired by Lord Rushcliffe[57] and comprised of representatives from a wide range of organizations[58] involved in healthcare and local government.

Frances was happy in her work for the family in Grantham, but when she was 17 she decided that she would give up domestic work:

> I applied to Grantham Hospital, which was on the Great North Road, opposite Mrs Thatcher's shop. I used to see Margaret Thatcher when she was a young girl, the same age as myself standing at the door with her two blond plaits ... I stayed there for – it must have been nearly a year ... At that time, because the war was on, they allowed you to enter at seventeen and a half without a good education, unlike now.

Although she had not been consulted about it, Frances' mother was delighted with the idea of Frances becoming a nurse. She thought of buying a large house in Dublin that she would set up as a nursing home, with Frances acting as a midwife. Unfortunately, Frances' career in nursing was short-lived:

> I failed the theory part of my exams – I was all right in the practical but I wasn't very good at remembering the theory ... That was terrible because I wasn't one for studying and we had a horrible sister tutor who didn't like me ... She was a little woman like Queen Victoria, and she had the white cap on tied under her chin and she made me write 'I will not be rude to Sister Tutor' one hundred times ... But I carried on then and if you wanted to register you could automatically register as an SEN[59] if you had taken the exam but our

wages were only six pounds ten shillings a month and it was three guineas to register, so you never registered. But I always got by being an auxiliary and that, but it's the piece of paper that counts that says you're qualified, no matter how much knowledge you've learned, that doesn't count. But I was a good practice nurse in my own way.

Even though she had not qualified as an SRN, Frances got a job in the fever hospital in Boston[60] where she was working during the polio epidemic that hit Britain in 1945.[61] During the polio epidemic, Frances said that the hospital was so short of staff that she was giving injections and other advanced forms of treatment, even though she had failed her first year nursing examinations.

Frances remembered that it was standard practice for the nurses to be locked into the nurses' hostel at night, regardless of the danger from fire or other emergencies. On the night the war ended, the nurses climbed out of the windows and over the hospital railings so that they could join the celebrations in the town:

> There was a camp at the back and we heard the soldiers all coming back shouting the war is over, the war is over, so we all came down, over the railings and down the town at two o'clock in the morning. There was a huge big bonfire going, it was the best night of my life.

Staff shortages during the war could create promotion opportunities, as well as additional responsibility. Six weeks after Meta started work at the evacuation centre, Dr Gawne called for her in the middle of the night from the County Hall to deal with a staffing problem:

> So I hastily got dressed and went down there and anyway, to cut a long story short, there had been an episode there with the matron and another older assistant nurse. I didn't know anything about the sort of relations, in my education there had been no mention of lesbians or such things, and of course, they left right away. So he said that anyway, she was leaving and he would like me temporarily to take charge. Well, I said I'm only just qualified and all that kind of thing and he said I will send someone out from the accounts department in County Hall to show you about the petty cash. Because it was a huge big house out in the country and with its own vegetable garden and all that, there was a cook came every day from Preston, there were three women from the village who were cleaners and did general work about the house and I had to pay them every week.

The evacuation centre dealt with children from poorer homes because, as Meta pointed out, the more affluent ones were evacuated privately and some were even sent to America. Many of the children had impetigo and scabies[62] and aneuresis[63] for which they were given treatment in the evenings. The aneuresis meant that someone had to be up during the night to take the children to the bathroom so the staff tended to work long hours, although they had a break if the children were attending classes. None of the children were under 5 and they could be aged up to 12 or 13. Parents could have access to their children if they were able to visit the area but, more often than not, the children had been evacuated on their own:

> But I often think now of all those little children marched down to the railway station with just a label on them and it must have been terrible for the mothers to part with them, not knowing where they were going to.

More than three million people were evacuated from British cities in the first four days of September 1939, most of them schoolchildren separated from their parents.[64]

Meta had met Godfrey, her husband to be, while she was training in Liverpool and he was called up for the army when the war started. He was in the Royal Engineers and was moved around quite a bit in the early years of the war. This had implications for their plans to get married because at least one of them had to have a permanent address. They decided to use Meta's address at the evacuation centre and were married in the Methodist church at Kirkham, which was the nearest town. Meta bought her wedding dress in Liverpool. It cost three guineas, which was more than her week's wages at the time, and she needed extra coupons which she got from her sister to enable her to purchase it.

Godfrey eventually ended up as an instructor at the army radio school at Petersham, which is outside Richmond, between Kingston and Petersham.[65] By this time their son David had been born, Meta had given up her job at the evacuation centre so she decided to move to Richmond to be with her husband:

> This was 1943 or 44 and anyway, I got a letter from the War Office or somebody saying you are very valuable as a trained nurse. Would you come back and do nursing in a hospital and you could relieve a single state registered nurse to go in the army, for a military hospital ... David went to a day nursery – he got priority in a day nursery ... Now those day nurseries were very well run in those days. It was an SRN who was in charge of it and David was quite happy there.

Meta was very pleased to be back at work. She was assigned to the casualty and outpatients' department because she was tied to the nursery hours, which were from half past eight to five. Although she had no previous experience of casualty, other than her nursing training, she found the challenge very stimulating, including the responsibility of overseeing the student nurses who were working in the department with her:

> We covered a very, very large area and the clinics were very busy ... There was one incident at Kew where one of those doodlebugs was a direct hit on Chrysler's car factory[66] and there were a lot of casualties in there. That was a dreadful episode.

When something happened to prevent Meta leaving the hospital at her usual time, her husband was able to collect David from the nursery. She also had an arrangement with the nursery that the local ambulance service would occasionally collect him and leave him at the hospital, where she put him in a cubicle to keep himself amused. All of the staff kept an eye on him and the matron and senior staff called in to talk to David when they were doing their rounds. Clearly they felt that it was more important to free Meta to do her work than to be very rigid about hospital rules.

Frances fell foul of the matron in Grantham hospital because of a friendship with a soldier who was one of the patients there:

> I went out to the pictures with one, he was married, a nice man, and I was told off about that. Someone saw me, the sister tutor saw me, she was Irish as well, she saw me and I was hauled over the coals for that; matron called me, because he was married. And we only went to the pictures; he never even gave me a kiss; he gave me some of his chocolate ration. Ever such a nice man he was, but that was wrong, you couldn't do that. It was very moralistic, in some ways. But you were told off and you accepted it and that was the end of it.

The rebuke seems to have been because the man was married, rather than because there were any strictures against socializing between the nurses and the patients, although Frances was reprimanded again because of another incident with a patient who also happened to be a soldier:

> I was in the ward and my suspender broke. We had suspenders then and my stockings fell down and one of the soldiers chased me round the beds ... and my hat, my veil came off and who came back into the ward only the sister. And there was uproar. I was taken to the matron's office and tore off a strip and moved to the women's ward.

In Sonya Rose's analysis of public concern about female morality, she describes how the term 'moral laxity' was repeated over and over again in letters, editorials and official documents.[67] It was a phrase that suggested weakness and a lack of will and women and young girls who were perceived to be straying from convention and overtly seeking entertainment and pleasure were given the ironic label of 'good-time girls'.

Moral outrage was accompanied by fears about the rising rates of venereal disease. There was sufficient concern about the matter for the Westminster government to set up a parliamentary committee to investigate the 'amenities and welfare conditions in the three women's services', under the chairmanship of a lawyer, Violet Markham.[68] The committee showed that the incidence of illegitimate births and venereal disease in the women's services was less than in the comparable civilian population – in some cases half the level. The committee also said that pregnancy figures were no guide to promiscuity, owing to the fact that condoms were issued to servicemen but, significantly, not to service women.

There had been several bombing raids on villages near where Kathleen was living, which she thought might have happened because of the proximity of the airfield, but the family agreed that there was not much they could do about them and they should just get on with their lives. Kathleen's husband did not get much leave from the British army but when he did they tried to behave as normally as possible. They would get a train to London and see whatever show was on, ignoring bombing raids if they occurred, because they felt they 'just had to get on with things':

> We used to go to Lyons Corner House; that was always open.[69] You might get a pastry there but we were very strictly rationed. It made shopping easier in a way, like for Christmas, because there just wasn't anything to buy. It levelled everybody.

Kathleen and her sister exchanged regular letters with their mother in Northern Ireland but few people had private telephones so keeping up with home news was not always easy and they were unable to persuade their mother to travel to England because of her fear of U-boat attacks. Nancy remembered that the only time she had difficulty getting home to Dublin for her holidays was in May 1944, when preparations were being made for the D-Day landings, although she did not know that at the time:

> There was a ban on all travel between Ireland and England in 1944, just before D-Day, but our hospital had a rule that if you started on the 1st June you had your holiday in May and you came back on the

> 1st June so that ... it was just that particular time there was a ban. But they made provision for me because there was a place up in Shropshire for nurses who couldn't go home – it was for convalescent nurses who were sick. There was one Irish girl and she had her tonsils out and she was going up and I went with her. I paid for myself but they made arrangements for me to go to this farm in Shropshire so I had a holiday. It was like being in another world it was so quiet.

The ban on travel from Britain was imposed in March 1944. Before that date, Irish workers in Britain had been entitled to one visit home every six months, subject to the various travel restrictions and the agreement of their employer in Britain.[70] The Irish government responded by suspending the labour exchange facilities for recruitment of war workers in Britain.

Olive remembered the great enjoyment she got from the opportunity to meet people from different countries. In the hospital where she was working, a lot of people came to get the sort of training in innovative procedures that had attracted her, including a large group from Australia and New Zealand:

> I loved seeing the interaction between the English and the New Zealanders and the Australians. They called them colonials. Now they were grand to me and only once did somebody say something to me about us being neutral during the war and I said well I wasn't old enough, you know, but it was an RAF hospital and of course there were Irish fellows in the RAF.

Olive was fascinated by the fact that the 'colonials' did not have a vote in the general election of 1945, whereas she did. She said that the reason the English in the hospital disliked the Australians and New Zealanders was because they got invited to all the garden parties in Buckingham Palace through their embassies and that they 'crowed' about it afterwards.

The numbers of Irish workers travelling to Britain diminished significantly in the final year of the war although 1944 had also seen a decline in the number of travel permits that were issued. Frances continued to send money to her mother when she remained in England but it did not improve the relationship. She finally returned to Dublin in 1947 because she was having health problems. Frances married an Irish man whom she had met in Dublin in the early 1950s but her husband was out of work and they decided to return to England. They moved to London and had two sons. When Frances' husband died of cancer in 1967, she decided to remain in England because she thought it was a more open society than

Ireland and she preferred to live there. It seems that, in this area at least, she had something in common with her mother, who had worked in England all through the 1920s, after going there during the First World War to work in a munitions factory:

> Sure my mother was the same ... at 18, she went to work on munitions, and she didn't like all the women around her effing and blinding and swearing. But she never went back to Ireland for years.

Kathleen also remained in England after the war, when her husband was demobilized from the army. They settled in the area around Maidenhead where she had lived with her parents-in-law during the war, although she returned to Ireland when her husband died in the 1990s.

When Letty returned to Ireland at the end of the war she moved back into the family home. Although she had enjoyed living in the hostel with the other workers from the munitions factory, she was happy to be home with her mother and felt no sense of restriction of her personal freedom. Letty lived in that house until recently and she looks back on the time she spent in England during the war as a youthful adventure. That her sister Josephine was able to contribute to Letty's account of the years in England suggests that the stories have been told in the family many times.

When Meta first moved to England in the late 1930s, she decided very early on that she would not return to Northern Ireland, because the 'bright lights of Liverpool' were so much more exciting than even the city of Belfast could offer and the hardships of war did not change her mind. She supported her husband when he went to college in the years immediately after the war and he eventually became a professor of chemistry in a British university. She is an active member of the local Ulster Society in the town where she lives.

When Nancy qualified as a nurse she decided to expand her skills and she went to London to do a course in midwifery. She returned to Dublin in 1946 and she went to the Cork Street fever hospital to be trained in combatting communicable diseases. After she finished her training she moved back to England and eventually she joined the World Health Organisation. Olive remained in England until 1950, working in the Queen Victoria hospital. She and her fiancée were saving hard to get married and buy a home. They travelled back and forth between Ireland and England for a few years to see each other and then she returned to Dublin:

> But then I came home and that was the end of my nursing career. I got married and settled down. That was that.

Research into the status of women in belligerent western states during the Second World War found that the potentially liberating aspects of the war situation for women were offset by the extra work that was generated for them by the expectation that they should continue to fulfil their traditional domestic function, in addition to taking up war work.[71] Although the question of equal pay was raised, considering that many women were taking on jobs that had previously been done by men, only in the United States was the principle conceded and then individual employers frequently ignored the government's recommendation on the issue.[72] No fundamental changes in women's public status resulted from their involvement in war work, although, in the long term, their emergence into the workplace in large numbers contributed to the undermining of institutional gender-based discrimination. The women who were interviewed for this book were not subject to conscription and their motivation for travelling to Britain to work during the war years was varied. They had a choice about whether to go or not, in terms of conscription, but for most of them their reasons for going were a consequence of a lack of other choices that were in turn related to a combination of their family's economic circumstances and the women's gender.

5

Joining up

You know it's not so long ago that somebody asked me why did I join up and I said I didn't want to see the Nazis coming here. He looked at me and said he had never thought of that – he just thought I was joining up for England and the English are dreadful. (Ethel)

For much of the history of western society, separate gender roles have been clearly delineated, especially in wartime. In the Second World War women were still firmly associated with supporting the military role of men and they were not expected to cross the gender boundaries by engaging in combat. For the governments that were trying to exploit women's capabilities in their war efforts, there was always a tension between that need and the deeply held belief that women's real destiny was as wives and mothers. Despite women's proven ability to work as hard as men, to organize themselves and their families in difficult and dangerous conditions and generally to cope with the hardships of war at least as well as men, the enduring image of women's role during the Second World War was as the inspiration for warriors, the keepers of the 'flame of humanity'.[1] While the women who chose to enlist in the auxiliary armed forces had many different reasons for doing so, not the least of them was that they could see themselves as very different beings from the fragile souls defended by their men folk that were usually propagated. The Irish women who enlisted in various arms of the Allied forces were not compelled to take part in war work but they chose to do so, regardless of the dangers. The women whose stories are quoted in this chapter were motivated by the desire for adventure as well as the belief that they could play a useful role in the Allied war effort. While all four were from Éire their stories are consistent with the experiences of other Irish women, some from Northern Ireland, who joined the armed forces during the Second World War.[2]

In wartime, the nursing profession allowed women to get close to the action without arousing any misgivings about their suitability as combatants. Florence Nightingale is well known particularly for her service in the Crimean War and the tradition that she established of employing female nurses in or near lines of combat. Following in her footsteps and encouraged by the patronage of Queen Alexandra, wife of King Edward VII, in 1902 Queen Alexandra's Imperial Military Nursing Service (QAIMNS) was formed and it was recognized from its foundation as an integral part of the regular armed forces.[3] The nursing sisters who joined the Army Nursing Service of the British army in the First World War served in base hospitals, stationary hospitals, casualty clearing stations and advanced operating centres from 1914 to 1918. There were similar bodies of nurses attached to the armed forces of other belligerent nations when the Second World War commenced.

Hilda completed her nursing training in the Adelaide hospital[4] in Dublin in 1940 and she and her friend Mary then went to Belfast to enlist in the QAIMNS.[5] She said that 'anyone who trained in the Adelaide at that time seemed to go to the forces anyway'.[6] QAIMNS officers had to be state registered nurses; they had to be 'British subjects of European descent'[7] and under the age of 35 at enlistment. Hilda and Mary qualified as British subjects because they had been born when all of Ireland was still ruled from Britain and under the terms of the 1922 Treaty the Irish Free State (Éire from 1937) was still a part of the British Commonwealth. Women who acquired British citizenship by marriage were accepted into the Air Raid Precautions service and some of the auxiliary services, but not into extensions of the army like the QAIMNS. The euphemism 'European descent' presumably referred to the necessity for applicants to the QAIMNS to be white, although the exclusion might also have included Jewish women as the regulations for admission were drawn up during a period of intense anti-immigrant and anti-Semitic activity in England.[8] The 1905 Aliens Act in Britain specifically targeted poor Jewish people, following a period of heavy immigration from eastern European countries.

Mary was called up immediately after enlistment, but Hilda got pleurisy and was forced to stay in Dublin for a while. When she recovered, she took a job as a ward sister in Cornwall while awaiting her call-up. Mary's letters had stopped some months after she left Dublin and Hilda hoped that she would get news of her when she went to her first posting in Tidworth, at the very elegant Tedworth House:[9]

> Well, my first station was Tidworth, I was there about six months and it was a very big military hospital. After the Adelaide, I must say I liked the way the military hospitals were run, they were always very correct, of course, after an Irish hospital – the teaching here in Ireland was very good, it was very strict as you can imagine.

13. Tedworth House. This recent picture of Tedworth House shows it looking from the outside much as it would have done when Hilda was there. With thanks to Rosemary Meek, *Drumbeat*.

All the nursing sisters were told when they joined the QAIMNS that they must be willing to go abroad at any time and this was one of the attractions of the service for Hilda. During peacetime, a sister would be expected to serve for two or three years in an army hospital in Britain or Northern Ireland but in wartime it was much more likely that they would be sent overseas very quickly.

With the absence of conscription in Northern Ireland, the armed services had to rely on persuasion rather than coercion to get women there to enlist. Even though women were being asked to join up voluntarily, there was an extra layer of bureaucracy attached to their applications that did not extend to men. Parents had to give their consent to their daughters' recruitment while married women had to have their husband's written permission. There is little evidence that women's role in the military had a major impact on challenging prescribed ideals about women's place in society. When military needs dictated that women enter spheres previously inhabited only by men, the terms were clearly dictated. They were there for the duration of the war only, and even then strict limits were placed on the extent of their involvement in these 'masculine' activities.[10]

Hilda was ranked as a lieutenant and the matron of the hospital was a major. All of the nursing sisters had officer rank. Larger hospitals had a matron in charge but many of the small hospitals were administered by a sister-in-charge.[11] This meant that many senior nursing officers got experience in running a hospital even before achieving promotion to the rank of matron. The sisters lived in special quarters and were responsible for running their own mess. The living quarters in Tedworth House were run as if it was still a stately home:

> The breakfast table was white linen everywhere; it had sideboards of food, everything you could think of, even though it was wartime. Huge silver lids on everything. They had told me to bring a silver napkin ring so I had that, everybody had that; there was so much silver and all these dishes, with their huge lids, and enormous table settings – all absolutely perfect.

At one point in her life, Sally thought she would like to be a nurse but a visit to the matron of Dublin's Adelaide hospital had convinced her that she was not suited for the job. She became a Froebel teacher[12] and worked in that capacity until early 1941, when she was persuaded to go to Northern Ireland and join the ATS:[13]

> My school friend came to me one day and said she was joining up ... We simply just left for Belfast and then we were sent up to barracks in Ballymena.[14] So everybody went on three weeks training, to learn barracks square and battle and all this kind of thing and then you were asked what you wanted to be. You could either be, in those days, you could either be a cook, a clerk or an orderly so I said I wanted to be a cook ... So anyway, I became a cook and was put into the kitchen and put to peeling potatoes and Brussels sprouts.

Sally was given a corporal's stripes and eventually she was put in charge of ordering and procuring the rations for the whole camp. She was serving in the kitchen under a rather domineering female sergeant, to whom she had to 'pretend to know everything'. She was the only woman in the barracks at the time given trousers for her uniform. This was because of the nature of the work that she was doing. When she had ordered in supplies she would often have to lift in sacks of potatoes or vegetables and it was reckoned that trousers were necessary for the work she was doing. She did have a man working with her but generally she was fairly isolated. Sally was eventually promoted to sergeant herself and in 1945 she was offered a post as quarter-master at Bangor Castle, where officers about to be demobbed were billeted:

> There were nurses and doctors and a mixture of Japanese and Germans, Chinese and whatnot, all in together and I was in charge of the officers' mess in Bangor Castle and I had a couple of Germans as orderlies, to look after the officers. And these two, I got very fond of them and I used to go on my bike, I had my bike up there, I used to go into the town at weekends and the officers would give you so much for mess money and you would go round the farms getting eggs or something that you didn't get on the rations, you know. They were still doing the rations then.

The lieutenant in charge of Sally's ATS section was surprised that Sally was not interested in trying to get an officer's rank, particularly since she had been a teacher in civilian life. There was an assumption that a professional person should not belong to the rank and file and Sally was considered to be very odd because she did not seek promotion. She did think of continuing in the army after the war and would have been given the opportunity to do it but family circumstances prevented her. An aunt in Wales became sick and Sally was the only female member of the family available to nurse her. Sally's two younger brothers had married while she was in Northern Ireland, but it does not seem to have been considered that they or their wives would accept any responsibility for the aunt's care. Even though Sally had initially joined the ATS at the invitation of her friend, she said she had been very influenced by Churchill's speeches and wanted to contribute to the war effort on behalf of the Allies.

Ethel had taken a close interest in the progress of the war from its commencement and she was attracted to the idea of enlisting in the auxiliary forces because she also wanted to contribute to the Allied war effort:

> I just said to my mother: 'I'm going to join up'. She just said: 'don't be silly, nobody would expect you to do that'. Being the youngest, I was very demanding, and I suppose I was used to arguing but for once, I just kept quiet and I thought I'll be 21 in February and there's nothing they can do to stop me. So I waited until I got over my twenty-first birthday and ... I got the day off and I never told the family I was going to Belfast. I just came back and said I've joined the WAAF.[15]

Ethel's family paid close attention to the progress of the war although she was the only one who enlisted in the Allied forces. Both of her brothers were in the Air Raid Protection service in Dublin. One of them was a pacifist and would not have enlisted in the armed forces in any case but the other one was prevented from joining because of poor health. Ethel remembered the family listening to radio broadcasts by Winston Churchill, despite the strict censorship in Éire.[16]

At her enlistment interview, Ethel was asked about her best subjects in school. She said that science, maths and English were her favourites and she also enjoyed mechanical drawing. She was selected to train as an electrician and she 'sailed through the exams' because she enjoyed the subject so much. 'So I did six months on that course and then I went to Honeybourne, it's near Stratford, and I was working on Whitleys then.' Ethel's job was to repair the electrical systems in the aircraft and the training started with wiring batteries, gradually moving up to maintenance of the bombing gear. Even though frequent misgivings were expressed about the suitability of women for combat roles, there were no restrictions on women maintaining and thereby being involved in the use of lethal weapons such as bombs.[17] The WAAF was set up specifically to provide female substitutes for RAF personnel in particular trades and, as far as possible, all ranks were administered, trained and controlled under the same regulations, regardless of gender. The rank badges and the colour and style of the WAAF, uniforms were identical to those of the officers and airmen of the RAF. This was intended to demonstrate the close connection between the WAAF and its parent service.[18]

The training course lasted for six months and then Ethel was sent as a group 2 electrician to Uxbridge where she was stationed with what they called 'works and bricks' – the civilian workers in the camp. She was one of the first women to do the advanced electricians' training course at Melsham,[19] which lasted for four months and from which she qualified as a group 1 electrician. In addition to the skill that she had acquired, which meant she was paid extra, she had also developed in terms of strength. She remembered working on Whitley aircraft[20] with other WAAFs:

> They'd had fixed undercarriages as far as I can remember and when you wanted to do repairs on them they weren't up high enough and somebody would shout 'two six' and that's a form to move anything in the RAF. So when somebody shouted 'two six' on the hangar floor we would drop what we were doing, go out and get underneath the aircraft and bend down and then somebody would say 'lift' and we'd

heave our backs up and lift the aircraft up and they had trestles that they stuck in at either end and to put the trestles in to hold it up.

The Uxbridge camp was where the planning for D-Day, the invasion of Europe, had taken place. Ethel was moved there after D-Day but she noted that the women in the signals section were still down there:

> They were pushing aircraft around a table – you know you'd see the girls doing them in films – and I'd have to put these lights up in their offices. I don't know whether you've ever heard of 'Cats Eyes Cunningham',[21] well I was sent along to his office one day because there was a bulb gone. I walked in and he just took one look and he said 'a girl!' He had a navigator with him and he said to the navigator 'you get up and do it'.

Ethel was amused by Cunningham's failure to recognize that she was well qualified to do this simple task but his prejudice was not unusual, particularly among older officers, both male and female. When women from the ATS were recruited into anti-aircraft batteries in 1941 much of the insistence that their role should be confined to plotting and aiming came from senior officers of the ATS, rather than the Royal Artillery.[22] Rather than argue with the clear evidence that women were capable of doing many of the jobs that men could do, recourse was taken in the claim that they were not as physically strong as men and that this justified the gender discrimination that was such an intrinsic element of women's wartime role.

Ethel had enlisted in the WAAF because she wanted to contribute to the fight against Nazism and she shared this motivation with many other women. Some women also wanted to break out of the confines of the usual 'rules' that governed their behaviour and employment and were not surprised when they were subject to inferior conditions.[23] Many women earned the respect of their male colleagues but many others found that older men in particular were disconcerted by the fact that these 'girls' did not need male protectors. Ethel recalled that she could cope very well with the dangers of wartime:

> It was extraordinary but the only time I was scared was when I was in Uxbridge and I was down in this underground, cellar sort of place and there was a big generator for generating the electricity. We'd switch that off and go on to batteries because we'd have to test it and when you switched that off and it was quiet, the buzz bombs were going over and the chimney, a kind of ventilator that went up out of it, you

could hear them go over and you just sat there and waited. Then you'd hear them go off and it wasn't beside you so that was all right.

When Hilda had completed six months at Tidworth, she was given the opportunity to go abroad to nurse in combat areas, which she was delighted to accept. When she and her fellow nursing sisters embarked they had no idea where they would be going:

> France had fallen, so we thought the obvious place was – this was before we got on the ship, when she asked us to sign the form if you wanted to go abroad – we thought, well, the only place now that they can fight is the Middle East, they were fighting there at that time, so we were pretty sure we were going to the Middle East. But we thought we wouldn't be any longer away than six months or a year, at the very, very most because that was the usual thing in the army, before the war, of course, that you'd go abroad and you wouldn't be any longer than a year at the very outside.

They did not find out they were going to India until they were well on the way from Durban in South Africa, where they had to tranship for the journey through the Indian Ocean. Hilda was permitted to send a letter to her parents, which was taken by the returning convoy, and when she reached Rawalpindi she was allowed to send a telegram giving an address for return post. This would have been the first communication to her parents for several months, during which they suffered considerable anxiety on her behalf. Hilda was very excited about her posting:

> I went to Rawalpindi and I was delighted I went because I saw what it was like during the Raj,[24] it really was just like Tidworth with all the silver covers and we had bearers with our crest on and we had a bearer between two rooms.

She spent some months there and then she was moved to Kashmir and later to Burma.

Although her parents were Irish, Pat was born in Liverpool and lived there until she was old enough for secondary school. Her mother brought her to Ireland to go to school there. Her father was still working in England when the war broke out in 1939 and he insisted that his family remain in Ireland, where he considered they would be safer. Pat's father was a banker and he was 'getting on for sixty' at that time so he was not likely to be conscripted. He was an ARP warden and her mother worried constantly about his safety. They did not see him very much during the early years of the war because of the difficulty associated with crossing the Irish Sea:

> It wasn't very pleasant travelling between England and Ireland and it was also very unsafe. This was because of the submarines and being bombed, it was very risky ... Nothing ever happened to my knowledge, but there was always that danger.

In 1942 Pat's parents decided that the whole family should return to Liverpool and shortly afterwards she reached her eighteenth birthday, which meant that she would have to volunteer for the forces or be conscripted for war work:[25]

> So I pleaded with my mum and dad to let me join the forces. Reluctantly they did because I said I didn't want to go into a factory and I didn't either. ... Well, I wouldn't have liked the work ... So they gave in, they had to ... I joined the ATS – the Auxiliary Territorial Service or something like that.

The formation of the ATS was publicly announced on 27 September 1938. Dame Helen Gwynne-Vaughan was appointed as director, answerable directly to the adjutant-general of the British army. In April 1941 the ATS was given equal military status with men, coming under the jurisdiction of the Army Act. However, when announcing this development, the Secretary of State for War told the House of Commons that women 'will, of course, be employed only on work for which they have a special aptitude, but the House should know that such work included duties at searchlight and gun stations'.[26] At the beginning of the war, members of the ATS could work as cooks, clerks, orderlies, storewomen or drivers. After conscription for women was introduced in 1942, the number of occupations was extended and women took on an increasing proportion of the technical work that had previously been done by men.

When Pat joined the ATS she was sent to Scotland for induction and training in the middle of a freezing cold winter. The training for ATS volunteers involved four weeks of drilling and marching, mainly intended to teach the recruits to obey orders. The women were paid two shillings per day, plus food and board, during this training period:

> It was a dreadful time. We all thought we were crazy for volunteering because to go from comfortable homes to chalets, yes, wooden chalets. You'd all go into the ladies room and there'd be all the hand

> This document is the property of His Britannic Majesty's Government
>
> Printed for the Cabinet, March, 1941
>
> SECRET.
>
> W.P. (41) 72
>
> Copy No. 26
>
> 29th March, 1941 TO BE KEPT UNDER LOCK AND KEY
>
> It is requested that special care may be taken to ensure the secrecy of this document.
>
> WAR CABINET
>
> STATUS AND FUTURE EMPLOYMENT OF THE A.T.S.
>
> MEMORANDUM BY THE SECRETARY OF STATE FOR WAR
>
> 1. For some time I have been considering the question of giving fuller military status to the Auxiliary Territorial Service. This is one aspect of a wide review of the conditions of service of this womens' corps, a review which has as its object to attract recruits to the corps in order to make up the serious deficiencies in its establishment. At the same time, I am anxious to tighten up the conditions of enrolment of the corps to something approximating more to the terms of service of the soldier. There is a pronounced shortage, as my colleagues know, in the womens' organizations of all three fighting services, and to some extent the remedies which the three Service Departments are seeking are on the common lines suggested by a common problem.
>
> 2. The matter has been brought to a head by proposals made in the report of Air Marshal Sir Philip Joubert's Committee on anti-aircraft re-organization, to utilise members of the A.T.S. for duties of an operational nature in connection with the Air Defences of Great Britain. The Joubert Committee, impressed with the need for economising man-power in the period that lies ahead, propose that members of the A.T.S. should be trained and employed in a number of duties in gun operational rôles such as Track Recorders, Plotters, Teleprinter Operators, etc., and also as complete reliefs for soldiers as Fire Control Operators at gun sites; further, the Committee consider women might appropriately be used for complete Searchlight detachments. It is estimated that in this way the services of some 30,000 women could be quickly utilised with advantage, with appreciable easing of our man power problem, which is becoming more and more insistent, and that eventually some 100,000 women would be employed with A.D.G.B. on operational and other rôles.
>
> The W.A.A.F are already largely employed on many similar types of duty in operation rooms, etc., but the suggested employment of A.T.S. members in operational rôles on gun and searchlight sites goes, I believe, further than anything now existing in the women's corps.

14. Memorandum from the Secretary of State for War, 1941. The status of the ATS was a matter of continuing controversy and debate throughout the war years. Courtesy of the National Archives, ref. INF2/85.

basins and you'd to get on and get washed. We often cried at night because you couldn't do anything.

Pat found the training quite difficult, not least because of the fact that uniforms were distributed with little care for size or comfort:

> Everything was thrown at you and maybe 'what size are you' and skirts and tops and bras and pants and stockings, and your greatcoat and cap.[27]

In 1941, a Wartime Social Survey report found that women registering at labour exchanges were reluctant to be assigned to the ATS because of the popular image of its members as the 'Groundsheet of the Army'.[28] Pat did not refer to any such anxiety and it is unlikely that her protective parents would have given her permission to enlist in the ATS if they had shared such concerns. In fact, none of the Irish women who spoke to me about their experiences in Britain and elsewhere mentioned being worried about how they would be perceived if they joined the armed forces and their parents' anxieties related to their physical safety rather than their moral well being.

The recruits had come from different backgrounds and areas and part of the challenge of the ATS for Pat was getting along with women with whom she had little in common. Angus Calder referred to the female volunteers in the ATS in the early stages of the war as 'girls' who tended to come 'from the better off sections of society and had put travel or adventure higher on their agendas than the dubious pleasures of marriage in wartime'.[29] This description contradicts the perception of ATS members identified in the Wartime Social Survey. However, the mixing of social classes that accompanied conscription was a recurring theme of social commentary during the war years.

Ethel remarked on the social background of other Irish women who enlisted in the WAAF at the same time as she did:

> There were a lot of girls from Jacob's factory.[30] They were characters and it was amazing when we got there, because of course, we all had to have medicals, and the number that had dirty heads! They had to be put into a billet on their own. You suddenly found there were a whole lot missing and then you heard where they were. Or you'd wake up in the middle of the night and hear one of the northern ones saying 'have you got a connection?' They were looking for a light for their cigarette. We never knew whether those northerns were

Protestants or Roman Catholics. You didn't think about it and you didn't care where they came from – you were just one of the gang.

Sonya Rose described how the wartime notion that there should be equality of sacrifice contributed to the construction of the war as a 'people's war'. This was tied in to the extent of civilian involvement on the home front and, of course, the role played by women and others who were usually seen as the object of warfare, rather than protagonists, and were seen to be making significant contributions to the war effort. Newspapers and magazines ran stories condemning 'immoral, self-interested behaviour on the part of elites but there was little criticism of the social order that privileged them in the first place'.[31]

Ethel experienced a milder abuse of privilege in the WAAF but the reaction to it emphasized the extent to which people from different social backgrounds can cooperate when faced with unreasonable behaviour by an authority figure:

> Another camp we were on, it was at Honeybourne and it was a big sprawling camp. We slept in one site and we ate on another and the working area was another – there were three sites. So we all had bicycles and we got a new CO and he didn't like the cyclists going at lunchtime cycling along the road to the mess, because it was holding his car up. So he told us we had to march from the working site to the mess. Like that, the word went round. You didn't hear anybody complaining or anything but we all formed up and we all marched up to the mess for lunch but we didn't go in. We dispersed and then, when the time was up, we marched back to camp again. There were cars flying up and down; they'd all this scrambled egg on their hands and they didn't know what to do about it. They didn't know whether to produce it again that night for supper or not. So we kept it up and the next day the order was rescinded. You could smell fish for miles around because they'd cooked all this fish for lunchtime and nobody to eat it … We didn't mutiny, we didn't break any rules; we just didn't eat.

When Pat completed her basic training in Scotland, she was posted to the Royal Air Force station at Farnborough[32] where she was appointed as secretary to a major who was second in command of the base. The secretarial course that Pat had attended before joining up qualified her for the job she was given, although she had further training relating to safety procedures at the station, as well as the normal range of drilling. She would have preferred to join the transport corps but training was only given to women who could already drive.

Pat enjoyed her time away although she was aware that her parents were not very enthusiastic about it:

> If I was to be quite honest, it was a chance to get away from home. Spread my wings. They [Pat's parents] were quite worried. That I would be caught out, maybe in an air raid and be killed, that was the thing.

One of the benefits of being away from home, from her point of view, was that it enabled her to meet people of many different nationalities. At the air force base, there were Danes, Poles and French men who had joined up and were identifiable by the shoulder band on their uniforms naming their home countries.

Pat could not remember any specific rules about the extent of socializing that was permitted between male and female members of the armed forces, and the ATS seems to have been very discreet when relationships resulted in pregnancy:

> All I ever knew was that if somebody was discharged under Paragraph 11[33] we knew then that they were pregnant. That was it but that only went up after they'd been discharged.

WAAF airwomen's sense of identity was informed by their ideas of service and duty.[34] They assessed the importance and value of their jobs by their proximity to combat operations and their direct contribution to the war effort. This was not a gendered analysis because there was no clear distinction between fighting men and supporting women, as there was in other services. Many of the ground crews were men who could not be used as flight crew owing to the nature of their particular skills and who were therefore not substituted by women. The integration of women into the RAF through their membership of the WAAF thus created a sense of identity that superceded gender and could be manifested in a variety of ways. Ethel remembered that when she was stationed at Honeybourne, there were Canadians flying the planes:

> There was an unwritten law that we didn't go out with the Canadians. We only went out with the lads that we worked with. You see, they had much more money and the girls went mad for these Canadians, or if there were Americans around they'd want to go out with them,

so we wouldn't go out with them. There was a real fellowship, you see, you just didn't do it. It was amazing.

The integration of the WAAF into the RAF was carried throughout all aspects of the service, including accommodation, as Ethel noted:

> We had these wooden billets and there was just a fence with three strands of wire along it and the men were in the next plot and there were some Americans there and they wouldn't believe it that the WAAF billets were beside the men's billets and there weren't guards on.

Clearly, normal relations between men and women did continue throughout the war and women, both married and unmarried, became pregnant. The WAAF policy was to discharge women at the end of the third month of their pregnancy, although an airwoman marked as 'suitable for re-enrolment' on her discharge could apply to rejoin six months after the birth of her child. The WAAF refused to accept responsibility for pregnant airwomen who were unmarried, on the grounds that such women were the responsibility of the Ministry of Health but also because it was feared that allowing them to stay in RAF hostels would adversely affect the service.[35]

Only one of Pat's friends in the ATS had a serious relationship with another member of the armed forces and that ended sadly. Pat thought the couple had divorced after the war. The husband had been with one of the first Allied forces to enter the Belsen concentration camp and he had become extremely depressed afterwards as a result of the experience. Pat enjoyed the social life at Farnborough, regardless of the restrictions, but towards the end of the war she was moved to another base in Wiltshire, which was much more isolated than Farnborough, being a long distance even from a bus stop:

> We were about seven miles from this town, Marlborough, which has a very well-known public school there, and on a Saturday, about six of us would get the bus into Marlborough and have chips and eggs and this was heaven to us ... We'd then sit there in this lovely bay window and have the chips and the eggs and bread and butter and I think it amounted to 2/6.

Many years later she tried to recreate this 'heaven' and she paid a visit to Marlborough with her husband. She was very disappointed to find that everything had changed.

Hilda enquired about her friend Mary whenever she was moved to a new station but it was not until she reached Ceylon that she finally got news of her:

> I was in a station once at Trincomalee[36] that's in Sri Lanka now, it was Ceylon then, and there was a sister there and when you arrive first, everyone is asking where did you come from, when did you come out, on what ship did you come, what was the last station you were at, all this – and I told her. Then, of course, at that time whenever I was sent to anywhere new I would always ask did anyone ever hear of Mary Cooper. Then there was a girl there and she said she did, that she was in Singapore with her at the Alexandra hospital in Singapore when the Japs came and they drew straws and Mary only got off on the last boat and it was torpedoed. They were washed up off Batavia[37] or somewhere like that and some of the sisters were shot by the Japs. Anyway, Mary ended up in a prison camp in Sumatra[38] where just before the war ended she died from the starvation and beatings.

Hilda was even more shocked when she and other nurses were sent to meet refugees from Singapore who had made their way through the jungle in Burma to get to India:

> After arriving at Rawalpindi the next day we were to go down to meet the train and help to sort out people. When we got there and saw, I couldn't believe it, all these people who got off this train bedraggled and looking terrible in rags. They had trekked up through Burma. There was one woman, she was a young person, she couldn't have been more than 20 and she had long hair and it hadn't been combed. She had this child and then one of the senior sisters called me and told me to bring it to matron's office because the woman wouldn't admit that the child was dead and she was carrying her baby. The sister told me to get the particulars and to get a tonga[39] and bring her to the hospital but she wouldn't give me any information and she didn't want to part with the child. So I had to bring her with the child to the matron and then we were able to take the child to bring it down to the mortuary.

Hilda was moved around between India, Ceylon and Burma. She found that travelling between the various hospitals was the most difficult aspect of her work, because it could take days to get from one place to another, often in appalling weather. When she first arrived in Asia, she had been nervous about travelling on her own but she learned to adapt to the conditions and found herself doing things she could not have imagined when she was still in Ireland, such as travelling to Kashmir by herself:

> This bus was supposed to arrive in Srinagar[40] the capital, I think it was due at eight o'clock and the girls said they would meet me there at the bus stop, wherever it was. But anyway, they were stopping here and there and they were throwing water on the wheels and they stopped at different tea houses ... We didn't arrive at the post office until after one o'clock and I did not know it but the two girls had been and gone. Now I discovered I didn't have the telegram with the name of their boat and the bus stopped at the post office and there were hundreds of Kashmiri fellows there, all men, no women. But someone had told me that if I was in trouble anywhere to go to the post master and he would probably see me right. So I went to the post master because there was nothing else to do ... So he said he would get me a tonga, that was a pony trap that they used out there and he told me what to pay for it and that was it. He said this was a very reliable man and I would be all right ... You couldn't see where you were going and when the clouds came over the moon, it got black dark and we only had a tiny little light and you could hear the pony trotting along. I didn't know where the hell I was or anything. The next thing, after some miles I thought, we stopped and now I see water. They said to get in a boat and I didn't know about this at all but I paid them and they said – there were two Kashmiris smoking their hookah in the boat. By this time, it was black dark and I was thoroughly frightened but there was nothing to do only get in the boat. When I was on the lake with these two I never thought I would see anyone again. I'd paid the tonga man and he told me what to pay the boat men and that at least was a good sign ... So anyhow, the next thing after paddling along in the boat for a couple of miles, suddenly we hear shouting from the houseboats. It was from what they called the donga, which was really a servant's boat behind the houseboat, where the servants stayed. The boatmen and the servants were all shouting now and the next thing I see the girls in their dressing gowns. I can tell you I was glad to see them.

The small number of European women in the area made the nursing sisters very popular when there was an opportunity for socializing. Hilda enjoyed herself but she was adamant that she would not have married any of the army men that she met in the Far East: 'I always said I would get married at home because you always felt you would never stay with one person out there.'

One duty was dealing with soldiers who had picked up venereal diseases after visiting prostitutes. Hilda was not in the least judgemental about this although she encountered one young soldier who was so ashamed of being infected that he could not stop crying when he was being treated. She remarked on how sheltered Irish people were from knowledge of the widespread abuses by the Japanese army who had forced Burmese, Korean and women of other nationalities into brothels. She had one difficult encounter in a hospital at Comilla[41] that reminded her of how vulnerable she was as a woman working virtually alone in a potentially hostile environment where she did not think the local workers would help her:

> I remember at night time there was a doctor who would come round between half past ten and eleven to sign up for things, drugs or if you had a patient who had to be seen. Every single night this happened but this particular time a Sikh man, a major, with his turban and all he seemed about six foot tall or more, a youngish fellow about thirty, very well built ... At half past one I was still telling him stories about Ireland because I was frightened about why he was hanging on there. I was keeping my composure but I couldn't get out because there was only a narrow doorway into a passage and he was standing in front of it. There were only the Sepoys, the Indian orderlies around and they were outside somewhere ... I knew the Indians wouldn't help me because they were more frightened of their officers than they would be of a British officer. They were really terrified of their own officers and they wouldn't dare interfere. I took the short cut over to the British wing, out through scrub jungle ... Then the next thing I heard the branches and everything breaking behind me and I knew he would kill me. He would rape me and then he would have to kill me, he would have no option. We did have a sister, by the way, who was raped by a Cypriot and he was shot ... I'll never forget when I saw the light and he must have seen it at the same time that I saw it so he stopped and realised the game was up.

On the following day, Hilda told the commanding officer what had happened and she said the Sikh major was never seen again at the hospital, but she did not know what had been said to him about the incident. She was upset that the matron, as the most senior female present, was dismissive of the incident, suggesting that since she had not actually been hurt that she should not register a complaint. Hilda's explanation of the matron's lack of interest was that she was a Red Cross nurse and not an army officer and 'she did not know the rules'.

The end of the war seemed unexpected for Hilda because she had become so used to the world she was living in:

> But then the war ended like a thunderbolt. I remember when I was told it was over I couldn't believe it. An officer came along and he said they've dropped the bomb on Japan. An officer came and told us they dropped one bomb and they wouldn't stop and then they dropped another one and now the war is over.

She was unable to come back to Ireland straight away because there were problems getting access to transport:

> I came back on a hospital ship – I didn't have to come back on a hospital ship and it was true, they said in the army never volunteer for anything because it will always be you, you and you …Then the next thing was there was a red line through our names because we didn't have any priority. We weren't married and we didn't have any children or anything but we got tired of that, we were knocked off about three ships. We were there over a fortnight and then somebody came along and said you can go home if you work your way home on a hospital ship. This was October 1945 and we thought about it and we thought well, the war is over since August, and these fellows going home won't be that bad and we'll have a bit of chat and that wouldn't be too bad.

There was a matron and ten nursing sisters and they worked twelve-hour shifts all the way home. On the ship, Hilda was aware of the tensions between army personnel and civilians who had been in prison camps and she attributed this to the class and national differences that had persisted even in the camps:

> It seems that the soldiers wouldn't stay in the wards if the civilian people were in the same ward. That was true too, that happened in Sumatra. The Dutch people there that had been residents out in Sumatra – they knew the language for one thing, and also, their homes – they had money and they were able to bring clothes … A bit of aggro went on in the camps because the young ones were made do a lot more than the usual. This was because you had all these superior

people, or they thought they were and this was the same thing with the men on board.

When Hilda got to England, she was posted to a place outside Bisterne[42] until she was demobilized. She was very unhappy there, not least because it seemed undisciplined after the army hospitals she had been used to working in and she was very bored. There were some attractions but not enough to make her want to stay:

> I'd got the Burma Star[43] at that time and another one and I had them on my uniform. I would go down with one of the other sisters, one of them would come down with me to a hotel in Bisterne in uniform, because now we'd got rationing and we didn't have any mufti to go about … it's a very posh part of the world round Bisterne, a lot of very well heeled people. They would see the medals, the ribbons, and they would come over and buy us drinks. But I didn't like it.

After the war, the QAIMNS was wound up and amalgamated into the Army Nursing Service. The orderlies had to qualify as state registered nurses and they were then given the same status as the nursing sisters:

> I wouldn't have fancied that, though some of the orderlies were excellent, there's no doubt about it. Especially now, the ones we'd trained.[44] Of course, we'd give them lectures and teach them and then they'd get really good and they'd disappear and you'd get some novice who would know nothing but obviously they had taken them for the field hospitals. Actually, they must have done that – the orderlies, and of course, the doctors too, they had a bad time. The first stage was first aid, then the field hospital and then they'd be sent to us.

Hilda returned to Ireland and after some months she received a request from the QAIMNS asking her to re-enlist but the thought did not appeal to her because her post-war experience in Bisterne persuaded her that the service had changed too much for her to fit in well. She found that the prospects for romance were much more restricted than they had been in India:

> Actually, I was home for a couple of months and the first time I met my husband he was with a girl. Of course, it was a different kettle of fish over here because there were a lot of girls after him. It was not like abroad, where there were no women.

Nevertheless, Hilda 'got her man' who was very impressed by her service abroad. He would have joined the armed forces himself but his father died and he had to take over the family farm.

Before being released from the ATS at the end of the war, Pat was offered an opportunity to sign up again and to travel abroad:

> My junior commander, she asked me would I like to go to Washington. 'Washington where?' I said. So I said I'd have to ring my parents so I rang home that night and my mother said this is very short notice. I just knew she didn't want me to go so I went back the next day and I told the junior commander. I've often wondered what would have happened if I had gone there. It would have been very nice.

Although Pat has often thought of how her life would have been if she had insisted on going to Washington, she does not regret her decision to leave the ATS as soon as the war was over. The army provided her with transport home and a small sum of money:

> That's what I got when I was demobbed, I got £25, which was my demob money and I bought two suits with it ... And they weren't cheap, I can assure you, they were beautiful.

Shortly after moving back with her parents in Liverpool, she decided to come back to Ireland and to live with her uncle again. This was partly because she wanted to be independent but also because she preferred Ireland, not least because her future husband was living in Carlow.

Pat remembered that at the end of the war, some of the older women who had been promoted were quite sad at having to leave 'because they would have no authority in civilian life, like they had in the army'. This observation is consistent with Dorothy Sheridan's research[45] into the memories of women who joined the ATS and became both a part of the military machine but at the same time remained separate from it, mainly because it was clear that it was a temporary role they were playing. Their dissatisfaction with relegation to the domestic sphere after the war did not manifest itself in any particular form of protest but may well have contributed to the gradual changes in social attitudes to women that eventually emerged in Britain.

When the war ended in June 1945, Ethel was assigned to work on Mosquito[46] aircraft that were needed for a new theatre of war:

They were the most beautiful, next to a Spitfire, to me they were the most beautiful aircraft, and we were tropicalising them for the Middle East. They were expecting the Jews, you see they were moving into Palestine, there was all that trouble going on and they were expecting great heat out there. We were fitting these with rockets – I spent most of my time soldering the plugs for them to plug in the rockets.

When asked how she felt about preparing weapons for use against the victims of the war, she said that way of considering the situation had not occurred to her: 'They were blowing up the British army; the Jews were blowing them up so we didn't think of them. The army were our boys.' Ethel extended her membership of the WAAF when the war ended, after joining the WAAF central band:

I actually signed on for an extra two years because I was having such a good time. I joined in '43 and the war was over in '45 and I wasn't due to be demobbed until 1946, so then I stayed on and actually it was '49 when I came out. I did enjoy it, yes, but I got to the stage when I thought 'I'm doing everything automatically; I'm not thinking for myself at all'.

When the war in Europe ended in May 1945 with the unconditional surrender of the German armed forces, a decision was taken to send the WAAF central band[47] on tours which took them from Denmark, through Holland and Belgium and finally to Germany. Ethel played the trumpet when she joined the station band after her work repairing aircraft was no longer necessary, but when she was moved into the central band she was assigned to the 'big drum' after the drummer got married and went to Australia:

When we finished with the Mosquitoes I went in to the band, the station band, and then the central band was posted in and I got squeezed into that. I couldn't play a note on the trumpet when they came but the warrant officer just said 'stand at the back, Paddy and keep blowing'. So I just kept blowing then and eventually I ended up on the big drum. But we did a lot of travelling with that because we were recruiting and also, we were sent over to Liège in Belgium for their victory parade and we went to Germany twice and we travelled around Hamburg and Hanover. In Hamburg, we did a march through the streets and it was just after the indoor tattoo for which we trained, the Royal Tournament, and we did a fifteen-minute demonstration

> at that – we were the first women ever to appear in the Royal Tournament, that was it.

Ethel kept her group 1 electrician's pay, which she remembered was much higher than she would have been entitled to earn as a band member. She had a curious reprise of the Cats Eyes Cunningham incident when the band was ordered to play in Scotland:

> There was to be a big celebration parade and there was no band available in Edinburgh so they sent us off and Eisenhower[48] was supposed to be inspecting us. But someone said that he looked at us and said 'they're just girls' and walked on and never inspected us! I never had time for Eisenhower after that.

Regardless of Eisenhower's opinion, the value of the WAAF to the war effort was recognized when in 1949 it was made a permanent and integral part of the RAF as the Women's Royal Air Force.[49]

Ethel's family was proud of her service, even her pacifist brother, who had joined the Air Raid Protection service in Dublin. She was never conscious of needing to keep silent about wearing a British uniform during the war, as many other Irish recruits reported doing. She did not go to many reunions with her former colleagues but when she did, it was a very positive experience for her:

> But after the war, I went to one – it was after I was married and it was nineteen years before I got back and it was a most marvellous day. It was in Eileen's house and I just walked in and they weren't expecting me because they always kept somebody as a surprise. And they just said 'Paddy' and I was made so welcome. I wasn't anybody's wife or anybody's daughter or sister, I was me, and it was really marvellous. It's nice to be yourself once in a while.

6

The home front

The term 'home front' is used in this chapter in the same way that it appeared in the government propaganda produced by several Allied states, meaning an extension of the battlefront that included 'keeping the home fires burning' not just by contributing to war industry and related involvement, but also by preserving the idealized 'home' for which the armed forces could be said to be fighting. Some of the aspects of home and family life that were examined in works about belligerent countries provide a framework for thinking about domestic life in Ireland.[1] Allied government propaganda identified the maintenance of the home front as the patriotic duty of women and older people in particular and the plans for post-war reconstruction and development outlined in the Beveridge Report in Britain, for instance, could be said to represent a *quid pro quo* for that contribution.[2] In that regard, the difference between the two Irish states in terms of their status in the war significantly affected the shaping of the post-war home front and the provision of services that especially benefited women, such as better housing, since they still spent more time at home than men.

In the 1930s and 1940s, local authorities in both Éire and Northern Ireland were forced to acknowledge the extent of poor housing stock and overcrowding in many areas of their capital cities, although the problem was by no means confined there. In Belfast, the bombing raids in April and May 1941 revealed the shocking state of many homes in the city's slum areas and a massive building programme was undertaken in the immediate aftermath of the war, as indeed was also the case in a number of cities in Britain. The background to housing policy in Belfast that was a consequence of the sectarian problems in that city must be considered when examining the status of the city as home front. In Dublin, slum clearance was already well under way when the Emergency started, but the shortage of raw materials for construction brought the programme to a virtual standstill in mid 1941.[3]

When Ivy got married in Belfast in the late 1930s, finding affordable property in some areas of the city was very difficult for young working-class couples on low incomes. She was born and raised on the Falls Road and could not envisage moving to another area, but the Falls was one of the city wards where overcrowding worsened during the war years:[4]

> and there were no houses then and I went to Leo's family and they let us have a room with them ... a week before I was married his brother got a house and he wanted to share it so I went into two rooms in that. You were very lucky when you got two rooms.

Despite the longer than usual interval between the census of 1937 and that of 1951 the increase in the number of houses was relatively small because the post-war building programme had not yet compensated for the destruction caused by the blitz (see Appendix 9). The denominational breakdown between the three main religious groups (Church of Ireland, Roman Catholic and Presbyterian) illustrated in Appendix 10 shows the extent to which co-religionists tended to live in the same areas. Segregated housing had been developing as a policy in Belfast since the nineteenth century, when the main providers of housing (speculative builders and developers and large employers, especially the mill owners) also tended to encourage it as a means of avoiding trouble between the two communities.

Maureen's family was Catholic, living in the Falls Road area of Belfast. She did not remember ever meeting any Protestants when she was growing up, probably because her school and social activities and her early working life were all situated in the Falls Road area, where more than 91 per cent of the population was Roman Catholic. Religious sectarianism was not the only reason for prejudice against neighbours, as Maureen recalled:

> My mother was an outsider, you see, she didn't come from the Falls Road. She came from Ballymakerrig, over the Newtownards Road direction. She was still a Belfast woman but she wasn't a Falls Road woman. She was very reserved – she didn't mix a lot with the other women in the street ... We were considered sometimes to be snobs. Because Mummy was very particular about how we dressed and on Sunday, you had to wear your hat and you had to wear your gloves and you know, people thought who did they think they are?

Dorothy Bates was an English civil servant who wrote for Mass-Observation from her home in Purley, Sussex and continued her diary when she was based in Belfast for five months in 1941. She described the evidence of overcrowded housing in her notes on a walk in the Falls area:

> Not having a map I just walked straight for it from the hotel. First through small squalid houses and across a dismal gap with an engineering works

on it. Hundreds of small children – some pretty, most stupid looking, and all dirty, were playing in the streets. I counted eighty-two in two minutes. I have never seen so many living in a small area.[5]

The poor housing was by no means confined to Catholic areas but efforts to deal with homelessness were not helped by sectarian suspicions. Even at the height of the blitz, while Catholics and Protestants sheltered together from air raids in the hillsides, when it came to finding billets for those made homeless by the bombing, there was invariably gravitation to co-religionist areas. Even if families were willing to offer accommodation or to stay with members of 'the other' religious community, the attitudes of social agencies discouraged this as a policy. Moya Woodside reported on one of the results of this attitude:

> Spent most of the morning trying to find lodgings for a temporarily homeless Catholic girl, who had left her employment on account of illness and was without relatives or friends. She had spent two nights at a Catholic girls' hostel at 6d a night, but complained that everyone was turned out on the streets at 7.30 a.m. and not let in again till 5 p.m. (not, it seems to me, the best way to keep young girls straight). I telephoned three other hostels (Salvation Army, Girls' Help Society and something else) but all of them, on hearing the girl was a Catholic, found they didn't have any beds ... Eventually we got on the track of a Catholic social worker who, we were assured, would find some lodgings for the girl in *the right religious surroundings*.[6] One forgets how wide the gulf between Catholic and Protestant is here until something like this happens.[7]

In both Catholic and Protestant areas of Belfast the local church was the centre of many social and sporting activities. In the Falls Road neighbourhood, there was a choir and parish dances and the parish priest also helped to manage the GAA[8] club in the area, where boys played football and hurling and girls played camogie. The association of the Catholic Church and Gaelic games was an important part of the mindset of nationalist areas in Northern Ireland and allowed local clergy to strengthen their social control in a manner that was not necessary for them in Éire, where Catholics were a majority and state institutions clearly fostered a Catholic ethos. Other forms of entertainment were connected to local Catholic churches, especially the street celebrations that were an intrinsic part of the Catholic Church rituals. Such occasions were celebrated by the whole parish and were also important family days. Maureen loved the sense of excitement generated by the Corpus Christi processions, when most people in the Falls Road area followed a statue of the Virgin Mary which was carried through the streets, singing hymns and praying aloud in unison with the clergy of the parish, reinforcing a sense of community:

> I belonged to St Peter's cathedral, it was a pro-cathedral then and we had processions around the church, round the streets, you know, and if you had just made your first holy communion you wore your first holy communion dress and veil or your confirmation, you wore the outfit that you wore. And they were big days, they were very big days ... Everybody joined in. I think anything that was going on people joined in because it was sort of the only entertainment they had, you know it was something to look forward to. They didn't have television or going away on holiday.

Religion was also important to Alice's family and her mother made sure that her children attended church every Sunday. When Alice was 17 she was permitted to stop going to Sunday school but only on condition that she went to a service at the city's YWCA[9] hall instead.

In Dublin, the areas of highest population density in the city generally corresponded to the areas of greatest poverty, particularly on the north side of the city, where large numbers of single-family residences were given over to multi-family tenement accommodation. Clare's mother ran a small grocery shop in the Mountjoy ward[10] of the city, which had the highest percentage of people living in overcrowded conditions, with nearly 57 per cent of the total population of the ward living in one-room dwellings:[11]

> I remember one family, they were living in a large room and I remember going in and seeing mattresses piled on top of each other which were taken down at night. They were young adults, they were not small children, a very large family ... That was in what's now Sean McDermott Street.[12]

In the city as a whole, there was a decrease in the numbers of persons living in extremely overcrowded conditions between the census of 1936 and that of 1946. These changes were mainly due to the slum clearance projects and the greater number of corporation homes becoming available. Appendix 11 shows the distribution of people in the Dublin county borough in dwellings classified from one room in size to seven rooms. The corporation managed to maintain the slum clearance schemes throughout 1939 and 1940 but shortage of materials had put an almost complete halt to building by 1941.[13] The increase of 23.3 per cent in the number of

15. Clare on her confirmation day in 1939

persons living in dwellings of six rooms or more is evidence of the scale of building of middle-class, private housing schemes.

The possibility of buying their own homes was beyond the capacity of most families during the Second World War years, even in middle-class areas, because of the shortage of mortgage finance. It was particularly difficult for working-class families, partly because they would have found it extremely difficult to raise sufficient money for a deposit and partly because they did not have confidence in their ability to keep up payments when work could be difficult to find. Dublin Corporation had instigated a rental-purchase scheme in 1926 that allowed tenants to use their rent towards the eventual ownership of their homes but without losing the advantages that accrued to corporation tenancy, such as the provision of free repair and maintenance.[14] Shortly before the war started, Sheila's parents bought a house in the new development of Marino under this scheme but when Sheila's father suffered a stroke, the opportunity to own their own home was jeopardized:

> They shared a house in Richmond Road[15] and then they bought – theirs was one of the first houses built – Dublin Corporation/Council

houses, built by the town commissioners in Marino – and you could either rent them or rent/buy them and they rent/bought them and everybody told them they were mad.[16] In those days, you didn't buy a house; you lived in one unless you were very wealthy. But through all her troubles, she continued to buy it, which was, you know, I think a tremendous achievement for her, because once Daddy had the stroke, there was little or no money coming in.

Letty and Josie's mother decided to move from the house in the North Strand[17] where they were both born when her health began to suffer as a result of living in a low lying area of Dublin where dampness was prevalent. The family moved to Dowth Avenue[18] which was part of the newly developed district of Cabra on the north side of the city:

They weren't long built at the time ... Through Sean T. O'Kelly, he was the man that forged all that along.[19] They rid Dublin of the tenements because there was such devastation in them. So that's how we moved up there, it was a purchased house in Dowth Avenue.

The house was purchased when a small legacy from an uncle allowed Josie's mother to buy out the interest of a previous corporation tenant. The rent paid was intended to cover the eventual purchase of the corporation's interest, while giving an affordable home to a working-class family who might not have qualified for a commercial mortgage. For the Dublin Housing Commission's *Report of the Inquiry into the Housing of the Working Class of the City of Dublin 1939–43* a survey was carried out of the rent-paying capacity of a random sampling of families. It showed that almost 30 per cent of the total had no income margin at all while another 25 per cent of the families had absolutely minimal levels of income over and above basic subsistence.[20] The survey covered 130,769 persons or 33,411 families, living in a variety of accommodation types, including corporation cottages and privately owned tenements. The *Report* concluded that 22,172 dwellings would be needed to re-house families living in unfit or overcrowded conditions and it recognized that many of those families would be unable to afford the economic rent set by the corporation. The corporation was not persuaded to introduce a differential renting system for tenants, even though the core of the corporation's housing problems was at all times linked to the pressing problem of poverty in Dublin.[21]

The census of Northern Ireland up to and including 1951 did not include rents in the information that was collected about the dwellings in which the population was living. Unemployment assistance rates included rent allowance but the reports of the Unemployment assistance Board do not give examples of the rents that were being paid, although the report for 1938 refers to a random survey of recipients of assistance in Belfast showing an average rent per household of 6/8 per week.[22] Reports were not published during the war years and the first composite report, issued in 1946, did not refer to rent allowances.

The precarious nature of tenancy for many working-class families was illustrated by the rules governing the house in which Josie's husband's family lived in Dublin. Her father-in-law was an engine driver and the house in Great Western Square in Phibsborough[23] belonged to the railway company for which he worked. The right to a tenancy in the house lasted only as long as the employment:

> When they came to retirement they had to get out. Indeed, it was dreadful, they had to get out. They only got six months and if they weren't out in six months their furniture was put out on the street. I remember seeing that as a young one, their furniture was put out if they weren't out in the six months. That's the way it was.

Access to public transport was also frequently curtailed by lack of money. When discussing with Josie and Letty their custom of handing their unopened pay packets directly to their mother, Josie told me that she would often walk home after a day's work from Grafton Street to Cabra[24] because she did not feel she could take the bus fare without her mother's permission. After she had given her mother the pay packet, the amount she was given back for her own expenses often did not cover the full bus fare:

> I always remember, I would walk sometimes from Grafton Street at lunchtime down to the, like, it was the Pillar[25] that was there at the time, and I'd get the number 10 bus as far as Doyle's Corner. I'd have to get out at Doyle's Corner[26] because I wouldn't have the extra halfpenny to bring me up to Cabra. It was three halfpence to Cabra – a penny and a halfpenny and your penny would bring you to Doyle's Corner and if you hadn't got the other halfpenny, you'd get out and you'd walk.

She would hope to meet a neighbour who was also going home and get a lift on the crossbar of his bicycle because that would save her the cost of the bus fare.

Bicycles were particularly useful as a means of transport at a time when petrol rationing curtailed access to public and private transport. Clare used her bicycle to get around Dublin, even travelling from Phibsborough to Rathfarnham on one occasion, a journey of about ten miles from one side of the city to the other. Clare and other women remarked on the difficulty involved in cycling during the blackout in the winter, when it would be quite difficult to see the road ahead. The blackout regulations required that bicycle lamps had to be dipped and pointing down to the ground, rather than straight ahead, so that light could not be seen from above, although the women insisted that they had felt safer in the dark in those days than they would now on well-lit streets.

In September 1940, Moya Woodside wrote that Dublin was much better lit than Belfast, despite the Dublin women's perception of how dark the city was in the blackout:

> In Dublin for a few days of bright lights and gaiety before settling down to the gloom of an Ulster winter. The streets after dark seem like daylight to our unaccustomed eyes – electric signs flashing, shop windows ablaze, large street lamps, cars speeding along the streets. One can actually see what people are wearing! ... But why is this neutral and so far unthreatened city putting up air-raid shelters and running classes in First Aid and ARP?[27]

When Woodside returned to Dublin in January of the following year, she noticed that preparations for war were further advanced, although there still did not seem to be any sense of urgency:

> Saw three air-raid shelters in O'Connell St. with wooden doors which were securely padlocked. It takes quite a time before you realise the cause of the different atmosphere in the streets – there are no uniforms. Blessed relief. Once down here, in this peace and plenty of normal living, you understand why the people of Eire want to stay neutral as long as possible. Coming out of the pictures at 11 p.m. was like awakening from a bad dream, to find again a normal world of light and colour, and carefree crowds strolling in the streets. True, the big standard lights have been dimmed a little on the top since I last saw Dublin four months ago, but otherwise everything is as brilliant as before.[28]

Writing in May 1941, Dorothy Bates shared Woodside's perception of Dublin as being much brighter and more appealing than Belfast, although ultimately she decided she was not envious of Dublin's apparent affluence.

WARNING
TO ELECTRICITY CONSUMERS

•

Remember that the restrictions are based on your average **DAILY** consumption of this period LAST YEAR. Check up and make certain you are carrying them out, as consumers are now being disconnected for infringement of restrictions.

REMEMBER:—

- NO ELECTRIC HEATING
- NO EXTRA ELECTRICITY FOR COOKING
- 50% OFF YOUR **DAILY** CONSUMPTION OF THIS PERIOD **LAST YEAR** FOR WATER HEATING
- 10% OFF MOTIVE POWER
- 25% OFF LIGHTING AND OTHER USES

These are the restrictions, and if you WERE using gas or coal or other fuel for any purpose this time last year and are NOW using electricity for this purpose you are infringing the restrictions, and in due course you will be disconnected from all electricity supply.

Issued by the

ELECTRICITY SUPPLY BOARD

16. Notice to ESB consumers. Rationing of electricity and gas was introduced by the Éire government in 1942.

I loved Dublin, which seemed much more attractive than Belfast. The hotel (the Gresham) was rather palatial in O'Connell St. – rather like Versailles inside – with chandeliers, murals, mouldings, but less expensive than I expected. It worked out at 12/6 for bed and breakfast ... It looked queer to see iced cakes and newspaper posters. I went to the Abbey Theatre to 'The Money Doesn't Matter'. A comedy, but quite serious with an Irish setting ... It was strange to come out at 11.00 and find street lamps full on and lighted shop windows and buses. Yet I had a feeling of depression – I couldn't live in such a precarious peace – purchased as it were, at other people's expense, while they were suffering.[29]

Moya Woodside also went to the theatre in Dublin, where she was reminded of another important difference between Belfast and Dublin:

In the theatre had another thrill to find Maud Gonne MacBride[30] accompanied by (presumably) a member of the famous Cumann na mBan[31] sitting in the same row! They were both in deep mourning, which I am told they wear 'for Ireland' and the sorrows of the Rebellion.[32]

One of the first measures of the war taken by the Westminster government in relation to rationing was the Motor Fuel Rationing Order 1939, which was passed on 3 September and applied to Northern Ireland as well as the rest of Britain. In the same week the Stormont parliament passed the Civil Defence Act (Northern Ireland) 1939 by which the Home Secretary was empowered to delegate officers or departments of the government of Northern Ireland to carry out many war functions, including the imposition of blackout arrangements. Moya Woodside noted that travelling to work was increasingly difficult for workers and shoppers, although she escaped some of the worst restrictions because her husband was a surgeon and doctors were exempted from the petrol rationing. In her diary, she drew attention to several aspects of the problem, which would not have been confined to Belfast:

> Everywhere one hears remarks: 'oh, I'm living out at so-and-so now' or 'I have to get up at six to be in time at the office' etc. The strain thrown on the transport facilities by all those unaccustomed commuters is terrific. Three and four buses run where formerly one sufficed; and buses have evidently been borrowed from Dublin, Glasgow and even Sheffield, judging from the licence plates. I believe that the railway stations at night are like a football match. Numbers of people, especially the lower-paid workers, must find it impossible to manage when railway or bus season tickets are suddenly added to their expenses. Then, too, if travel to and from work takes perhaps an hour or 1½ hours instead of 15 minutes, and with maybe billets instead of a home, discontent and weariness is bound to be manifest.[33]

Emily had to leave her home on the Falls Road at six o'clock in the morning to walk to the railway station, where she caught the train for Bangor. Her NAAFI office in Chichester Street[34] was bombed in the April 1941 raid and all of the staff were moved to Bangor. It was not possible to stay in the town because of a shortage of accommodation and she and other staff members who lived in the city were forced to spend long hours every day just travelling to and from work.

Despite the concentration of industry in Belfast's docklands, the large number of ordinary residents in the area had virtually no shelter protection.[35]

By June 1940, when British cities were being bombed and it was clear that Belfast was a potential target, Belfast homes had been given only four thousand free domestic shelters, out of a potential six thousand homes that were eligible to receive them. Although funds were allocated for the construction of several public shelters, these were very unpopular and generally not used for their intended purpose. Jean's husband purchased an Anderson shelter for their home but like many people, she had ambivalent feelings about its security:

> It was about the size of that rug only twice as much across [indicating rug about 8 feet x 6 feet] and it was sitting in the living room. We crawled under it ... They were very small; you had practically no room ... Some people felt secure, others felt trapped under them. You know, too, if the house fell down on some of them – the walls – you'd be smothered.

The shoddy quality of the housing in working-class areas was reflected in the relatively high number of people killed outright in the poorer areas. Even in more middle-class areas, such as where Jean and her family lived, there were significant numbers of fatalities:

> There was a coal merchant lived – I think he had eight of a family, four girls and four boys, and seven of them were killed and only one lived from that night ... The following morning I got up, very tired, and went to the window to look into the garden and the place was all gone. My mother's house was gone too, and the strange thing, there was a pantry, I can see it yet, there was part of a windowsill sitting and part of the house was still standing with no room left behind it, and there was a bright blue teapot sitting on the windowsill.

Fortunately, Jean's mother had been staying overnight with friends and she escaped the bombing but the shock of seeing the destruction of her mother's home stayed with Jean for many years.

Because of the danger of bombing, people had to look at their homes in a new way, assessing them for their capacity to protect the family. Alice's home was on the Donegall Road, in a very vulnerable position:

> right up opposite it was Maguire and Paterson's match factory[36] a big, big building, just opposite to it on the other side, which meant that as soon as the sirens went we had to get out immediately because if an incendiary had hit the match factory, well it would have blown the

> Donegall Road[37] to kingdom come ... No, we didn't go into shelters; we always went up [to the Black Mountain]. There was no shelter really, if there was any danger and you thought there might be something and you didn't have time to go out, everybody had something. We had a place underneath the stairs, for instance.

It was not true that there were no shelters but Alice clearly shared the general antipathy of the Belfast population to the public shelters that were provided. They were considered to be too small for their intended purpose and were frequently used by 'courting couples' and even as public conveniences, so that people were very reluctant to enter them.[38] In any case, the shelters were too few in number and too flimsily constructed to offer adequate protection against heavy bombing.[39] Moya Woodside was frustrated by the failure of the local authorities to keep householders properly informed about civil defence:

> If the propaganda authorities want something sensible to do, why don't they survey results of different methods of window protection in already bombed areas and publish their findings for the benefit of those in remoter parts? As all but the vaguest reference to raids and their effects is chopped out of letters from England, people over here are completely in the dark as to what is effective and what isn't.[40]

Bombing could create other hazards for residents of Belfast, as Alice discovered when she was going out to work one morning:

> one night coming back over the Albert Bridge[41] on the bicycle, you know there were tramlines in those days? Well a land mine had fallen on Cromac Square[42] ... I had this racing type bike coming over and the front wheel, the narrow wheels you see, went in to a tram line, into the dent the tram line made and I shot over into the hole the landmine made in Cromac Square. And the army you see, they were all there, and so a few of the soldiers got in the hole and got me out. And I didn't even know where the bike was, but I could see the soldiers with the bike between their knees taking the buckle out of the wheel and everything.

Road accidents were a common feature of the blackout because few city people were used to getting around in darkness. Road signs were also obscured or removed, with the intention of causing confusion in the event of invasion.

Many Belfast people preferred the safety of the hills, rather than staying in shelters in the city.[43] Just as Alice's family used to go to the Black Mountain for safety in a bombing raid, they regularly joined hundreds of other people who did not feel any safer there than in their homes:

> Well, they weren't sleeping really, just all standing, watching out. They had put up sort of tents, sort of pole things with what do you call them, big tarpaulins over them, because it would be raining sometimes, you see. And people were just all crowding in, just standing, keeping one another warm, type of thing. And then the 'All Clear'. As soon as the 'All Clear' would sound, we'd go the way back. When you got back down it was hardly worth while getting into bed because the first thing you'd want was a cup of tea and then it was work time.

In areas where people had been settled for many years, the threat of being bombed brought them closer together, even where they had little in common with each other:

> We were fairly young at the time, they were all middle aged. I remember about three or four o'clock in the morning, in between the bombing you would get a lapse of maybe ten or fifteen minutes, maybe longer. There was a man next door – there was a knock, and there was the husband at the door with a jug of tea ... My neighbour at the other side, they were older too, than us, and her husband, he was a bit panicky. Years afterwards, we laughed because they had two sons and a daughter and as soon as the sirens went, he said – and her name was Minnie – and he said, Minnie get next door and bring that baby in next door, bring that baby in to us here. He thought she would be safer with them than with us.

On the other hand, Jean also remembers people who were not so concerned for the well being of their neighbours:

> You know, at that time, we didn't have a car, and we had bought the house so we had very little money then, but there was quite a lot of people had cars and we called them the hillbillies. The minute the sirens went, they were in their cars and they were away to the hills. We said those were the hillbillies when at one o'clock you'd hear the sirens going and they started up ... Certainly, we were never offered a lift.

Many neighbourhood networks were disrupted by the dispersal of people following the destruction of their homes in the bombing raids, as Susan recalled:

> In that particular house where I lodged, she had another lodger ... a lady working in the factories had been bombed out and she had very reluctantly agreed to take her in, and this poor woman, really she was wretched because she was from a different part of the town altogether, and she didn't know any of the people round about and she missed her neighbours and she missed her own home as well. The lady that we were lodging with was really very eccentric and wasn't very kind to this other lady. I don't think she felt she came from a good background and that kind of thing.

Susan's story was echoed by Moya Woodside's observations about the 'culture shock' experienced by bombed out families from the slum areas who were temporarily re-housed in middle-class homes. The families who played host were often equally stunned by the disparity in lifestyles, although Woodside believed that it was about time for exposure of the extreme poverty and poor housing in Belfast's slum areas. She welcomed the fact that complacency and/or ignorance had been shattered in the course of the blitz:

> My mother telephoned to say that she took in eight evacuees last night, two mothers and six children. Says one mother is about to have another baby any minute; that they are all filthy; the smell in the room is terrible; they refuse all food except bread and tea; the children have made puddles all over the house, etc. She is terribly sorry for them, and is kindliness itself, but finds this revelation of how the 'other half' lives rather overpowering ... Went up to see my mother, who has now discovered to her horror that several of the evacuee children are T.B., and two have skin diseases on their hands.[44]

Woodside's comments about the Belfast evacuees were similar to the problems outlined in a report called *Town Children through Country Eyes*, which was prepared by the Women's Institute from the experiences in 1,700 of their branches. The report concluded that:

> the dirt and low standard of living of the evacuees from big industrial cities of Leeds and Hull has been an eye-opener and an unpleasant shock to the inhabitants of an agricultural county like Lincolnshire, who had no idea that such terrible conditions existed.[45]

Official policy on evacuation throughout Britain was based on the assumption that the poorer sections of the city populations would be the most likely to panic under air attack. Even though they were classified as 'priority evacuation classes', parents of children from slum areas were expected to provide their children with a very specific range of clothing and equipment, most of which was beyond both their income and their experience.

Alice believed that because people had to take houses wherever they could be found, it had the effect of breaking up many neighbourhoods and the community spirit did not recover until years after the war. She also believed that in the long run this was in the interests of the people, because the Housing Trust and later the Housing Executive replaced the destroyed homes with better buildings. The German bombing raids on Belfast in April and May 1941 provided the impetus for a major programme of slum-clearance in the city. In 1944 a Housing Bill was introduced which provided for new subsidies and for the establishment of the Northern Ireland Housing Trust, which was originally given the dual objectives of providing employment and improving housing conditions. Objectors in the Unionist Party saw these aims as a reflection on the competence and integrity of the local authorities. They succeeded in obtaining a number of assurances from the government, which ensured that the trust was to be no more than an auxiliary to the local authorities without power to coerce them into action. The Minister of Finance decreed that the Housing Trust's costs must determine the rents. Everything was to be paid for out of the subsidies received from the Stormont government. The task of providing housing was to be shared between the private sector, building almost entirely for sale rather than for rent, the local authorities and the Housing Trust.[46] Unlike other housing authorities in the United Kingdom, the Northern Ireland Housing Trust could not spread the rent-load over old housing stock, built when costs were not as high, nor could they use the rate fund to subsidize rents. This meant that when post-war building costs began to rise sharply and interest rates rose, the trust was never able to charge rents low enough to meet the needs of the worse-housed and lowest-paid and it was forced to build to a lower standard than that adopted in Britain.

As well as being the most overcrowded dwellings in the county borough of Dublin, the majority of the houses without a private water supply or fixed bath were to be found in the 'inner city' area, for example Arran Quay and Ballybough wards on the north side of the city and Merchant's Quay and Pembroke East wards on the south side. Many dwellings, whether they were houses, flats or rooms in tenements, still had only minimal sanitary facilities. Flats and tenements constituted 43.5 per cent of the number of private dwellings and 75 per cent of these had shared sanitary facilities, compared to 35 per cent in houses. As late as 1946, nearly 40 per cent of private dwellings had no indoor lavatory while very few working-class homes had bathrooms, making the public bathhouse a feature of the urban landscape in both Belfast and Dublin. Bathhouses had swimming baths as well as bathrooms, which could be hired for short periods of time.[47] Some families filled a tin bath in front of the fire but this involved heating so much water and carrying buckets from the fire or cooker to the bath that it was often not considered worth the bother. While the lack of adequate, or even indoor, sanitary facilities made life difficult for every member of a family living in poor housing conditions, it was especially difficult for women, particularly those with young children.

Although Mary's family were middle class and used to a comfortable home, the cottage in Coney Island to which her mother moved them for safety during the war years had only primitive facilities:

> The bedrooms were tiny and there was no water, no electricity, no inside toilet. The toilet was down, quite a distance away – we used to call it The Ivy House – over a stream and it was always kept spotless and smelling of Jeyes Fluid and all sorts of things. It was just a wooden bench with a hole in it and my grandfather was very interested in everything Irish and he used to called it 'Tondragee' which apparently means 'back to the wind'. When you were sitting on the bench this was pretty obviously why it was called that but it was fine because the stream carried everything away and every year one of the locals came and dug out everything ... of course, the toilet paper was always bits of newspaper cut up and put in on a handle.

Housework was very hard for women who had few labour-saving devices. Water had to be heated for washing clothes, most of which was done by hand in a bath with a scrubbing board. This involved lifting heavy pots of water on and off the range or cooker before emptying them into whatever container held the clothes, as Catherine explained. She had moved into a new corporation house in Drimnagh in 1942 when her husband became ill and they could no longer afford the rent for the house where they lived previously, which she thought was a much better house. She had six children and her daily routine was difficult, even before her husband died in 1944 and she had to take a cleaning job in Guinness's brewery:

> I had no washing machine, the washing all had to be done in the big zinc bath, and a scrubbing board which I still have, for washing, and

> I'd do the clothes in that ... I'd have to heat the water ... I'd rub them up and down, and leave them for a while to soak in, you know, and keeping putting in more hot water and rub up and down, like.

Mary's mother also used a zinc bath for the washing, which was done on a Monday. It was a 'huge chore' to heat the water so Mary's mother found other uses for it when the clothes had been washed:

> We were children underfoot at that stage and obviously they'd give you something to keep you occupied because we didn't have many toys. So they always gave us coloured chalks on a Monday and the floor of the kitchen was flagged and we used to draw to our heart's content on the kitchen floor. Then the water that had been left over from the clothes, that was the day that the kitchen floor was cleaned and it was cleaned so that all your chalk marks were washed away by the water.

Alice's widowed mother was out at work at her cleaning job all day and she allocated household chores to her two daughters and her son. Because of the pressure on her own time, she was very strict about ensuring that those chores were completed within a tight schedule:

> We had a mangle and I had to turn it while she put the clothes through. Thursday was ironing night and I had that to do. We had pulley lines, you know, for the clothes. Oh no, as I say, they don't know about hard work now, so they don't. My mother had a really hard life but we all had to help, our jobs were all laid out for us. She had to go back to do an office always on a Monday night. She washed on Tuesday nights so Thursday night was ironing night and that was my job. I had the ironing to do, even when I would be 18, 19 and maybe I used to say to my mother I've got a date and she'd say that's all right, after you get the ironing done.

Electric washing machines became available in Ireland in the 1920s but they were prohibitively expensive as well as being inconveniently large and unwieldy to use and it was not until the late 1960s that they were looked upon as a necessity for average homes. Washing clothes was a difficult household task and many advertisements for a range of products alluded to this in their imagery and texts, including frequent references to 'times of extra work and strain'. Newspaper features aimed at a female readership stressed that it was a woman's duty to make the most of the raw materials available to keep herself and her home looking attractive, particularly at such a time of crisis. Many advertisements for household services (such as carpet cleaning) were written in the guise of news columns and 'household hints' about the most effective ways of coping with the shortages. While the following paragraph is taken from a newspaper article published in Éire, the content and tone were reproduced in similar features in Northern Irish journals and were applied equally to food preparation, personal grooming and housework as tasks for which women were deemed to be responsible. The implication was clear that women who failed to 'make do and mend' efficiently were guilty of letting down their country as well as their families:

> The woman who is going to make or retain a reputation for a fashionable appearance in 1941 is she whose own natural flair tells how to make best use of old and familiar things, and how to place small innovations so that they will be of the best possible advantage to the whole picture. From this, I dare to prophecy a new art will develop, the art of improvisation, and its developments will be a fascinating and absorbing pursuit for all those who are not too lazy or unenterprising to give serious consideration to a matter of such vital personal interest.[48]

Maureen's home on the Falls Road was typical of artisans' dwellings in both Belfast and Dublin. Individual fireplaces heated the rooms, but having a fire in the bedroom was a special treat reserved for cases of illness, because the cost of fuel was too high for most working-class families to have fires anywhere other than the family room downstairs, even when it was available. The main kitchen was where the family lived and ate and where the mother cooked the meals on the range. The scullery had an earthenware sink or 'jawbox'[49] with one coldwater tap – there was no hot running water in any of the houses. There were no plumbed-in baths and toilets were usually in outhouses in the back yard. Local employers with large numbers of workers owned many of the houses and tenants could expect to have the rent deducted from their wages before they received them.

Only the largest and wealthiest homes had any form of central heating, and this meant that a common daily chore was cleaning out and lighting the fires or stoves that provided heat. While girls were expected to help with cooking and cleaning, carrying coal and turf to and from household bunkers was generally a task for the boys in a family. However, the household dirt that resulted from burning fires was a constant source of extra work for women, who were primarily in charge of domestic cleanliness. Coal dust has a tendency to leave a fine deposit over every surface of the room in which the fire is burned, not only leading to extra cleaning work, but also eventually damaging the various textiles in the room. In Éire, when coal had to be replaced by turf as a consequence of wartime rationing[50] the problem was exacerbated, because turf dust was even finer and more difficult to control.

Due to the shortage of coal and the subsequent restrictions on gas and electricity, the Dublin government commissioned the Turf Development Board to look into the mechanization of turf collection so that it could be exploited on a commercial scale, as opposed to the very unwieldy and inefficient methods used prior to the Emergency.[51] Turf dust was also burned in order to generate electricity. By 1942, in most homes in Dublin, coal had been replaced by turf, which was fetched directly from the storage area in the Phoenix Park[52] or delivered by local horse and cart drivers. It had been brought to Dublin in open rail carriages and stacked in the open air to dry. It had generally not been dried for a sufficient length of time to make it burn efficiently and people developed various strategies for helping it along, as Josie recalled:

> It was always soaking, most people couldn't use it, it would be so smoky ... I remember a man, he worked in C.I.E. and whatever part of it he was in he'd pick up the bits of coal from the trains, and I remember he was using the lining of his coat, to put bits of coal down the lining of the coat and he'd be walking from side to side with the coal ... He'd be bringing home the coal from the railway for a bit of fire.

When turf began to replace coal as the domestic fuel the government issued an order to fix the price of turf at 64 shillings per ton[53] but the poor often had to put up with overcharging because they could only afford to buy in small quantities. By 1942, some families were so in need of help that the government decided to introduce the winter fuel scheme for necessitous households in November 1942. This ensured that one hundredweight of turf was supplied weekly to needy families, either free of charge or at rates ranging from one shilling to two shillings per hundredweight, which compared very favourably with the fixed retail prices of commercial suppliers. In practice, 66 per cent of recipients were charged at the rate of 6d or less for their fuel. Moreover, the operation of the scheme led to the opening of more local depots throughout the city and although the collection of fuel from these centres was frequently a trying experience for many people, they reduced the need to travel and improved the distribution network.[54]

Another drawback of turf was that it was frequently flea ridden, as Clare and other women recalled. Clare's mother sent the family's bed linen to a laundry for cleaning, and she recalled how the white sheets were often covered with tiny blood spots where the fleas had bitten sleepers:

> But with the turf came fleas, by the million. Everybody suffered from the fleas. We became expert at checking our blankets at night. We would look at them before we got into bed ... They would have been in the house from the turf. I don't think we lit fires in the bedrooms; because Irish people were not accustomed to heat in the bedrooms. But the fleas would get into the bed, probably on our clothes. They were just endemic. Because of this turf, they lived in it, and everybody suffered from them and we used to squash them between our thumbs and fingers, our thumbnails.

In Northern Ireland, the Divisional Coal Officer controlled retail prices and set rations for the domestic consumer, but there was no real shortage, due to the maintenance of regular imports from Britain.[55] Before the war the Northern Irish government had accumulated reserves of coal and this allowed the Divisional Coal Officer some latitude in controlling retail prices. As in the case of food rationing, advisory committees were set up to oversee pricing and rationing so that coal merchants could not take advantage of the situation, although Moya Woodside thought the committees were unsuccessful:

> Coal prices have been on the up and up since before the war, and this morning I see the Northern Ireland Coal Owners Association are adding yet another 2/6 per ton, the reason given being increases in wages and in freight charges. This means that 1st and 2nd grade coal will now cost the frightful sum of 67/6 a ton – I'm perfectly sure the miners are getting little or no benefit.[56]

Restrictions on gas and electricity affected cooking just as much as the shortage of rationed foods. Many households used a trivet over their turf fire, on which a kettle could be left to boil. Letty remembered that her mother used the 'glimmer' of gas left in the system to keep her teapot warm because she couldn't bear to be without a pot of tea. The glimmer men[57] were officers of local gas companies, whose job was to check that the regulations concerning gas usage were strictly observed. Josie remembered being sent out by her mother to watch for the glimmer man so that she could be warned if he was coming to her house and ensure the gas cooker was cool if he came in. The glimmer man also assisted in checking that blackout regulations were enforced. The Department of Supplies issued newspaper advertisements advising on alternative means of cooking, making use of easily obtained objects, as Clare recalled:

> During this period, my mother was very skilful at cooking in unconventional fashion with what we called a 'sawdust' cooker. It consisted of a strong biscuit tin, which was actually square. It was given out by Jacobs Biscuits[58] through shops. You would try and find one of these and you would fill it with sawdust. In the middle while you were filling it with sawdust you would put down a very strong bottle. My brother reminded me it was a champagne bottle; we didn't drink champagne but that's what it was.[59] So then the sawdust was packed tightly around this bottle in this twelve-inch square tin and dampened, and through some method it became congealed, I suppose, and then it was ignited and it burnt very slowly, in a manner like a slow cooker and it was extremely efficient. Apparently, there were other systems known as hay box cooking, for keeping food warm, because gas was rationed in the Dublin area. You got one hour for cooking and then you must turn off the system and people, the glimmer men went around checking for gas, whether it had been used in the off period. It was extremely limited in the amount you could use every day so this haybox system would keep food warm where people came in for a late dinner or whatever.

In January 1943 the Dublin Gas Company drew attention to another aspect of the rationing of gas that was the cause of some concern, when a warning was issued to gas users urging them to exercise more care in seeing all gas taps were turned off at night. Several instances of gas poisoning had been reported in the city and there were even some deaths. The problem was that in the blackout, many people were going to bed very early but forgetting to turn off the gas taps. When the daily rationing period ended at 9.30 p.m. the gas started flowing through the pipes again and could seep through a house very quickly, leading to carbon monoxide poisoning.[60]

Delivery vans and carts were a common feature of the streets during the Second World War years. Since few people at the time had refrigerators, storing food could be problematic, especially in warm weather, and shopping had to be done frequently, even daily. A regular delivery of perishable foods such as milk, eggs, meat and bread allowed women some relief from the pressure of having to shop every day, as Mary described:

Everything could be delivered. It was a good walk up to Ardglass but the bread man called daily and we dealt with – you see interestingly, when you talk about the Protestant/Catholic thing – there were two shops in Ardglass, two grocer shops. One was Milligan's, that would have been a Catholic family and the other was Hunter's, and it was very prim and proper. My grandmother always dealt with Hunter's and you went up with a list to Hunter's and they just took the list and charged you and delivered. You didn't have to carry shopping or anything like that, so that was easier in a way.

Alice was the only one of the interviewees who remembered wartime vacations and that was because the wartime conditions made the memory more vivid for her. Moya Woodside and her husband were able to travel away from the routes served only by public transport because of the petrol allowance his job afforded him and this made it possible for her to see less developed areas of Éire. They spent several wartime holidays in a luxury hotel in Donegal[61] where they met other people from Northern Ireland who were in a position to escape the privations of war for a time:

> This hotel provides an extraordinary oasis in a wartime world. Catering must be a nightmare (for geographic reasons alone – 135 miles from Belfast, 215 from Dublin, no other towns and a scanty and uncertain train service) yet food remains at pre-war luxury level; and a band plays during tea and dinner and later for dancing; people golf solemnly most of the day and bridge with equal seriousness at night. All around are sand dunes, mountains, sea and the poverty stricken country people, whom one does not dare to approach because of being ashamed (to speak for myself) of staying in such a place.[62]

Following the introduction of rationing in Northern Ireland in September 1939 the newspapers featured allegations of profiteering, and it was agreed that the Ministry of Food would place advertisements in the press giving the controlled prices of food as set out in the Emergency Powers Orders. There were some difficulties as regards the advertising, with complaints that only city newspapers carried the advertisements, putting people from rural areas at a disadvantage:

> As a matter of fact, the general attitude of the Ministry of Food to press advertisement is negative, as they have told me in the course of correspondence which I have had with them on the subject. They say that the Press is publishing from their Orders quite sufficient for the

general guidance of the public. After the War itself, as I pointed out to press representatives who came to see me here the other day, food is supremely 'news'.[63]

The effect of this was to cause confusion for ordinary people, although it is clear from the following correspondence that those responsible for policy in the Ministry of Food in London were more concerned about the enormous logistical task they faced than they were about publicizing food orders: 'I quite agree that it must be a matter of some difficulty for the "average housewife" to keep track of controlled retail prices. If it would be any consolation to her, you might tell her that it is not an easy matter for the Divisional Food Officer!'[64]

The cost of living index in Northern Ireland was not differentiated from the cost of living index for the rest of the United Kingdom, which was calculated from statistics compiled by the Ministry of Labour in Westminster. In these figures, the indices for rent and rates in the working class cost of living index did not rise significantly until 1947, which suggests that the housing shortage created by the bombing raids on many areas of the United Kingdom, including Belfast, did not cause rent prices to rise, most likely because of the anti-profiteering measures adopted by the Ministry of War in London.[65] Despite the very sharp rise in the cost of living index generally in the course of the war, the fact that rationing reduced the social inequities in consumption acted as a boost to the poor and low paid, who had not enjoyed much purchasing power in the pre-war years.

In Éire, the shortage of basic essentials led to a rise in the cost of living during the Emergency, particularly in the early period between 1939 and 1941 when the absence of rationing arrangements increased the opportunities for exploitation of the need for scarce goods. In February 1940, the cost of living index number was five points (or 3 per cent) above that for November 1939 and 23 points (or 13 per cent) above that for February 1939, which was 'altogether attributable to war-time conditions'.[66] Between August 1939 and August 1945, the cost of living index for food alone rose by 120 points or 70 per cent.[67]

Appendix 12 compares the average cost of several basic but essential foodstuffs through the period from 1938 to 1945, derived from information collected in 120 towns, large and small, throughout Éire. The effect of the rising cost of basic necessities obviously had a greater impact on the low paid than on families with reasonable incomes. Given that women workers earned considerably less than their male counterparts in most industries, the effect of rising costs on their wages was disproportionately greater. Sheila's mother had her own methods of ensuring that her family was fed properly:

17. Kathleen, Mary and Sheila in the garden of their Marino home. They are surrounded by Mary's hens.

> She kept hens, she grew potatoes, she grew everything. She grew lettuce, we had apple trees, she was amazing in that way; and I mean we always had fresh eggs, so that we were quite well fed. Funny, I remember my sister, I remember Maureen saying that, you know, when things were probably quite bad, that she remembers the actual slices of bread being rationed. Like, Mammy would butter the bread on the table and there were two slices each, but I don't remember that, I really don't. I must have been maybe sheltered, I don't know, but I don't remember that.

As shortages in a range of products became more widespread, shopping took up a significant portion of the average woman's day as she had to search for everything, including items that were common before the war. This was difficult enough for the full-time housewife but must have been a nightmare for the woman who was also in employment outside the home, as Moya Woodside commented:

> One wastes so much time, running round from place to place, begging for ½ lb. of this and ¼ lb. of that, and mostly being told 'no'. Rationing, which of course [sic] inevitable, does put one at the mercy of the shopkeepers so, who are in a position to grant or withhold scarce commodities and who know that this customer can't go elsewhere.[68]

Various strategies were adopted for making better use of existing foods, as more and more items disappeared from the shelves. The newspapers were full of helpful hints for economies, many of them carrying columns headed 'For Women'[69] or some similar title which made it clear who had the responsibility for ensuring the nation's well-being despite the shortages. The monthly *Model Housekeeping* magazine had a column entitled 'Housekeeping for January' (or the appropriate month) which suggested menus for every day of the week. Recipes for the various dishes were also included in the magazine, although economy of scale or the unavailability of many foods does not seem to have been an important influence (see Appendix 13).[70]

The Ministry of Food produced a 'food facts' leaflet on a regular basis that suggested recipes for healthy eating. The fact that the restricted diet was healthier in many ways than traditional Ulster high-fat cooking was of little consolation to some people:

> I am very much grieved at receiving my notice to only give one sixth of an ounce of butter to men for breakfast, tea etc. I enclose this quantity just to let you see the size of butter for a man's breakfast – and have some soldiers[71] who call in occasionally for these meals and I think it would be an insult to any man who was going out to fight for us and also fight for both King and Country. The man who made this law has little faith in God and does not seem to know the 23 Psalm, The Lords my Shepherd I'll not want, if these men who make the laws of the land lived on the laws of God they would be a shepherd to the flock who have to go out when trained to meet and fight the enemy. I was told by a Belfast man on Saturday that he knew that lots of butter was stored up until stinked and then it had to be sold to the soap factorys. I'd like very much to know if this is true and perhaps you would find out and ever so much oblige.
>
> Signed Mollie Lee.
>
> P.S. Years ago I read a speech made by Miss Pankhurst I don't know if she is alive yet she was trying to get votes for women and in her

speech she said I'd be willing to do six months in gaol to get sense boxed into men's heads.[72]

Susan's landlady in Belfast clearly did not understand the basis of the rationing system and the intention to equalize access to scarce commodities:

> I was in lodging with an elderly lady who didn't really understand much about rationing. She thought that if the food was there she would take it. I had to share her larder and one day I came home from work, well, I don't think we got much butter at all but we had marg, and I had my marg ration in the larder and when I came home from work that evening there was 1/6 there or something instead of the marg and a little note from her saying 'I have taken your marg.'

The rationing system recognized that some people had special needs and children under five, pregnant women and nursing mothers had one pint of milk daily and twice the normal ration of eggs. They also had first choice of any fruit. Cod liver oil, fruit juices and vitamin supplements were also allocated to expectant mothers and children under five.[73] As food became scarcer, prices rose so that even if essential items, such as fruit, became available, they were out of the reach of women on low incomes:

> At usual weekly case committee of Welfare Society. Case after case asking for 'extra nourishment', 'clothing for the children'. Local U.A.B. and P.A.'s scales of relief make it impossible for people to provide even the barest of minimum diets (£2.2s.0d for a family of 11 was one sample) and clothing replacements are almost out of the question. In this war, the very poor will suffer the worst.[74]

The southern government also made special provision for pregnant women and young children.

Throughout her diary, Moya Woodside referred to the prices of individual items of food and she wondered often who could actually afford to pay for them, even though she herself seems to have enjoyed a reasonably good income. She noted that the shortages had the further effect of closing down small businesses like groceries and fruit shops, whose trade was cut back to such an extent they could no longer afford to stay open.

The majority of the shop assistants in these businesses were women. The Ministry of Food did make efforts to maintain profit margins for food retailers and, in virtually every case, the margins allowed under the various price orders for food were slightly in excess of the profit levels before the war. The Ministry of Food (Defence Plans) Department in London made a comprehensive series of orders during the period from the end of August to early October 1939 in which control was assumed over the sale of virtually every form of foodstuff.

During the Emergency, the government of Éire assumed wide-ranging powers in response to the demands of security and the need to ensure the continuation of essential services. The Emergency Powers Act 1939 was the basis of the blackout regulations, censorship, food and clothing rationing and travel restrictions until its expiration in September 1946. Although the Northern Ireland parliament's powers to legislate were restricted by the terms of the Government of Ireland Act 1920, most of the laws passed during the war years were enacted to enable the agency arrangements whereby departments of the Northern Ireland government were deputed to act on behalf of wartime ministries in Britain. The emergency legislation passed by the Westminster government concerned most areas of civilian life, including restrictions on travel between Éire and Britain. The impact of the war on the lives of women in Éire and Northern Ireland in the shape of the wartime laws passed by their respective governments was manifested to a significant extent in the effect that the various Emergency Powers Orders had on their domestic responsibilities. In their domestic lives, particularly for women with families to look after, the war led to a significant rise in the cost of food and fuel and this had an immediate impact on their capacity to make their incomes cover all of the basic necessities. The rationing introduced by both the Northern Ireland and the Éire governments enabled a fairer distribution of scarce goods and this benefited lower paid women, but the queuing for rations and the 'making do and mend' policies promulgated by those governments also entailed an increased domestic workload which was mainly borne by women. In this regard, even though the two 'home fronts' were distinguished by the difference in the belligerent standing of their respective governments, the impact on the women who were so intrinsically identified with the home was essentially identical.

7

Health in wartime

> Then I got a bit of chicken and other patients used to say, oh did you get chicken? That was a sign you were going home; that meant you were dying, you know? Oh Josie, did you get the bit of chicken, you must be going home. (Josie)

Throughout the nineteenth and twentieth centuries, the only time that preventive medicine really flourished was during wars, when the need to prevent people from falling sick, as distinct from curing them when they did, was urgent.[1] Health care was not a priority for the Northern Ireland government in the inter-war years. There was no Ministry of Health until 1945. Before that date, the Ministry of Local Government controlled health matters. Similarly, in the Irish Free State and Éire, health was the responsibility of the Department of Local Government and Public Health, rather than a dedicated ministry, which was not established until 1947.

Dr R.H. Trinnick was a Mass-Observation diarist in Belfast, and many of his reports concerned his patients and the affect the war was having on their health. Writing in February 1942, he categorized the physical and emotional manifestations of the wartime conditions that were bringing patients to his clinic. The different types of patient that he identified were suffering from many of the same conditions recalled by the women who took part in this project and also described by Moya Woodside in her own Mass-Observation diary, although he did not mention any particular difficulties associated with maternity:

> I don't think the war has affected my physical health, but I have to deal professionally every day with people whose health has been so affected. The following are some examples:
> 1. An entire group (members of related families) living together, some of them bombed out, who used to live in the same small cottage. There were 14 of them and although it must be a physical impossibility, the whole lot of them used to shelter in an Anderson when raids were on. Almost all of them got bronchitis.

18. Advertisements for tonics were a common feature of newspaper and magazine advertising during the war years. There were frequent references to women's 'nerves'.

2. Although perhaps not strictly physically ill, there is a large group of women who are listless, nervous, and inclined to weep easily as a direct result of war circumstances. They come from what is in peacetime an underfed and badly housed section of the populace, and may be divided into:–
   (a) wives of privates and equivalent ranks who seem to be lost and helpless without their husbands, and fairly frequently ask for medical certificates on insufficient grounds for a grant of leave for their husbands.
   (b) ... mothers whose sons and daughters (civilian) are back with them on account of being bombed out or of the call-up of the husband. The extra homework and responsibility frequently leads to 'nerves' in this group.
3. Workers, men and women from all walks of life in factories and offices who are either working too long hours or under grossly unsatisfactory conditions of ventilation, lighting, both or worse.

> For example, a group of Home Defence workers who in their spell of night duty are shamefully overcrowded in a small brick building with inadequate ventilation in which they sleep *situated on the banks of a sewage farm*. About half these men have had influenza, bronchitis, or heavy colds ...
> 4. There is an increase in minor skin infections such as scabies and impetigo, due to the poorer housing conditions, and the general movement and mixing of population groups – evacuation, bombed outs, etc.[2]

The main causes of infant death in Northern Ireland during the war years were identified as premature birth and injury at birth and bronchial and gastric disorders.[3] In Belfast in particular, these causes were related to the poverty and inadequate nutrition of the mothers, although it is likely that the food rationing operating during the war years operated to the advantage of poor mothers and their children in that many of them received a guaranteed and balanced diet, possibly for the first time in their lives. Nevertheless, Northern Ireland had the worst record in the United Kingdom in respect of taking advantage of free vitamin products, with the result that in a survey of rickets[4] in the United Kingdom and Éire, Belfast had the poorest record of any other city.[5] This state of affairs would not have been improved by the scarcity of fresh fruit during the war.

In the 1939–40 report of the Department of Local Government and Public Health, the Medical Officer of the Dublin County Borough Maternity and Child Welfare Scheme is quoted as citing the failure of mothers to breast-feed their infants as a causative factor of infant mortality:

> He believes that this failure is due to a large extent to some form of malnutrition or diet deficiency and to the increased pace of life conditions in the city but has no relation to housing accommodation.[6]

In a study of infant mortality in the city of Belfast conducted in 1944, James Deeny and Eric Murdock noted that the significance of income as a deciding factor influencing infant mortality is clear, where income was considered as the amount, less rent, available to the mother for household purposes per head per week.[7] They found that certain dispensary areas in Belfast showed an unduly heavy mortality rate and this was associated with the concentration in those areas of a larger number of people with low incomes living in crowded conditions.

By 1942, the shortages caused by the war were exacting a heavy toll from many sections of the population in both Belfast and Dublin, particularly for families on low incomes. Although rationing of food and fuel ensured a fairer distribution of vital commodities to the poor and low paid, people involved in providing services often ran into obstacles unrelated to the cost of food, as Susan recalled about her work in the Rotunda hospital:

> At that time, we would have been seeing, well, we would have been seeing the in-patients but we were seeing a lot of the out-patients and helping them make arrangements for the care of their children when they came in to have their babies or various things like that, and arranging for them to have any charitable assistance that they needed. For instance, the St John's Brigade, they ran dinners in Dublin and it was they we dealt with at that time because a lot of the women really needed the extra food and most of our patients would not take the dinners because they served too much fish and in war time, because of all the people who were being drowned, the fish were feeding on the drowned people, therefore they just would not eat fish. They certainly were very adamant about that, but they also served a lot of cheese dishes and Irish people in those days wouldn't eat much cheese.

Some women had their own methods of ensuring that their families stayed healthy, regardless of the hardships of war. Clare's mother gave her children cod liver oil and a drink called 'Parrish's food' which was iron based and which she made them take every morning, despite their protests about the terrible taste.

One of the most serious consequences of the bread shortage was the increase in the cases of rickets in Éire, particularly in Dublin, which was attributed to the government order to make 100 grammes of bread from 95 per cent extraction flour. While it is generally considered that a wholemeal loaf is more nutritious than a white loaf, the phytic acid contained in the wheat grain and incorporated in the wholemeal loaf operates to destroy calcium in the normal diet.[8] Children from poorer homes were more likely to have bread as a high proportion of their diet and it was estimated that an individual whose bread intake was twelve ounces per day would lose approximately 230 mg of calcium. In the 1946 national nutrition survey carried out by the Department of Health (which covered the Emergency years) 'bread and spread' meals counted for a much larger proportion of the meals eaten by families living in slums than of artisan families and the middle class.[9]

Finding a solution to food shortages during the war, on both sides of the border, forced the authorities in both states to take a much more proactive approach to devising social policy than had been the case in the 1930s, particularly in Northern Ireland, and rationing and anti-profiteering measures meant that state control was exerted over previously unregulated areas of productivity. In Britain, the concept of total war that characterized the national mobilization raised domestic problems to the same level as military strategy. The result of this influence on social policy was a recognition that after the war there would have to be important changes. Northern Ireland's role in the war guaranteed that the benefits (embodied in the recommendations of the Beveridge Report) would be extended to that part of the United Kingdom and the kind of poverty and malnourishment that was exposed after the Belfast blitz would be eliminated. Éire's neutrality did not preclude this radicalization of social policy and while it was not as wide-ranging in the long term as in the North, the assumption by the state of responsibility for improved nutrition as part of a number of measures to prevent ill health was not very different from the approach taken by its belligerent neighbour.

For many working-class women, whether employed or unemployed, bad health was the order of the day. Poverty and overcrowding in many areas increased the likelihood of poor health, but women were particularly vulnerable because of the heavy demands made on them by childbirth and their domestic responsibilities. They had to face the problems of raising children, making ends meet, doing most of the housework and often doing paid employment as well, as Moya Woodside observed:

> Interviewed a woman at Welfare Office this morning, whose husband had had no work for the past 7 years. She was 33, tubercular, and had a 'bad heart' and was the mother of nine living children. Four other children had died. She came to us asking for baby clothes, as she was shortly expecting her 14th confinement, just a year after the last.[10]

According to a study conducted during the war, tuberculosis was particularly prevalent among the unemployed, where the two factors that most favoured the development of the disease were very likely to be found – insufficient food and overcrowded housing.[11] In the 1930s the Irish Free State had the worst annual percentage reduction in deaths from tuberculosis out of twenty countries in Europe, Australasia and North America.[12] Within Ireland the reduction rate in Dublin was the lowest, coming second only to Rome in a list of major European cities.[13]

Tuberculosis continued to be the most widespread of the contagious diseases into the 1940s, despite the strenuous efforts that were being made to combat infection. Counihan and Dillon concluded that the main operative factor for the difference in the total death rate between Belfast and Dublin was the persistence of unemployment in the latter city.[14] Josie was one of the casualties:

> I got very sick with TB at the time ... I had it in the hip and I was away four years there. I had to learn to walk again, after that. I would have been about 18 when I got that, you know. Thank God I made a great recovery. I had wonderful care but at the time it was very hard.

Josie was not living in overcrowded conditions although she was unable to find work in Dublin during the Emergency. None of the rest of her family got the disease, although she had two sisters and her mother at home when she was diagnosed.

In November 1942, the formation of the National Anti-Tuberculosis League was announced in Dublin. Its aim was to unite all classes in society in a nation-wide campaign against the disease but it ran into opposition from the Catholic Church in the person of the Archbishop of Dublin, Dr McQuaid, who insisted that the Irish Red Cross should be in charge. Dr John Shanley, chairman of the Red Cross at the time, suggested that Archbishop McQuaid was alarmed by the Protestant flavour of the leadership of the proposed league and he preferred the predominantly Catholic Red Cross.[15] In any case, measures to tackle tuberculosis were adopted by the government and pushed through under the stewardship of Dr James Deeny[16] who was appointed chief medical officer in September 1944. The potential for conflict between the Church and the state emerged as other schemes for over-hauling the health system were proposed. These would give the minister a more direct role in allocating services. An alliance developed between the Catholic Church and the medical profession in resisting what they saw as the encroachments of politicians and bureaucrats.[17]

Medicines were also in short supply and the Department of Local Government and Public Health concentrated on controlling outbreaks of the most infectious diseases. In addition to the problem of widespread tuberculosis, other contagious diseases, such as diphtheria[18] and scarlet fever,[19] were particularly dangerous in overcrowded housing conditions because they were passed on by personal contact. Even without overcrowding, once a virulent infection got into a family it could spread very quickly, as Catherine recalled:

> I had one little girl when I lived in another house, far away from here, and she died ... she got scarlet fever and he [the general practitioner] left me to look after her and I was expecting another baby at the time and the little girl, 4 years old, she died ... Then she was buried this day

and I got the scarlet fever and of course, I was expecting a baby that very day. So when they took away the hearse and the funeral went off I was taken in the ambulance to Cork Street fever hospital[20] and I had a baby girl. Of course, I had to stay there till the scarlet went off, the scarlet fever. They treated it and that, and then when I came home there was a couple of the other children after getting it too.

In 1941, the year that Catherine's little girl died, there were thirty-two deaths from scarlet fever in the Dublin county borough.[21] Betty also remembered the way the disease swept through their family, partly because she associated the event with another trauma in the family:

We all got the scarlet fever together. My sister got it first and they didn't treat her properly for it. Now my brother, my eldest brother that's away, he was ten years old then, and about two months before she died he fell off a wall and broke his neck and he was in plaster of Paris from here to here and all you could see was his two eyes, his nose and his mouth ... Now the day he got the plaster off his neck my sister died of scarlet fever. That was on the Saturday, and she was buried on the Monday morning, And my sister that's away now, she was born in Cork Street fever hospital, she was the only baby ever born in Cork Street.

Betty and the other children had to be quarantined when they got the fever and she remembered being in Sir Patrick Dun's hospital[22] over Christmas and a doctor playing Santa Clause for the benefit of the patients.

Quarantine regulations were very strictly enforced and could lead to very difficult situations for a family. Clare was sent to hospital when she contracted diphtheria after sharing a friend's lollipop. Her friend developed the infection just before her and Clare was put into quarantine and was unable to see her family:

I was in for eight weeks. It was isolation, in the Hardwicke Hospital.[23] I was in it for seven weeks without contact with my family. I thought they had died in a fire in the house and they were all gone. After one month I used to be allowed to go down to the garden where my father could see me. My mother never came, because she might have brought it back to the rest of the family.

In 1940 and 1941, the Éire government was concerned about the possibility of invasion and plans were drawn up to evacuate 70,000 children from the

Dublin county borough and Dun Laoghaire. It was intended that eligibility for evacuation would include the condition that children be inoculated against diphtheria. Clare had been released from hospital by this time but, in any case, immunization appears to have been the key to eradication of the disease and the decline in the number of deaths was directly attributable to the inoculation programme.[24]

When Nancy finished her nursing training in England, she returned to Dublin for a while to take up a job in the Cork Street fever hospital. She was horrified by the conditions in the hospital but she did not know if they were typical of Irish hospitals or just the result of the fact that the hospital was nearly 150 years old:

> The conditions were terrible ... It had been there for donkey's years. It was in very bad shape and the medical superintendent of the hospital, he said there was a diagram in the front hall of a model of the new hospital. He said do you see that laundry down there, and all that steam going to waste up the chimney there, that should be piped up into the hospital for poor children with the croup and what have you. But he said I'll never live to see that. But they started building soon after I left, out at Cherry Orchard. The poor man had a heart attack so he didn't get to see it.

Most of Nancy's patients were from the slum areas of Dublin, and having to go out to collect patients in an ambulance gave her an insight into the dreadful conditions in which some people in the city were living:

> They came from, if you saw some of the houses, because they were all infectious diseases, or reputed to be infectious diseases, we had to go out and collect them in our own ambulance from Cork Street and there we had two drivers who also were a pantomime. So we had to go out and bring them in and you couldn't even bring in their clothes so you had to wrap them in a blanket and bring them in so that nothing came in.

The Northern Irish health authorities were also concerned to contain any outbreaks of potentially epidemic diseases. The executive sanitary officers, later known as public health inspectors and environmental health officers, were responsible for the purity of the water supply, as well as working with the medical superintendent officer of health in carrying out whatever measures were necessary to prevent the spread of disease.[25] A diary entry by Moya Woodside refers to an epidemic of scabies[26] that swept through

What a difference Sunlight makes—

Homes brighter—
Clothes whiter

What a blessing Sunlight is to the busy housewife! Its rich, active suds soon get to work making the home spotless, the wash as white as snow. And the cheerful, natural golden colour of Sunlight is a guarantee. A guarantee that Sunlight is all pure soap, safe to use for every washing job in the home and so very gentle both to the hands and clothes. Let your home be happy with the radiant cleanness Sunlight gives!

19. Advertisement for 'Sunlight' soap. This was a very popular product in Ireland and Britain.

Ulster in late 1940 and which she felt the authorities were slow to deal with, possibly on account of embarrassment about the extent of the epidemic and their uncertainty about how to combat it. While her response is a personal one, she does highlight a problem that was consistent with the Northern Ireland government's cautious approach to taking action:

> Apropos of this epidemic, a refugee doctor from Vienna, who for years had made scabies his special study, and who had been in charge of a Viennese hospital with one block set apart solely for the treatment of this disease, went off recently (after months of idleness and in spite of an English degree) to waste his talents doing G.P. in the Midlands. What might not a progressive public health administration have done with this man, cast up on their own doorstep just when his knowledge and experience were needed?[27]

Scabies was very common in Éire as well, and the public health authorities seem to have adopted very strict methods to deal with an outbreak, as Clare recalled:

> In this period, children developed a disease called scabies and every family had to go to the Iveagh Baths to be washed down with a white liquid, immersed in the public bath, to our absolute shame and horror to be stripped down in front of everyone.[28] We had to be immersed in this solution because scabies became rampant.

There was a shortage of cleaning materials, for personal and domestic hygiene, because so many of those products had to be imported and there were no ships to bring them. Scabies became widespread throughout Dublin. The infection was particularly likely to appear where families were crowded together and where clothing was not regularly laundered. This did not necessarily apply only in very poor households, as Clare explained, because her mother used a local laundry for bed linen and regular cleaning did not help them escape either the scabies mite or the fleas that infested the turf that was burned for heat:

> Our soap was very basic. Sunlight soap that we buy today, that was the main soap, you'd to wash your face in that. Then there was carbolic soap; that was like a red soap and the soap that was supposed to be for washing floors – that was called 'Dirtshifter', a grey soap. You could wash the clothes in it if you hadn't got the other one ... All the bed linen went to a laundry and it got what they called a 'full finish', which meant it came back ironed and starched. The bed linen went and table cloths, and I think, maybe towels, anything of that nature.

Although during the early years of the Emergency scabies was not a notifiable disease under the terms of the Public Health (Infectious Diseases) regulations, the government was forced to deal with the outbreak as a matter of urgency because the British government decided that every Irish immigrant would have to undergo a health inspection before being allowed to enter the country. Both scabies and lice were treated at the same time. Clare's recollection of the shame associated with the cleansing procedure was based on the lack of personal dignity in the treatment, during which the infected person was subjected to washing and shaving of the under-arm and pubic areas and then painted with benzyl benzoate, a noxious blue dye.[29] In October 1943, the government made scabies a notifiable disease under the Public Health regulations.

The dispensary doctors who operated local clinics in both Northern Ireland and Éire were severely overworked and were sometimes unable to see all the patients registered with them. Similarly, as there were no vaccination programmes against childhood diseases in either jurisdiction, these could often develop into serious illness, as Minnie's family discovered to their cost:

> She was 3 years old when we went down the country for our summer holidays. Every year when we got our school holidays Mam took us down to her mother's and Catherine with us and she got pneumonia and died. She got measles and took the pneumonia from the measles. She died down there; she's buried in Castleblayney.[30]

Most of the women who were interviewed remembered family members who died prematurely but they did not think that they could have been saved, given the level of medical knowledge during the Second World War period. The Guinness brewery where Catherine's husband worked (and where she went to work after his death from a septic ulcer) had a very well resourced medical centre for staff and employees, where free medical and dental care was offered to family members as well as workers. It is not clear how usual that sort of service was at the time, even in large companies. Alice enjoyed free medical care in the Ormeau Bakery, although it seems that sick pay was not extended to all members of staff. When she had an accident on her bike, she went into work the next day, despite feeling very unwell:

> There was a doctor, not on the premises but just in the next block. Dr Young, he was the bakery doctor and another ... I was so scared I wouldn't get out on the bike again I got up and went to work the next morning. When I went in and Mr Curson, one of the managers, came in on business into the chocolate room and he saw me. So when I told him what had happened he sent me to the ambulance room and then Dr Young was sent for and I was sent home. I was concussed ... But I was well taken care of in the bakery – it was in the middle of the week and they told me to stay off until the following Monday ... Yes, I was paid for that.

The Women's Voluntary Services called upon women who were not normally employed in the health service to train in elementary first aid as part of the WVS brief to assist the local authorities. In Northern Ireland, the organization worked under the general direction of the Ministry of Public

Security until its dissolution in May 1944; subsequently the WVS operated under the auspices of the Ministry of Home Affairs. The WVS volunteers also trained in fire-fighting techniques and assisted with local air raid precautions, although their most common occupation was running canteens and administering evacuation services and rest centre services. Voluntary work seems to have been undertaken mainly by middle-class women, who claimed it was their patriotic duty. Moya Woodside felt that their eagerness to do 'jobs which at home they would have left to maid or charwoman' would have been better given to unemployed women who needed the work and could be paid for doing it.[31] Her observation underlines the difficulty in securing improved pay and conditions for women health workers, particularly in time of war, when the traditional argument that nurturing was its own reward could be combined with appeals to the national interest.

In a study carried out in 1945 to assess the means of improving the health services in Belfast city, it was recommended that better maternity services were the most urgent requirement.[32] There was a further suggestion that home helps should be recruited in sufficient numbers to help the many women needing assistance at home. One of the difficulties in this regard was recruitment of sufficient numbers to do this work. There was a presumption that only women would be applying for the jobs but nevertheless the poor pay and conditions were clearly a barrier to recruitment:

> The present conditions of service apparently are not attractive enough to enable us to get a sufficient supply of women for the work. The present rate of pay is 8/- per day and the hours worked are from 8 a.m. to 6 p.m., Sundays excepted, save where Sunday falls within four days of the confinement. These hours seem to be too long with insufficient off duty time ... Another disadvantage of the existing conditions is that employment may be irregular, and the Home Helps do not qualify for unemployment benefit. To get over this difficulty, I suggest that we pay a retaining fee of 4/- per day after three months service.[33]

Many working-class women still chose to give birth at home, particularly when they had more than one child: 'Well, it was more or less handier with the others, to have them in the house. Gertie was born at home, and Maureen ... So Gertie and Maureen and Paddy, three were born at home.' Mothers might have found it easier to have births at home, although this was not necessarily because they could expect assistance from the fathers, but because they needed to be around to make sure the children were looked after and domestic chores were attended to properly. Susan recalled a case she came across in her work at the Rotunda hospital:

> In those days, husbands didn't attend the birth or the delivery room ... I don't think they [the mothers] were given too much advice at all. I don't think they were given a lot of help in any way. They mostly had swarms of young children at home and very inadequate housing, a lot of them ... I was visiting a woman who'd had her twenty-first child and it was in a tenement house. The staircase was all gone; I had to practically crawl up the last few steps on my hands and knees. Her husband was unemployed ... and the doctor said, he's not unemployed, if he's got twenty-one children.

The women who had their children at home usually called on local midwives to assist at the births. Dublin was better served by maternity hospitals than the rest of the country and the maternal mortality rate tended to be lower than in the rest of the country, although there has been some argument about whether this was due to the hospitals themselves or the fact that the only extensive maternity and child welfare scheme in the country was operating in the city.[34] In 1944, the annual report of the Department of Local Government and Public Health paid tribute to the Rotunda, Coombe, and National Maternity hospitals in Dublin, crediting them with playing a significant role in the reduction of maternal morality rates in the country as a whole. Cormac Ó Gráda notes that the high mortality was in part the product of repeated childbearing, and the associated high blood pressure and anaemia. He credits the combination of smaller families with improved medical care for the huge reduction in maternal mortality since the 1930s and 1940s.[35] The Department of Local Government and Public Health report attributed the improvement to increased use of measures to combat puerperal sepsis, which had been responsible for many maternal deaths in earlier decades.[36] The quality of care depended on the standards of the staff as much as the facilities and Jean's experience of puerperal sepsis in a nursing home in Belfast underlined the fact that childbirth could be very dangerous:

> Well, I was three days in an emergency room, which was next to the delivery room and the other miracle is that we both lived thanks to my own doctor having to come in at five o'clock in the morning. He saved us both ... The problem was that the night nurse who was on was incapable; she didn't give me an enema when she should have ... then the doctor wouldn't risk her giving me a sedative or an anaesthetic so he looked after me himself and called in a consultant.

Unqualified midwives were forbidden to practise in Northern Ireland, just like in Éire, although some women still preferred to rely on local women who were trusted to assist with family crises, including childbirth. These 'handywomen', as they were known, were attractive to mothers because they would help with the housework and the other children, as well as delivering the new baby, as Maureen recalled:

> there was always a woman in most streets and if anyone was sick you went for her – childbirth and everything. Mrs Craig it was in our street and when you were sick everyone went for Mrs Craig ... We were all born at home. My mother always had a nurse come in. If there was complications, probably a doctor would be called but usually the nurse would come in when you called her.

The Midwives Act 1917 (predating the partition of Ireland and the establishment of the two states) made it illegal for an untrained person to assist at a birth if a trained person was available. The provisions of this Act were strengthened in the South by the Midwives Act 1931 and the Registration of Maternity Homes Act 1934 and in the North by the Midwives and Nursing Homes Act (Northern Ireland) 1929, although the latter dealt primarily with the registration of midwives working in private nursing homes.

Moya Woodside made a diary entry in 1940 which cast light on a phenomenon also noted in Britain in the early years of the war:

> A friend told me yesterday afternoon that she has started her 2nd baby, to arrive in September. Has 1st only 13 months old, but 'we wanted to get on with it' she said. I admired her faith in the future, belief that there would always be enough to eat for these children. It's rather curious that people married during the last three or four years tend to believe in children again and to start families right away; while those who got married from six to ten years ago frequently held that the world was in no fit state to bring children into, and postponed parenthood – when indeed, the world was considerably more liveable in than it is now! I can't explain this unexpected change of outlook, but it's a fact. I know many examples here and elsewhere; and some Czech refugee friends tell me it was the same with people there.[37]

It might seem that it would be more likely that the birth rate would fall in wartime but in *The People's War*, Angus Calder also remarked on the popularity of marriage and childbearing in the first two or three years of the war, although he attributed it to the greater fluidity of social relations. Woodside was still preoccupied with the phenomenon late in the following year:

> Talked to a friend about the astonishing popularity of babies at the moment. We could think of dozens of people known to one or other of us who were either having or have just had an infant, and many of them barely a year married. We decided that it must be that so many young wives expected their husbands to be sent out East, and wanted to have something to occupy them selves with while they were away![38]

Between 1941 and 1942, 57 per cent of all births registered in the three Dublin maternity hospitals occurred within the first year of the mother's marriage, suggesting that very few women were using contraception.[39] Moya Woodside gave regular talks on birth control to women's groups, particularly in Protestant working-class districts of Belfast. Although she does not refer to it directly, it is unlikely that such talks would have been encouraged in Catholic areas, where most welfare work was channelled through the local priest. Her account of one meeting where she gave a lecture gives a good indication of attitudes that were shared by the women who spoke to me, particularly in regard to their reticence about the subject:

> Gave talk on birth control to Co-Op Women's Guild meeting ... Response to my talk much as usual – older women (in the majority) inclined to repeat they had eight (or ten or twelve) children and were none the worse for it. One woman (60ish) enquired 'doesn't all this bother with birth control make you neurotic?' I told her how it soon became as automatic as your dentures, which amused the others greatly. Younger women are more receptive, although shy of asking questions in front of people. Although I have no children myself, I find that at these meetings, I am always made the recipient of intimate gynaecological and obstetrical histories, once the ice has been broken.[40]

If a woman wanted to exercise some form of mechanical birth control, she had to make arrangements to get supplies from Britain, although organizations like the Marie Stopes family planning clinics in London had local agents in Belfast, like Moya Woodside herself,[41] who would arrange to import some medical supplies. Detailed information about birth control also was available through mail order from Britain.[42] Northern Ireland was part of the United Kingdom and no attempts were made to ban birth control, despite disapproval and opposition from both Catholic and Protestant sources.

Greta Jones' research on the operation of the Marie Stopes Mother's Clinic in Belfast suggests that it was not only local women who were using the services.[43] The admittedly limited evidence, because most of the case files were destroyed, suggests that women from Éire were asking for advice and information about birth control. Sections 16 and 17 of the 1929 Censorship of Publications Act banned the printing, publishing, distribution or sale of publications advocating contraception or abortion as means of birth control while Section 17 of the 1935 Criminal Law Amendment Act prohibited the import and sale of contraceptives. Nevertheless, information was available through the Marie Stopes clinic or in British newspapers and magazines, which were still accessible, despite the stringency of the wartime censorship. Investigations of sexual relations in other countries in the early and middle years of the twentieth century also emphasized the reluctance of people to talk about such an intimate aspect of their lives.[44] Many of these studies concentrated on birth control as an issue of interest primarily to women, although the oral history interviews conducted by Kate Fisher[45] make it clear that contraception was at least of equal concern to men and that, in many cases, it was men who were better informed and more likely to make decisions about the method used. Fisher's interviews illustrate the extent to which euphemism was used in discussing sexual intimacy and how the women respondents tended to equate ignorance of the mechanics of sex and birth control with femininity and respectability. The women who responded to my questions also equated lack of knowledge with innocence.

The extent to which matters of family planning were normally kept very private is reflected in the following entry in Moya Woodside's diary, when she also drew attention to an aspect of Northern Irish political life that was unique in terms of comparison to both Britain and Éire:

> Astonished to see the report of our annual public Birth Control Clinic meeting yesterday given large headlines and more than half a column in each of the local papers, instead of being relegated to a few lines in an obscure column, if indeed it is noticed at all. Reason: the speakers dealt largely with population problems and mentioned that in Eire (where all contraceptive information is illegal) the birth rate is lower, and has been falling longer, than anywhere else in the world. This piece of news falls pleasantly on Ulster Unionist ears, hence the headlines and verbatim report.[46]

As part of the initiative to improve maternity and paediatric services in Belfast, it was also recommended that arrangements should be made with the Society for the Nursing of the Sick Poor (a society affiliated to the Queen's Institute of District Nursing) to provide home nursing facilities for children up to 2 years of age suffering from acute bronchitis, bronchial pneumonia or gastroenteritis. Nurses employed by the society were paid less than Queen's Institute nurses because they did not undertake maternity work and they had definite hours of duty, although their qualifications were the same. They were answerable to the matron of the homes run by the society, rather than local doctors, and their salaries were paid by the society. Discipline in the homes was quite strict and there were various reports in the minutes of the society during the 1940s of difficulties in recruiting new staff, partly because of the requirement that they should stay a minimum of eighteen months.[47]

Medical personnel and the Westminster Ministry for Health raised concerns about the danger of the increased spread of sexually transmitted diseases because of wartime conditions. Both the local authorities and the military authorities were aware that the presence of large numbers of American and British troops billeted in Northern Ireland from 1941 until 1944 was a potential cause for difficulties arising out of 'fraternization'. The handbook issued to the United States soldiers explained that they should be aware of local differences in approaching young women: 'Ireland is an Old World country where the woman's place is still to a considerable extent in the home ... Quite probably the young lady you're interested in must ask her family's permission before she can go out with you.'[48] The military authorities also recognized that some fraternization might have unwanted consequences, and part of Susan's job in the sexually transmitted diseases clinic in the Royal Victoria hospital was to deal with the prostitutes who might have passed on a venereal disease to a soldier:

> Of course it was wartime still and the American soldiers were here and there was a special nurse attached to the American forces, one of their own nurses, and she was following up their contacts so she worked very closely with me. She would advise them on the use of condoms and she would be aware if someone needed to be treated and bring them to me. We worked together whenever we could without breaching too much confidentiality, you know. It had to be done and also, in those days, at that time, there were special regulations. I don't remember the name of them, and if the partner didn't turn up for treatment, she could be taken to court. So this American girl she told me about these girls who were having treatment, and which of her soldiers were being infected or vice versa. I didn't have anything to do with the men; I only had to deal with the girls.

Susan's position in the Rotunda hospital in Dublin often involved quite sensitive dealings with patients in difficult circumstances so she was quite used to keeping confidences and respecting the privacy of the women whom she was assisting. When she moved to the Royal Victoria hospital in Belfast, she encountered an unexpected difficulty with one of the senior medical personnel:

> Well then, when I came up here, I came specifically to work in the STD department and that was a very difficult job because I was the first social worker ever to work in the hospital ... I wasn't either a nurse or a doctor and the question of confidentiality was what was bothering them ... I remember the first morning when I went in, he [the senior doctor] called me into his private office and he took me aside and read me the story from the bible of the woman taken in adultery and he said, now I don't want you to condemn any one who comes in here. I said I wouldn't do that, it's not my job to condemn, I'm here to help and it's completely outside my training to make any moral judgements.

Susan explained how she had made the consultant recognize her professionalism and accept her standing in the hospital. She did not believe that the doubt about her ability to keep confidences was due to her being a woman, but was due to a misunderstanding of her role as a medical social worker, which was not yet a widely recognized profession:

> There were a lot of children in the hospital, particularly in the wards, who had been passed the diseases by their mothers, they should have been in children's hospitals, but because of their problems they were there ... I said I would like to do something for all these children and I said how would it be if I asked the ladies who visit to give each child two tickets for the pantomime ... they also gave me a lot of toys which they sent to a party ... and this all worked very well and some little time after, I found a picture on my desk, entitled the Good Fairy, of me with a wand and wings. So after that I had no opposition at all.

In Britain, the early years of the war had seen a sharp increase in the number of syphilis[49] cases being reported for treatment and there was also a rise in the cases of gonorrhoea.[50] Since neither disease was a notifiable one, the Westminster government introduced Defence Regulation 33B, which provided that any person suspected of having infected two or more patients might be compelled to undergo treatment.[51] The provisions of this regulation were extended to Northern Ireland. In theory, Regulation 33B was supposed to be applied equally to both sexes but, in practice, it was focussed almost exclusively on women, so much so that the annual conference of the National Council of Women in October 1943 formulated the following resolution:

> The NCW repudiates as fallacious the prevalent opinion that it is the conduct of girls and women that is mainly responsible for the present increase of Venereal Disease, and desires to emphasise the fact that in the great majority of those fleeting and irresponsible sex relationships by which the disease is spread both partners must be held responsible, and a recall to moral responsibility must necessarily be made to both sexes.
>
> The NCW therefore calls upon the government to consider afresh its whole approach to this problem, and to initiate a bold and positive education campaign which will bring home to every citizen and every household the conviction that all who indulge in sexual promiscuity not only may be responsible for the spread of VD, but are lacking in good citizenship.[52]

An information campaign was launched in Britain in February 1943 and the Northern Ireland government followed suit. Newspaper advertisements were placed to give the 'plain facts' about venereal diseases and their likely prevalence in wartime, how they were caused, and the urgent necessity for early treatment and where advice and treatment could be obtained. This was quite a significant move and indicated the level of concern about the problem because, before the war, newspapers had refused to carry any information about sexually transmitted diseases and there was a social taboo against any public reference to 'sexual intercourse'. In Northern Ireland, the advertisements were sent to the *Irish News*, the *Belfast News Letter*, the *Belfast Telegraph*, the *Northern Whig* and a range of provincial papers for insertion each Friday 'for about four to five weeks'. A requisition was also sent to London for two hundred copies of the series of seven booklets, issued by the United Kingdom Ministry of Health, which the Northern Ireland ministry intended to over-stamp and distribute.

Officials in the Northern Ireland Ministry of Local Government seem to have been ambivalent in regard to the VD awareness campaign and were reluctant to be too explicit about the nature of the problem. The Royal Hippodrome cinema in Belfast suggested that they use the first showing of the information film *Social Enemy No.1*[53] as part of an anti-VD campaign but this initiative was rebuffed by the ministry[54] despite the agreement with the Odeon chain that had been worked out by the Ministry of Health in Whitehall. Part of the reason for refusal seems to have been based on concern about the audience, although the precise nature of this concern was not spelled out. A possible reason may be suggested by the plans for a photographic display on VD, which was produced by the Ministry of Information on behalf of the Ministry of Health. A circular from the Ministry of Health in London was forwarded by the Northern Ireland Ministry of Health under its own stamp to hospitals and workplaces in which it was announced that the photographic display had been 'prepared for private showing to those who wish to see it, and to members of the two sexes separately'.

Up to the 1940s, women in Northern Ireland had a shorter life expectancy than women in Éire but this situation was reversed in the period 1950 to 1952, when Northern Irish females could expect to live to an average of 68.8 years, compared to 67.1 years for women in the South.[55] It seems likely that the reversal was a result of the significantly increased level of investment in Northern Ireland in public services that followed the Second World War, and in particular, the National Health Service. Generally, the health services north and south of the border in the inter-war years seem to have been equally beset by problems of funding and dealing with the legacy of domination by special interest groups. In this regard, women were no worse off then men and, in fact, when attention was paid to the need for improvements, it was the areas of maternal and child welfare that benefited first from reforms in both practice and funding, although with considerably greater success in Northern Ireland than in Éire, and later in the Republic.

While the Fianna Fáil government that came to power in the Irish Free State in 1932 did immediately attempt to reform the health service, in Northern Ireland there were no wide-ranging efforts to improve matters until after the war, when the impact of the Beveridge Report and the willingness of the Westminster government to provide funding combined to facilitate the setting up of an efficient National Health Service. In terms of access to decent health care, women were no more systematically discriminated against than men, although the additional demands of their domestic lives tended to take a greater toll on their health. Their increased vulnerability was recognized in Northern Ireland in that the first major improvements to the public health service were based on maternal and child welfare. In Éire, reforming impulses were devoted particularly to dealing with universal threats to health, such as tuberculosis.[56]

Interviewees from Éire and Northern Ireland were equally reluctant to discuss such intimate areas of domestic life as sexual relations and birth control methods and there was plentiful evidence to suggest that this stemmed from society's attitudes to such issues during the war years. This reticence was also discernible in governmental approaches to sensitive topics, particularly in the necessity to publicize the danger of sexually transmitted diseases. The Westminster government's information campaign was deemed sufficiently urgent to overcome pre-war taboos on public discussion of the subject. While the official policy in approaching the subject was intended to be even handed, in practice the regulations about inspection and reporting of sexually transmitted diseases were focussed primarily on women and most of the publicity tended to suggest that women were mainly responsible for the spread of infection.

In Belfast and Northern Ireland generally, a variety of poor health conditions were attributed to the war. Nervous exhaustion was to be expected during and after the blitz, but the Mass-Observation diarist, Dr Trennick, identified many of his female patients as suffering because of the absence of their husbands in the forces and consequent anxiety about their safety. Overcrowded conditions in housing, but also in the close confines of bomb shelters, contributed to an increase in respiratory diseases. Similarly, contagious skin diseases, such as scabies and impetigo, were more easily passed on when large numbers of people were forced to come together in small spaces for hours at a time. Poor nutrition was identified as the cause of the poor infant mortality rates in both cities, and the fact that improved economic performance in Belfast in the later years of the war coincided with a decrease in infant mortality, particularly compared to Dublin, underlines the cause and effect. Rationing of food certainly evened the burden for poor families and contributed to an improvement in nutrition, but the evidence of malnutrition and related illness that was revealed after the blitz, in particular, provided considerable impetus for post-war changes in social policy in Northern Ireland, not least in terms of the benefits of the implementation of the Beveridge plan. In Éire, while the changes were not as dramatic, social policy was focussed more directly on improving nutritional standards for poor families and consequently health overall. In both Northern Ireland and Éire, tuberculosis was a scourge before the war and continued to be throughout the war years with the mortality rate actually increasing between 1939 and 1941. The relationship between poverty, overcrowding and the disease was manifest when improvements in access to work in Belfast in the second half of the war was accompanied by a decrease in the mortality rates, whereas in Dublin they continued to rise. Concern about the ravages of the disease was widespread and led to a post-war determination to eradicate it together with the conditions that helped it to flourish.

8

Conclusion
Plus ça change, plus c'est la même chose?

> As one who has had some experience in sensing the mind of the ordinary man or woman I can positively say that the most popular thing you could do, as well also as the very best thing nationally, would be to make it known that your desire was to send women back to the home where they belong.[1]

The attitude to a woman's place in society, that is explicit in this extract from a letter to Eamon de Valera, reflected the widely-held conviction in the period prior to the commencement of the Second World War that women's primary role was a domestic one. This identification of women with the private world of the family unit provided a context for the questions raised in this book. Were Irish women (in both Northern Ireland and Éire) subject to institutional discrimination regarding employment, social welfare and equality of opportunity as were women in Britain, Europe and the United States in the years before the Second World War? To what extent was the war's impact on them differentiated by the fact that Northern Ireland was actively at war, while Éire remained neutral? Did the war have an effect on all aspects of their lives – on their domestic responsibilities as well as their paid employment?

The evidence of a female-centred approach to the history of the Second World War demonstrates the extent to which the traditional view of men as combatants and women as the symbols of the 'home front' – the protective focus for which the war was being fought – both dominated the integration into the war effort of the social policies of the Allied governments and survived into the post-war years. The wartime role of women in a belligerent state like Britain shows that many women overcame the boundaries of those social policies and broke through the barriers of social expectation, even if it was only for a limited period of time.

Even in belligerent states that did not have to deal with occupation by hostile forces in the course of the war, such as the United States, the public rewards for the valuable role played by women, on the home front and in war work, were of a temporary nature. After a sustained campaign to persuade women into traditional male areas of work during the First World War, inequality in pay and conditions continued to be a feature of the workplace in the post-war years, so far as women workers were concerned. The potentially liberating outcome of such employment for women was offset as soon as the First World War ended by reiteration of the notion that women's 'natural' place was in the home. In Britain and Ireland, there was little or no public acknowledgement of the paid employment that many women had undertaken to provide or supplement their family income and the dismissal of the work of many other women under the census heading of 'engaged in home duties' denied the value of such activity to the household and the public economy. The demand by belligerent governments during the Second World War that women should continue to play their private domestic role while they were called upon to make a public contribution to the war effort resulted in a heavier workload for many women. Women in Northern Ireland were formally excused from playing such a part because conscription was not imposed on the state but the wartime conditions still created problems for them in their domestic lives. Women depending on social welfare payments could also find themselves being forced to take up work outside Northern Ireland when they did not choose to do so.

Most of the recent research that focussed primarily on women's role in both world wars refuted the claim that those wars acted as liberating forces for women. Nevertheless, the evidence of specialized research on this topic is that many individual women welcomed the opportunity to become part of the war effort and expand their personal horizons and this includes Irish women. Oral history interviews were instrumental in airing positive interpretations of women's wartime experiences in much of that research. Similarly, the testimonies of most of the women quoted in this book subvert the conclusion that the absence of economic and legislative change suggests that the war made no difference to Irish women in either jurisdiction. Their stories show that the effect of the war on their individual lives was mainly positive, particularly for those women who grasped the improved opportunities for personal development, employment, friendship and travel that were offered by the wartime situation. This is an impact of the Second World War as it affected Ireland that has not been given any attention in previous Irish historiography.

The immediate influence of the war on the daily lives of women in Ireland was manifested in the effect that state responses to the situation had on both their domestic role and their paid employment. The government in Éire declared a state of emergency and assumed wide-ranging powers to secure territorial and political integrity while ensuring the continuation of essential services. The pressure on women in Éire that was created by the rising cost of living and shortage of household goods was a result of the presumption that budgeting and allocation of family resources was their responsibility, regardless of the changes in income that accompanied higher levels of unemployment and the restrictions on pay increases dictated by the Wages Standstill Act of 1941. Employment opportunities for women improved in Northern Ireland in the course of the war, and consequently offered increased incomes, but the difficulties caused by rationing and other wartime restrictions contributed to a much heavier workload for many of them. The war provided opportunities for some women to broaden their horizons by travelling outside Ireland to work (and this was the main reason for the positive recollections of some of the women quoted in this book) but for the majority of women in Ireland, north and south of the border, access to paid employment continued to be governed by pre-war conceptions about appropriate occupations and levels of pay. Nevertheless, it is clear that pride in survival and 'making do' is an element of the wartime experience that cannot be ignored. It is consistent with research in other countries, particularly in Britain, where investigation of the 'people's war' relates as much to the collective memory of resistance to attack and invasion as to the actual narrative of the war on the home front.

The emergency powers adopted by the British government that were extended to Northern Ireland concerned most areas of civilian life and had a similar impact on women's lives as comparable statutory instruments did in Éire. Wartime measures such as rationing of food and other commodities, blackout arrangements and billeting of armed forces were all put in place by the Northern Ireland government, but the politically motivated decision not to extend conscription to the state was probably the most important one made by the Stormont and Westminster authorities. In terms of its impact on women, it meant that there was no need for the kind of ongoing debate about recruiting women that engaged the Ministry of Labour in Britain, when the determination not to offer hostages to fortune in terms of definite promises of post-war legislation to change women's status had to be balanced with the immediate need to persuade women to adopt a public role as well as their usual private and domestic one.

John Blake's history of the war in Northern Ireland, which was commissioned by the government, postulates a united response to the war by the loyal unionist population of the state. He included women's voluntary engagement in war work as evidence of the commitment of the majority of the population and claimed that the post-war prosperity of

20. WAAF baby care classes. When WAAF members were being demobilised at the end of the war they were provided with classes in baby care. It was clear that their future occupation was presumed to be in the home. Courtesy of The Imperial War Museum, ref. TR2660.

Northern Ireland, in comparison to the economic situation south of the border, was a reward for widespread involvement in fighting for a just cause. Even writing in 1956, this was a considerable stretching of the truth of the matter, as more recent research has shown just how divided was Northern Ireland's response to the wartime conditions.[2] The 1941 bombing raids on Belfast caused enormous death and destruction but they also led directly to recognition of the levels of poverty in some parts of the city that resulted in major post-war changes to the physical fabric of Belfast, as well as widespread social welfare reform. The sectarian divisions in the city were not changed by the shared hardship, although some temporary identification of interests seems to have occurred. Nevertheless, all of the women remembered the war years as a time of positive social cohesion when there was a much greater impulse for neighbours to look after each other. While the target of the bombs dropped on Éire remains open to question, the consequence was a strengthening of support for the state's policy of neutrality that was seen as a significant contribution to establishing an international and independent identity in the post-war years.

CONCLUSION 171

How do the memories of the youth and young adulthood of the women who took part in this research, which have been filtered by the subsequent sixty years of understanding, compare with the testimony of Moya Woodside, also a young woman in 1939 but writing about her daily experience of wartime as a self-conscious recorder for the Mass-Observation organization? Woodside's political interests and social outlook were just as important to her as her domestic responsibilities and her viewpoint was shaped by the circumstances of her life at the time. So too were the opinions of the interviewees, but their lives have changed in the intervening years. Their concerns now are not necessarily those that preoccupied them during the war years, whereas Woodside was writing about events that were immediate to her. Her diary entries generally supported the evidence given in the interviews, particularly when they referred to the practical impact of aspects of the situation. On the other hand, most of the interviewees needed to be prompted by specific questions about different aspects of their experiences during the war years simply because so much has happened in the intervening period that it cannot be as vital to them as it was to Woodside, writing her observations on an almost daily basis through 1940 and 1941. Although their memories were very clear about the issues that interested them, these varied according to how they defined themselves at the time – as housewives or workers, schoolgirls or independent figures.

While it is obvious that the women who were interviewed were aware that there was workplace gender discrimination in terms of pay and conditions, this is not something that concerned them very much at the time they are recalling or that is of much more than peripheral interest now. The recurrent theme in most of the women's recollections of their entry into their various workplaces is of satisfaction about securing a job and earning a wage that would allow them to keep themselves and contribute to the family income. The women's sense of self-worth was linked to their capacity to earn, although most of them had considerable pride in the high standard of their work, which they pointed out often exceeded the demands of their employers. It is also important to note that most of them agreed that even if they had been conscious of structural gender discrimination in the workplace, due to the exigencies of the period they would have been much less concerned to do something about it than simply getting on with the task at hand.[3]

Recollection is a process of selection. Psychologists agree that information about a specific event is interpreted in the light of a person's general background knowledge and interests.[4] In the phenomenon recognized by psychologists as 'life review' the desire to remember is accompanied by a candour that goes with the belief that life is nearing its end and achievement is completed. In this phase of life, informants display great continuity between their past and present in their basic activities, interests and values. It was, therefore, not surprising to find that the interviewees mainly remembered the war years in terms of their personal and family stories and had not thought of that time in the context of a more general bearing on the status of women in society, either Irish or international, because that was not something in which they were especially interested. To the extent that they are the products of the society in which they were educated and in which they reached adulthood, their growing realization over the years that they had been discriminated against in the past was synchronized with changing social attitudes.

> In one sense we compose or construct memories using the public languages and meanings of our culture. In another sense we compose memories that help us to feel relatively comfortable with our lives and identities that give us a feeling of composure.[5]

In examining this aspect of the women's memories, the immediacy of Moya Woodside's diary provides a double contrast, not just in terms of the lapse of time, but because she was a political campaigner and her observations were filtered through the prism of her activism.

Women's involvement in both world wars in the twentieth century eventually contributed to changes in the sexual division of roles within the family unit. This is evidenced in the wide-ranging research into post-war women's lives, which has not been examined in this book.[6] It was not immediate, but the public recognition of women's emergence from the home to the workplace for the duration of the war eventually undermined the idea that a woman's natural place was in the home and a man's job was to enable her to stay there to fulfil her maternal destiny. This did not happen after the First World War but there was much less time for such a process to occur, with only twenty years between the two conflicts. After the Second World War technological developments in many areas diluted the need for strength in many traditionally male areas of work so that women were more attractive to employers. Technological developments also changed the home front, with better access to labour-saving domestic appliances giving more time to women in the home. Technological developments in the area of health also contributed to change, particularly in the area of pregnancy and childbirth, with improved access to contraception. Changes in familial organization and the allocation of domestic responsibilities were much slower in Ireland than in the rest of Europe but one consequence of the wartime concern of both governments with the poor state of public health was the increased attention paid to maternal and child welfare and the state's acceptance of a measure of responsibility for providing adequate nutrition for all citizens. The latter concern was of particular importance in Éire because the method adopted – the implementation of a children's allowance payment – outlasted the Emergency and was passed by the Dáil despite the prevailing economic caution. It was not only popular with the electorate but it complied with the Catholic social teaching that was so influential on policy makers at the time.

Many of the women's attitudes to how they lived their lives were derived from the certainties of their religious beliefs, which had been inculcated through church attendance from an early age, in both Catholic and Protestant churches. The extent to which their religious education influenced the women seemed to depend on the fervour of their families. The women who maintained the certainty of their youth had mothers who were considered to be very 'religious' and had faithfully passed on religious principles and values to their children.

Family relations shaped many women's consciousness about their place in society, particularly where they saw their mothers assuming authority in the home that they might not have been able to command outside it. Most of the women who took part in this research remembered their mothers as strong characters who shouldered responsibility for their family's welfare. Some of the mothers were forced to manage as single parents as a result of early widowhood or their husband's illness and their daughters grew up with a keen awareness of women's capacity to surmount personal and financial difficulties. Although the school system in which they were educated generally prepared them to assume a domestic role in adulthood, in which their position was defined as being secondary to the male breadwinner, the personal experience of most of the women (especially the example of their mothers) inspired them with the determination to do their best in whatever role they assumed. The curricula in both educational systems were designed with the domestic role of women as a basic tenet, regardless of the religious ethos of individual schools.

The research for this book was prompted by similar work carried out in countries that had a belligerent role in the Second World War. If the impact of the war on women in those countries is assessed only by an examination of the economic and legislative consequences of women's emergence into a public role in the course of the war, the conclusion must be that the reward for answering the call of their governments to participate in the war effort was very limited and did not result in significant change until several decades later. Women in Northern Ireland were not called upon in the same way as the women in other belligerent states so that there was no question of a specifically female-oriented *quid pro quo* from the Stormont or the Westminster governments, but the war did affect their status as workers and citizens because of the altered employment situation and the increased opportunities to broaden their horizons. Women in Éire were similarly affected and it is clear from the travel records in the war years that significant numbers availed of those opportunities.

All of the interviewees who chose to travel to England during the war were enthusiastic about their experience, so much so that some of them did not return to Ireland. Of the women who remained in Ireland, whether in Northern Ireland or Éire, most were nostalgic for what they recalled as the more caring and ethical communities to which they belonged then and they regret the loss of the moral certainties that they remember ruling the country of their youth. While it may have been that the impact of the war was not apparent in terms of immediate change in the culture and society of mid-twentieth-century Ireland, the positive memories of most of the women suggest that it had a very beneficial effect on their lives. Self-continuity depends wholly on memory and recalling past experiences links us with our earlier selves, however different we may since have become.

Maureen referred to the small numbers of trade union activists who took responsibility for fighting the battles of their fellow workers. While she acknowledged that there can be frustrations attached to seeing the majority of people sitting back while a few people do the work, it had never prevented her from fighting for the rights of her fellow workers and she can look back on her years as a shop steward knowing that she helped to bring about beneficial change in her workplace. Moya Woodside also fought for change, although there are fewer references to that aspect of her life in the Mass-Observation diaries than there were to the more immediate concerns occasioned by the war. Nevertheless, people like her and Maureen provided the context for the wider social changes that came about because of the efforts of other small numbers. These changes could not have happened without the impetus created by women who survived and even thrived within the institutionalized inequalities that they faced simply because of their gender.

The women whose testimonies formed the core of this research did not focus on the rights of women as a social category and they did not actively fight for social change. They did, however, grasp whatever opportunities came their way, including those created by the Second World War, and in doing this they helped to erode the legal and social barriers that had been erected around them. It would be easy to conclude that the Second World

War had little impact on the lives of women in Ireland because there is little objective evidence to indicate what that impact might have been. There were few legislative or social changes and the Northern Irish government and the government of Éire paid no more attention in the immediate post-war years to the rights and status of women than they had in the period between the two world wars. Nevertheless, it is clear from the stories told by the women interviewed for this research that their experiences during the Second World War were an important subjective factor in their lives. Minnie echoed most of the other women when she said:

> After the war anyway, it was beginning to be a bit better, and women could see that it wasn't the right thing, you know, that there was something missing. I suppose they saw elsewhere, you see, women getting into jobs and that and thinking ... They'd want to be as equal as the men and they started the whole business then.

Notes

INTRODUCTION

1. Captain W.E. Johns wrote a series of books about Captain James Bigglesworth (known as 'Biggles'), a fictional pilot and adventurer, commencing in 1932. Many of the books were based on Biggles' exploits during the Second World War. Johns wrote nearly one hundred books between 1932 and his death in 1968.
2. *The Victor* was a British comic book published from 1961 until 1992. It featured many heroic characters and always ran at least one story based on the Second World War.
3. It may well be that other nations were included but my recollection of the Second World War 'enemy' was that they were either German or Japanese and other nationalities did not register.
4. Karl Marx's theory of historical materialism focussed on material conditions as the basis of class consciousness but he (and later Marxist theorists) recognized that categories of class are subject to change as historical conditions are altered by shifts in the processes of production.
5. E.P. Thompson, *The Making of the English Working Class* (London: Penguin Books, 1991 – first printed Victor Gollanz, 1963).
6. The terms 'working class' and 'middle class' will be used colloquially throughout this book because they are concepts open to considerable debate, particularly in terms of the context in which they are being used. There are many different influences that shape what is understood by definitions of class, including culture and education, but the terms are not defined either academically or sociologically in this context.
7. This research will be explored in greater detail in Chapter 1 and specific studies of women and the Second World War will be referred to throughout this book.
8. Bunreacht na hÉireann, the Constitution of Ireland, provides in Article 4 that the name of the state is Éire, or in the English language, Ireland. Normal practice dictates that Ireland is used in all English-language texts, while Éire (and its grammatical variations) is used in Irish-language texts. Corresponding translations are used for texts in other languages. The Republic of Ireland Act of 1948 provides for the description of the state as the Republic of Ireland but this provision has not changed the usage Ireland as the name of the state in the English language. Prior to the 1937 Constitution, the territory was known as the Irish Free State. The territory of the twenty-six counties will be described as 'Éire' or simply 'Ireland' throughout this book, whereas the six northern counties that are part of the United Kingdom will always be referred to as 'Northern Ireland'.
9. Alison Morrow wrote an excellent doctoral thesis in 1995, in which she used the evidence of oral history interviews to examine women's paid work in Northern Ireland over a thirty year period that included the Second World War. Sadly, she does

not appear to have published her work (A. Morrow, *Women and Work in Northern Ireland 1920–1950* [Unpublished D.Phil. thesis, University of Ulster at Coleraine, 1995]). For Éire, the Women's Oral History project in University College Cork studied Munster women's stories of their paid work between the years 1936 and 1960. Several valuable articles have emerged from the project and a book based on the project is being published: Learne, M. and Kiely, E. *Women and Working Life in Munster 1936–1960: A Feminist Oral History* (Dublin: Irish Academic Press, 2007). The Women's Oral History project was funded by the Higher Education Authority in 2000 to use oral histories to document the working lives of women in Cork, Kerry and Limerick between the years 1936 and 1960. (The Women's Oral History project, http://www.ucc.ie/wisp/ohp/).
10. R. Doherty, *Irish Men and Women in the Second World War* (Dublin: Four Courts Press, 1999). There is a companion volume, *Irish Volunteers in the Second World War*, also published by Four Courts Press, 2001.
11. B. Grob-Fitzgibbon, *The Irish Experience during the Second World War. An Oral History* (Dublin: Irish Academic Press, 2004).
12. D. Ferriter, *The Transformation of Ireland 1900–2000* (London: Profile Books, 2004).
13. This phrase is used by Caitriona Clear to replace the term 'housewife' in describing women who worked full-time in the home in C. Clear, *Women of the House. Women's Household Work in Ireland 1922–1961* (Dublin: Irish Academic Press, 2000).
14. Short biographies of the interviewees are presented in Appendix 1(1).
15. A short biographical note is included in Appendix 1(2). References to Woodside's diary will be made using the number assigned to her by the Mass-Observation Organization – MO 5462 and the date of the diary entry. Mass-Observation's policy is usually to preserve the anonymity of the diarist but Woodside had already been identified by Brian Barton in his book *The Blitz. Belfast in the War Years* (Belfast: Blackstaff Press, 1989).
16. An introduction to the Mass-Observation organization can be found in Appendix 2.
17. James Hinton's study of the leadership of the Women's Voluntary Services is particularly useful in this discussion. J. Hinton, *Women, Social Leadership and the Second World War. Continuities of Class* (Oxford: Oxford University Press, 2002).
18. These included the public service marriage bar, which was implemented in 1932 and the Conditions of Employment Act that became law in 1936.
19. 'In particular, the State recognises that by her life within the home, woman gives to the State a support without which the common good cannot be achieved. The State shall, therefore, endeavour to ensure that mothers shall not be obliged by economic necessity to engage in labour to the neglect of their duties in the home.' (Article 41.2(1) of Bunreacht na hÉireann, the Constitution of Ireland.)

CHAPTER ONE

1. John Dunn, father of the family which was the case study at the core of Alexander Humphreys' book about Dublin in the 1950s. A.J. Humphreys, *New Dubliners. Urbanization and the Irish Family* (London: Routledge and Kegan Paul, 1966), p.98.
2. Adam Smith, *The Wealth of Nations*. Quoted in J. Scott, 'The Woman Worker' in G. Duby and M. Perrot (eds), *A History of Women in the West. Vol. IV Emerging Feminism from Revolution to World War* (Cambridge, MA: Belknap Press, Harvard University Press, 1993), pp.399–426.

3. The Fifth Amendment to the Constitution, passed on 5th January 1973, removed the special position accorded to the Catholic Church by the 1937 Constitution.
4. A papal encyclical is a document written by the Pope, as head of the Roman Catholic Church, which is sent to all the members of the church via the bishops and priests. The word comes from the Latin 'encyclia' meaning 'general' or 'encircling'. Since the nineteenth century, when the theory of papal infallibility became part of the dogma of the Roman Catholic Church, papal encyclicals are considered to be 'holy writ' and must be obeyed by all Catholics.
5. M. Cousins, 'The Introduction of Children's Allowances in Ireland, 1939–1944', *Irish Economic and Social History*, XXVI (1999), pp.35–53.
6. Ibid., p.51.
7. William Beveridge produced a *Report on social insurance and allied services* in 1942, following lengthy discussion and consideration of social policy in Britain. The recommendations in the report were intended to form the basis of legislation for the post-war welfare state.
8. P. Summerfield, 'Women and War in the Twentieth Century', in J. Purvis (ed.), *Women's History. Britain, 1850–1945* (London: UCL Press, 1995), pp.307–32.
9. B. Barton, 'Northern Ireland: The Impact of War, 1939–1945', in B. Girvin and G. Roberts (eds), *Ireland and the Second World War. Politics, Society and Remembrance* (Dublin: Four Courts Press, 2000), pp.47–75.
10. C. Beaumont, 'Women, Citizenship and Catholicism in the Irish Free State, 1922–1948', *Women's History Review*, 6, 4 (1997), pp.563–85.
11. There are some useful accounts of the ways in which women were conditioned in the following books, although there are many more equally valuable examinations of this process, which can be found in the bibliography: C. Clear, *Women of the House. Women's Household Work in Ireland 1922–1961* (Dublin: Irish Academic Press, 2000); E. Roberts, *A Woman's Place. An Oral History of Working-Class Women, 1890–1940* (Oxford: Blackwell, 1984); J. Bourke, *Working Class Cultures in Britain 1890–1960. Gender, Class and Ethnicity* (London: Routledge, 1993); J. Lewis (ed.), *Labour and Love: Women's Experience of Home and Family 1850–1940* (Oxford: Oxford University Press, 1986); L.A. Tilly and J.W. Scott (eds), *Women, Work and Family* (London: Holt, Reinhart and Winston, 1978); N. Cott, 'The Modern Woman of the 1920s', in F. Thébaud (ed.), *A History of Women. Toward a Cultural Identity in the Twentieth Century* (Cambridge, MA: The Belknap Press of Harvard University Press, 1994), pp.76–91; R.R. Pierson and N. Chaudhuri (eds), *Nation, Empire, Colony: Historicizing Gender and Race* (Bloomington, IN: Indiana University Press, 1998).
12. Labour market forces play a stronger role than family or home influences in determining women's labour market position. S. Walby, *Theorizing Patriarchy* (Oxford: Blackwell, 1990).
13. Oral history-based research has attempted to fill in the gaps but there is always the *caveat* in interviews that the viewpoint being expressed is likely to have been influenced by events subsequent to those being discussed.
14. G. Braybon and P. Summerfield, *Out of the Cage: Women's Experiences in Two World Wars* (London: Pandora, 1987); Bourke, *Working Class cultures in Britain 1890-1960*; A.-M. Sohn, 'Between the Wars in France and England' in Thébaud (ed.), *A History of Women*, pp.92–119.
15. Arthur Marwick was one of the foremost proponents of this viewpoint which is articulated in a number of books, but particularly in the following: A. Marwick, *The*

Deluge. British Society and the First World War (London: The Bodley Head, 1965); A. Marwick, *War and Social Change in the Twentieth Century* (London: Macmillan, 1974).
16. Braybon and Summerfield, *Out of the Cage*; P. Summerfield, *Women Workers in the Second World War: Production and Patriarchy in Conflict* (London: Croom Helm, 1984); H. Smith, *Britain in the Second World War* (Manchester: Manchester University Press, 1996); H. Smith, 'The Effect of the War on the Status of Women', in H. Smith (ed.), *War and Social Change: British Society in the Second World War* (Manchester: Manchester University Press, 1986); S.O. Rose, *Which People's War? National Identity and Citizenship in Wartime Britain 1939–1945* (Oxford: Oxford University Press, 2003).
17. C. Clear, 'No Feminine Mystique: Popular Advice to Women of the House in Ireland, 1922–1954', in M. Valiulis and M. O'Dowd (eds), *Women and Irish History, Essays in Honour of Margaret MacCurtain* (Dublin: Wolfhound Press, 1997), pp.189–206.
18. M.E. Daly, '"Fanatacism and Excess" or "The Defence of Just Causes": the International Labour Organisation and Women's Protective Legislation in the Interwar Years', in M. O'Dowd and S. Wichert (eds), *Chattel, Servant or Citizen. Women's Status in Church, State and Society* (Belfast: Queen's University, Institute of Irish Studies, Historical Studies XIX, 1995), pp.215–27.
19. Mary Daly points out that while the preoccupation with protective legislation for women workers might be seen as reinforcing patriarchal attitudes, it can equally be interpreted as indicating a cohesive effort on the part of the working-class family as a whole to improve overall working conditions.
20. Roberts, *A Woman's Place. An Oral History of Working-Class Women*; Lewis (ed.), *Labour and Love*.
21. M. Mitchell, 'The Effects of Unemployment on the Social Conditions of Women and Children in the 1930s', *History Workshop* 19 (Oxford University, Spring 1985).
22. M. Spring Rice, *Working-Class Wives. Their Health and Conditions* (London: 1939. Reprinted London: Virago, 1981).
23. Tilly and Scott, *Women, Work and Family*.
24. D. Gittens, 'Marital Status, Work and Kinship, 1850–1930', in Lewis (ed.), *Labour and Love*, pp.249–67.
25. N. Lefaucheur, 'Maternity, Family and the State', (translated by A. Goldhammer) in Thébaud (ed.), *A History of Women*, pp.433–52.
26. B. Brooks, 'Women and Reproduction, 1860–1936', in Lewis (ed.) *Labour and Love*, pp.149–71.
27. This term is used in Clear, *Women of the House* and was widely used in rural Ireland to describe uncertified midwives who assisted at births. In Roberts' research in the north of England there are many references to 'wise women' or women known in neighbourhoods for their willingness and ability to help women in labour who could not afford the services of a doctor, with similar evidence of women active in this regard emerging from the work of Nancy Cott, particularly in N. Cott, *The Grounding of Modern Feminism* (New Haven, CT: Yale University Press, 1987).
28. Roberts, *A Woman's Place. An Oral History of Working-Class Women*.
29. The majority of references will be to the United Kingdom and the United States because these countries are the subjects of most of the research about women and the Second World War that will be cited in this book.
30. P. Summerfield, '"My Dress for an Army Uniform": Gender Instabilities in the Two World Wars'. An Inaugural Lecture delivered at the University of Lancaster, 30 April 1997.

31. Rose, *Which People's War?*; S. Rupp, *Mobilizing Women for War: German and American Propaganda, 1939–45* (Princeton, NJ: Princeton University Press, 1978).
32. Summerfield, *Women Workers in the Second World War*.
33. D. Sheridan, 'Ambivalent Memories: Women in the 1939–45 War in Britain', *Oral History*, 18,1 (Spring 1990), pp.32–40.
34. Rose, *Which People's War?*
35. Ibid., pp.136–8.
36. Engineering and shipbuilding were especially vulnerable to skill dilution, when jobs that were previously carried out by craftsmen were broken down into their component parts and carried out by a number of unskilled or semi-skilled workers. Women could be brought into the workforce quickly by this process because less time was required for training but it also meant that claims for equal pay could be denied on the grounds that there was no parity with the work that skilled men had performed.
37. C. Lang, *Keep Smiling Through. Women in the Second World War* (Cambridge: Cambridge University Press, 1989).
38. P. Summerfield, *Reconstructing Women's Wartime Lives. Discourse and Subjectivity in Oral Histories of the Second World War* (Manchester: Manchester University Press, 1998) and '"My Dress for an Army Uniform": Gender Instabilities in the Two World Wars'.
39. Richard Von Weizäcker, President of the Federal Republic of Germany, speaking in May 1985 on the fortieth anniversary of the German surrender, quoted in C. and E. Townsend (eds) *War Wives. A Second World War Anthology* (London: Grafton Books, 1989), p.xi.
40. Summerfield, *Women Workers in the Second World War*, p.190.
41. S.M. Hartmann, *The Home Front and Beyond. American Women in the 1940s.* (Boston, MA: Twayne Publishers, 1982).
42. M.S. Schweitzer, 'World War II and Female Labour Force Participation Rates', *The Journal of Economic History*, 40, 1 (March 1980), pp.89–95.
43. Ibid., p.90.
44. International Labour Office, *The War and Women's Employment. The Experience of Britain and the United States* (Montreal: I.L.O., 1946), p.276.
45. Survey undertaken by the US Department of Labour Women's Bureau, 'Women Workers in Ten War Production Areas and their Postwar Employment Plans', Bulletin 209, Washington DC, Government Printing Office, 1946 quoted in M. Honey, *Creating Rosie the Riveter. Class, Gender and Propaganda during World War II* (Amherst, MA: University of Massachusetts Press, 1984).
46. K. Anderson, *Wartime Women: Sex Roles, Family Relations and the Status of Women during World War II* (Connecticut: Greenwood Press, 1981), p.5.
47. Ibid., p.6.
48. Honey, *Creating Rosie the Riveter*.
49. Advertisement for Icilma Beauty Aids, *Daily Herald*, December 1939. Advertising and War Themes, Box 1/B [359]. Mass-Observation Archives, university of Sussex.
50. Ibid.
51. A. Calder, *The People's War. Britain 1939–45.* (London: Pimlico, 1992 [First published 1967]), pp.331–5.
52. Hartmann, *The Home Front and Beyond*.
53. Calder, *The People's War*, p.389.
54. Mass-Observation Archives, Day Nurseries file, Box 1[245].

CHAPTER TWO

1. Moya Woodside, MO 5462, Mass-Observation Archive, University of Sussex, 30 October 1940.
2. J.S. Torrie, 'Preservation by Dispersion: Civilian Evacuations and the City in Germany and France, 1939–1945'. Paper presented to the *Power, Knowledge and Society in the City*, International Conference on Urban History, Edinburgh, September 2002 (http://www.esh.ed.ac.uk/urban_history/text/TorrieM6.doc).
3. Le Corbusier was the pseudonym of Swiss architect Charles-Edouard Jeanneret. J.-L. Cohen, *Le Corbusier, 1887–1965: The Lyricism of Architecture in the Machine Age* (London: Koln, 2004).
4. D. Deriu, 'Cities through the Viewfinder: The Airborne Gaze and the Urban Target'. Paper presented to the *Power, Knowledge and Society in the City* (http://www.esh.ed.ac.uk/urban_history/text/DeriuM4.doc).
5. N.J. McCamley, *Secret Underground Cities. An Account of some of Britain's Subterranean Defence, Factory and Storage Sites in the Second World War* (Barnsley: Leo Cooper, 1988), p.2.
6. Ibid., p.3.
7. A. Calder, *The People's War* (London: Pimlico, 1992), p.22.
8. B. Barton, *The Blitz. Belfast in the War Years* (Belfast: The Blackstaff Press, 1989), p.28.
9. M. Brown, *Evacuees. Evacuation in Wartime Britain 1838–1945* (Stroud: Sutton Publishing Limited, 2000), pp.3–4.
10. Ibid., p.25.
11. Extract from Ministry of Home Security leaflet, dated October 1939, quoted in S. Hylton, *Their Darkest Hour. The Hidden Story of the Home Front 1939–1945* (Stroud: Sutton Publishing, 2001), p.112.
12. Torrie, 'Preservation by Dispersion', p.2.
13. J. Keegan, *The Second World War* (London: Hutchinson, 1989).
14. P. Summerfield and C. Peniston-Bird, 'Women in the Firing Line: the Home Guard and the Defence of Gender Boundaries in Britain in the Second World War', *Women's History Review*, 9, 2 (2000), pp.231–55.
15. The B Specials were auxiliaries recruited to the Royal Ulster Constabulary after 1920. They were part-time, usually on duty for one evening per week and serving under their own command structure, and unpaid, although they had a generous system of allowances. They gained a reputation for brutality and were viewed by most Roman Catholics in Northern Ireland as a Protestant vigilante force. They were disbanded in April 1970 after several notorious incidents, including attacks on civil rights marches.
16. B. Barton, *Northern Ireland in the Second World War* (Belfast: Ulster Historical Foundation, 1995), pp.33–5.
17. Woodside, Mass-Observation diary, MO 5462, 20 October 1940.
18. Barton, *Northern Ireland in the Second World War*, pp.194–202 *et seq*.
19. D. Campbell and R. Jensen, 'Defence Forces and Civil Defence', in J. Keegan (ed.), *The Oxford Companion to World War II* (Oxford: Oxford University Press, 2001), pp.928–9.
20. Irish Shipping was incorporated in March 1941 to provide the state with merchant shipping that would be independent of British vessels for supply.
21. The live register referred to the number of registered unemployed who were insured under the Unemployment Assistance Act 1933. Registration was compulsory for

receipt of unemployment benefits but the Act excluded domestic servants and workers categorized as 'assisting relatives'. This would account for part of the discrepancy between the numbers of unemployed on the live register and the number in the census, which looked at those out of work on a particular date, regardless of their entitlement to unemployment benefit.

22. J.F. Meenan, 'The Impact of the War upon the Irish Economy', *Journal of the Statistical and Social Inquiry Society of Ireland (JSSISI)*, 93rd session, Vol. XVI, 1939–40 pp.17–22.
23. Extract from the long title of the Emergency Powers Act 1939.
24. Section 4(1) of the Government of Ireland Act 1920 also retained to Westminster the exclusive right to deal with merchant shipping, submarine cables, wireless, telegraphy, navigation by sea or air, lighthouses, buoys and beacons (with some minor qualifications), the 'defence of the realm' and all 'matters arising from a state of war'.
25. Section 63 of the Government of Ireland Act 1920 enabled any department of the United Kingdom government to enter into an administrative arrangement with an officer of the Northern Ireland government for the discharge of specific functions.
26. J. Blake, *Northern Ireland in the Second World War* (Belfast: HMSO, 1956), pp.18–19.
27. For example, under regulation 22, the Ministry of Home Affairs became responsible for billeting in Northern Ireland; under regulation 50, the Ministry of Commerce was made responsible for urgent supplies of electricity arising from the war and under regulation 55, the Ministry of Agriculture was responsible for the control of seeds, crops, foodstuffs and agricultural machinery.
28. Woodside, MO 5462, 21 March 1940.
29. Part VII Section 49 of the Civil Defence Act (Northern Ireland) 1939.
30. Cushendun is a seaside resort on the coast of Co. Antrim.
31. Section 3(1) allowed the censor to revoke any certificate which he had granted under Section 7 of the 1923 Censorship Act before 3 September 1939, if he felt that the film contravened the provisions of the new Emergency Powers Order.
32. Woodside, MO 5462, 8 January 1941.
33. D. Ó Drisceoil, *Censorship in Ireland, 1939–1945. Neutrality, Politics and Society* (Cork: Cork University Press, 1996), p.256.
34. Uinseann MacEoin was interviewed in B. Grob-Fitzgibbon, *The Irish Experience During the Second World War* (Dublin: Irish Academic Press, 2004), pp.238–48.
35. Ibid., p.240.
36. Woodside, MO 5462, 18 March 1940.
37. P. Taylor, 'Censorship in Britain in the Second World War: an Overview', in A.C. Duke and C.A. Tamse (eds), *Too Mighty to be Free: Censorship and the Press in Britain and the Netherlands* (Zutphen: De Walburg Pers, 1987), pp.165–6. Quoted in Ó Drisceoil, *Censorship in Ireland*, p.285.
38. Woodside, MO 5462, 27 December 1940.
39. This was done under Section 2(2).
40. The 1911 Act gave penalties for spying, wrongful communication of privileged information, and unlicenced entry into prohibited places such as naval yards or storage places of secret information. The 1920 Act added penalties for the unlawful use of uniforms, possession of false documents, communication with foreign agents, and generally extended and strengthened the provisions of the 1911 Act.
41. The foods listed in the Emergency Powers (Control of Prices) (No.1) Order, 1939 were as follows: tea; coffee; cocoa; sugar; butter; margarine; bacon and ham and other

pig products; fresh meat; fresh fish; cured fish – unpacked; fresh pork; sausages and black and white puddings; lard; flour and other cereal products for human consumption; bread; fresh milk; cheese; patent and proprietary foods for infants; jams; packed, tinned and bottled foodstuffs; biscuits; ale, beer, porter, stout, wines and spirits and cider; corn-cakes and meals; maize and maize products. The other goods listed were bran, pollard and other animal feeding stuffs; coal and coke; tobacco and cigarettes; hardware and ironmongery for household use; paraffin oil; candles; soap; leather; footwear of all descriptions and personal clothing and wearing apparel.

42. The women were Andree Sheehy Skeffington, Marguerite Skelton, Nancy Simmons, Sheila Mallagh and Hilda Tweedy and they eventually founded the Irish Housewives Association. H. Tweedy, *A Link in the Chain. The Story of the Irish Housewives Association 1942–1992* (Dublin: Attic Press, 1992).
43. Ibid., p.17.
44. Food Control Committees (Constitution) Order 1939.
45. Section 22(1) and (2) extended the Act to Northern Ireland.
46. Woodside, MO 5462, 10 January 1941.
47. Ibid., 3 November 1940
48. Ministry of Health, *On the State of the Public Health during six years of War*. Report of the Chief Medical Officer of the Ministry of Health, 1939–45 (London: HMSO, 1946).
49. The appropriate number of coupons required for specific goods were listed in the schedules of consumer rationings which were issused regularly throughout the war years.
50. This particular column appeared in the *Irish News* on a daily basis and it included items on making and mending clothes, recipes and household hints. The other main Belfast newspaper, the *NewsLetter*, carried a column called 'Mainly for Women', which added gossip from 'Mayfair' and the British Court to the domestic economy articles.
51. Woodside, MO 5462, 6 June 1941.
52. Although it was decided not to extend conscription to Northern Ireland, arrangements were made to ensure that Northern Irish citizens who volunteered for the armed forces were not financially disadvantaged by their war service. The first of these was the passing of the Local Government Staffs (War Service) Act (Northern Ireland) 1939, which was enacted on 7 September to allow local authorities to make up the balance of pay of someone serving in the forces whose war service pay might be less than they were normally entitled to be paid. This act also protected the pension rights of any such local authority employees. Similar provisions were made in the Teachers' Salaries and Superannuation (War Service) Act (Northern Ireland) 1939, which was enacted on 6 December. Other workers were protected by the Superannuation Schemes (War Service) Act (Northern Ireland) 1941, which was passed on 1 July, and enabled provision to be made for preventing loss of benefits under certain superannuation schemes by members of those schemes who had joined the armed forces or were involved directly in other war work.
53. Blake, *Northern Ireland in the Second World War*.
54. M. Davis, *Comrade or Brother? The History of the British Labour Movement 1789–1951* (London: Pluto Press, 1993), pp.186–7.
55. The approved ports for civilian traffic in Northern Ireland were Belfast and Larne. Derry was used only for naval traffic.
56. Blake, *Northern Ireland in the Second World War*, pp.19–22.

57. Ibid., pp.171–3.
58. Woodside, MO 5462, 4 March 1940.
59. Ibid., 16 October 1941.
60. Ibid., 2 May 1941.
61. Barton, *The Blitz, Belfast in the War Years*, p.100.
62. Woodside, MO 5462, 30 April 1941.
63. Ibid., 6 May 1941.
64. The situation was so difficult that the Northern Irish government requested help from De Valera and fire brigades and ambulances from south of the border were sent north to assist. Although this action was perfectly permissible in terms of humanitarian assistance, it was perceived in many quarters, not least in Fianna Fáil circles, as a breach of Éire's neutrality and it was even suggested when Dublin was bombed that this might have been retaliation by Germany.
65. James Doherty, *Post 381. Memoirs of a Belfast Air Raid Warden* (Belfast: Friar's Bush Press, 1989).
66. Ibid., pp.101–2.
67. E. O'Halpin, *Defending Ireland. The Irish State and Its Enemies Since 1922* (Oxford: Oxford University Press, 1999), p.157.
68. Ibid., pp.151–71.

CHAPTER THREE

1. Open letter to the members of the Oireachtas (Éire government) from the Laundresses' Strike Committee, 9 October 1945; this letter was sent by Margaret McGrath as chair of the strike committee in the third month of the strike by laundry workers (all women) to secure a fortnight's annual paid leave. The strike was successful and subsequently the paid holidays of all manual workers were extended to two weeks.
2. Moya Woodside, MO 5462, 26 March 1940.
3. This rate compared well with most of the wages for women set by trade boards.
4. A. Morrow, *Women and Work in Northern Ireland, 1920–1950* (unpublished PhD thesis, University of Ulster at Coleraine, 1995), p.104.
5. Ministry of Commerce, Training of Women for War Work, correspondence in October 1941. Public Records Office Northern Ireland (PRONI) Com.61/13/649.
6. Letter from W.P. Kemp, Short & Haarland Limited, Queen's Island, Belfast to E.H. Cooper, Ministry of Commerce, dated 14 April 1942. PRONI Com.61/113/649.
7. Morrow, *Women and Work in Northern Ireland*, p.111.
8. Ministry of Labour, Recruitment of married women for war work in 1943. PRONI LAB 4/22/10.
9. J. Blake, *Northern Ireland in the Second World War* (Belfast: HMSO, 1956), p.396.
10. Ibid., p.61.
11. Woodside, MO 5462, 20 January 1941.
12. J.F. Meenan, 'The Impact of the War upon the Irish Economy', *Journal of the Statistical and Social Inquiry Society of Ireland (JSSISI)*, 93rd Session, Vol. XVI, 1939–40 pp.17–22.
13. The marriage bar was laid down by Statutory Order of the Minister for Finance under Section 9 of the Civil Service Regulation Act, 1924. The rule applied mainly to established posts and not to 'subordinate situations' such as office cleaners.

14. The phrase was used in a memorandum from the managing director, W. Haldane Porter, to the Registry Department, dated 18 July 1935, setting out the entrance procedures for lady clerks. The procedures were still applicable when Colette joined the brewery in 1941. (Guinness Archives File No. GDB/PEO.103/00300/2 concerning lady staff.)
15. Ibid.
16. HM Government report of proceedings of the National Conference of Women, Tuesday 28 September 1943, London, p.40. (Mass-Observation Archive.)
17. Thompson's (Belfast) Limited was established in 1847 as 'Purveyors, Restaurateurs, Caterers, and Confectioners'. Their premises at 14 Donegall Place and 31 Castle Lane, Belfast had luncheon, dining and afternoon tea rooms and could cater for private parties. They also had a hiring department, from where all the cutlery, glass et cetera necessary for any size of party could be obtained. The confectionery department, where Alice worked, also supplied wedding and christening cakes. *The Belfast and Province of Ulster Directory* (Belfast: Anderson and Company, 1946).
18. The processes specifically mentioned by the Trade Board were:
    (a) the mixing of flour, eggs, sugar or other ingredients into dough or batter;
    (b) the manipulating, moulding, or shaping of dough by hand;
    (c) the ovening of bread, pastry or flour confectionery;
    (d) decorating, icing or piping; or
    (e) any other similar operations incidental to or appertaining to the manufacture of the above-mentioned articles.
19. Ministry of Labour, Orders under the Trade Boards Acts, Baking Trade, NIBk (32) and Sugar Confectionery and Food Preserving Trade NIF (21).
20. Ibid.
21. Ministry of Labour files, August 1940, PRONI.
22. Ibid.
23. Department of Labour, File TIL 120, Draft Survey of Minimum Wage Regulations, p.2.
24. In her biography of Louie Bennett, Rosemary Cullen Owens argues that Bennett's personal attitudes were consistent with conservative public opinion of the time and she quotes her presidential address to the Irish Trade Union Congress in 1932, when she claimed that the increasing tendency to draw women into industry 'is of no real advantage to them. It has not raised their status as workers nor their wage standard. It is a menace to family life, and in so far as it has blocked the employment of men it has intensified poverty amongst the working class.' R. Cullen Owens, *Louie Bennett* (Cork: Cork University Press, 2001), p.91.
25. Report of the Executive to the Annual Convention of the Irish Women Workers' Union, 3 May 1939. IWWU files, Archive of the Irish Labour History Society.
26. This was a magazine produced by the *Irish Times* between 1943 and 1945. It had a number of regular columns, including the 'Four Corner Survey', ranging from 'Molly Bawn suggests', which was a household hints item aimed at women, to gardening advice and a children's page, as well as articles on politics and current affairs.
27. *Pictorial Weekly*, 8 May 1943, p.2.
28. I have no evidence for the sex of the author but the tone of the column as a whole strongly suggested it was written by a man.
29. Junior Assistant Mistresses.
30. Extract from strike leaflet produced by the Amalgamated Transport and General Workers Union, February 1940, reproduced in D. Bleakley, *Saidie Patterson. Irish Peacemaker* (Belfast: Blackstaff Press, 1980), p.37.

31. Report of the Registrar of Friendly Societies for Northern Ireland, HMSO, Belfast, 1947. PRONI.
32. C. Wrigley, *British Trade Unions since 1933* (Cambridge: Cambridge University Press, 2002).
33. T. Moriarty, 'Mary Galway', in M. Cullen and M. Luddy (eds), *Female Activists: Irish Women and Change 1900–1960* (Dublin: Woodfield Press, 2001), pp.9–36.
34. A. Boyd, *The Rise of the Irish Trade Unions* (Dublin: Anvil Books, 1985, 2nd edn); E. O'Connor, *A History of the Irish Working Class* (Dublin: Gill and MacMillan, 1992).
35. Reports of the Registrar of Friendly Societies for Northern Ireland, 1939–1945, HMSO Belfast.
36. The Irish Women Workers' Union had a total of 5,558 members in 1939 and between that year and the end of the war the membership was maintained at approximately five and a half thousand, not varying by more than one or two hundred in each year. *Annual Reports of the Irish Women Workers' Union, 1939–1945*, IWWU files in the Archive of the Irish Labour History Museum.
37. Guinness's policy was to stay ahead of the average pay rates in Dublin city and this practice was applied to both male and female employees. In regards to tradesmen working for the company, the practice was to pay a rate 'which to the nearest sixpence will be 2/6 above the "City Rates"'. (Memo from Registry Department concerning minimum wage rates for tradesmen, dated 13 March 1940. File No. GDB/ PEO3.01/0048, Guinness Archives.)
38. Memorandum dated 18 April 1941, Registry Department File No. GDB/ PEO3.01.0048, Guinness Archives.
39. Revised Classification for Lady Clerks, Board Memorandum dated 8 February 1939. File No. GDB/PEO.103/00300, Guinness Archives.
40. Woodside, MO 5462, 8 October 1940.
41. Half a crown was 2s.6d.
42. Flora's wages of 27/6 did not compare well with the weekly female rates paid under various trade board agreements, where only one rate was lower than Flora's – that of the Aerated Waters Trade Board.
43. A 'bob' was one shilling.
44. Between 1941 and 1942, the Irish National Teachers' Organisation applied on a number of occasions for a war bonus, referring to the fact that the teachers were the only body of public servants who had received no increase in pay since 1939, despite the fact that the cost of living had doubled since the beginning of the Emergency. They cited a figure of two thousand whole-time teachers earning salaries varying from 32/6 to 48/- per week, with more than 50 per cent of the whole teaching body earning less than £4 per week. This was compared to a civil servant on Executive Officer grade who would have been earning a basic salary of £5 per week, plus a cost of living bonus of £138/17 (£2/13/4 per week). T.J. O'Connell, *History of the Irish National Teachers' Organisation 1868–1968* (Dublin: INTO, 1968), p.209.
45. The Rotunda Hospital for the Relief of Poor Lying-In Women was founded in 1745. There were two distinct hospitals, the maternity or 'lying-in' wards and the gynaecological wing, which had 151 beds between them when Susan worked there in the early 1940s. The hospital had over 3,000 maternity cases during 1940 and nearly 1,000 gynaecological cases, with over 5,000 women attending the external maternity department. *Thom's Directory for the year 1940*, p.1,116.
46. This hospital is situated on Grosvenor Road in Belfast. It was founded to commemorate the diamond jubilee of Queen Victoria and was opened on 27 July 1903.

47. B. Walsh, 'Marriage in Ireland in the Twentieth Century', in A. Cosgrove (ed.), *Marriage in Ireland* (Dublin: College Press, 1985), pp.132–50.
48. *Census of Population 1946* (Dublin: Stationery Office, 1949), Vol. I, p.130.
49. In Britain, for example, more people married in six years of war than would have been the case if the pre-war trend had continued, although the peacetime inclination towards marriage at a younger age was consistent, with nearly three war-brides out of ten being under twenty-one. A. Calder, *The People's War* (London: Pimlico, 1969), p.312.
50. L. Earner-Byrne, '"In Respect of Motherhood": Maternity Policy and Provision in Dublin City, 1922–1956' (unpublished PhD thesis, University College Dublin, 2001).
51. The company also ran a scheme entitled 'Employees Benefit Trust' which had set up a trust deed on 13 March 1918 to provide weekly payments for employees incapacitated by illness or disability. The scheme also provided for payment of pensions to male and female employees and lump sum payments on the death of employees, their wives and children. In the event of an employee leaving the bakery before pension age all the contributions made by that employee were repaid together with compound interest. Ministry of Labour Files, PRONI, LAB/4/24/6.
52. This rule was introduced in 1938 as a means of reducing the number of young teachers who were unemployed. It was not until 1948 that the regulation was overturned after a prolonged campaign by the INTO against the inequity to older women teachers, whose pension rights were adversely affected.
53. Guinness had premises at 101 James's Street that was set up for the night clerks to sleep in.
54. Guinness did set up a transport service for the cleaners in the 1950s, but Catherine had left the brewery by that point, although Mary benefited from not having to walk long distances to work in the early mornings.
55. *Report of the Committee on the Shops Act*. PRONI, CAB 4/539.
56. In January 1943 the Ministry of Home Affairs ordered that, with certain variations, the hour fixed for weekday closing was to be 5.00 p.m., with the exception of Saturdays, when the closing time was extended to 7.00 p.m. On the early closing day, shops were ordered to shut at 1.00 p.m. The excepted businesses were barbers, tobacconists, off licences, premises where refreshments were consumed, pharmacies selling medicines and surgical appliances and newsagents. *Belfast Telegraph*, 1 January 1943, p.5.
57. Woodside, MO 5462, 31 December 1940.
58. *Irish Trade Journal and Statistical Journal*, XXI, 4 (Dublin: Government Stationery Office, November 1946).
59. B.R. Mitchell, *European Historical Statistics, 1750–1970* (London: MacMillan, 1975), p.187.
60. *Irish Statistical Survey 1948–49* (Dublin: Government Stationery Office, 1949).
61. Staff Booklet edited by C.K. Mill, revised edition, May 1960. File No.GDB/PEO3.01/0604, Guinness Archives.
62. The Guinness board first voted a subsidy for the show in 1927, when the grant was £60. There were several increases in subsequent years. The subsidy was £90 in the 1940s. File No.GDB/PEO3.01/0159, Guinness Archives.
63. St Mary's College of Domestic Science was based in Cathal Brugha Street in Dublin. It later became one of the constituent colleges of the Dublin Institute of Technology.
64. St James's Gate Fanciers and Industrial Association Annual Report 1944. File No.GDB/PEO3.01/0159, Guinness Archives.

65. James Wilson was managing director of the Ormeau Bakery. He was the son of Robert Wilson, founder of the bakery in 1875.
66. The Employee Benefit Trust was the Ormeau Bakery pension scheme.
67. Soldier's Dorcas was an organization that specialized in mending uniforms and darning socks for the troops billeted in Northern Ireland. 'Darning for Victory', *The Belfast Telegraph*, 24 April 1940.

CHAPTER FOUR

1. P. Summerfield, '"My dress for an Army Uniform"': Gender Instabilities in the Two World Wars'. An inaugural lecture delivered at the University of Lancaster on 30 April 1997; D. Sheridan, 'Ambivalent Memories: Women in the 1939–45 War in Britain', *Oral History*, 18, 1 (Spring 1990), pp.32–9; C. Lang, *Keep Smiling Through. Women in the Second World War* (Cambridge: Cambridge University Press, 1989); S. Hartmann, *The Home Front and Beyond. American Women in the 1940s* (Boston, MA: Twayne Publishers, 1982); K. Anderson, *Wartime Women: Sex Roles, Family Relations and the Status of Women during World War II* (Connecticut: Greenwood Press, 1981); M. Nicholson, *What did you do in the war, Mummy? Women in World War II* (London: Chatto and Windus, 1995).
2. Sheridan, 'Ambivalent Memories: Women and the 1939-45 War in Britain', pp.32–9.
3. E. Delaney, *Demography, State and Society. Irish Migration to Britain, 1921–1971* (Liverpool: Liverpool University Press, 2000) and S. Lambert, *Irish Women in Lancashire 1922–1960: Their Story* (Lancaster: Centre for North-West Regional Studies, University of Lancaster, 2001).
4. Delaney, *Demography, State and Society*.
5. T. Connolly, 'Irish Workers in Britain during World War Two', in B. Girvin and G. Roberts (eds), *Ireland and the Second World War. Politics, Society and Remembrance* (Dublin: Four Courts Press, 2000), pp.121–32.
6. Delaney, *Demography, State and Society*, p.120.
7. J.B. Wolf, 'Withholding their due. The Dispute between Ireland and Great Britain over Unemployed Insurance Payments to Conditionally Landed Irish Wartime Volunteer Workers', *Saothar 21* (Dublin: Irish Labour History Society, 1996), pp.39–46.
8. T. Connolly, 'Irish Workers in Britain during World War Two' in Girvin and Roberts (eds), *Ireland and the Second World War. Politics, Society and Remembrance*, pp.121–32.
9. J. Blake, *Northern Ireland in the Second World War* (Belfast: HMSO, 1956), p.340.
10. Quoted in A. Morrow, 'Women and Work in Northern Ireland 1920–1950' (Unpublished D.Phil. thesis, University of Ulster at Coleraine, 1995), p.105.
11. Diarmaid Ferriter cited Gerard Fee, 'The Effects of World War II on Dublin's low income families' (Unpublished PhD thesis, University College Dublin, 1996) for this information. D. Ferriter, *The Transformation of Ireland 1900–2000* (London: Profile Books, 2004).
12. Ibid., p.383.
13. Reading is noted as the county town of Berkshire, with a history as a settlement that stretches back more than 2,000 years. P. Llewellin and A. Saunders (eds), *AA Book of British Towns* (London: Drive Publications Limited, 1982), p.334.
14. D. Sheridan (ed.), *Wartime Women. A Mass-Observation Anthology 1937–45* (London: Phoenix Press, 1990).

15. Ibid., p.168.
16. M. Lennon, M. McAdam and J. O'Brien (eds), *Across the Water. Irish Women's Lives in Britain* (London: Virago, 1988).
17. Ibid., pp.94–5.
18. Frances' mother was very religious and although she was sending her away in wartime, she was concerned that her daughter's religious practices should be observed. Consequently, she only looked in the Catholic newspapers for job advertisements. Frances thought it was *The Universe* where her mother found the notice that a woman living in Dublin would be interviewing for the position in Birmingham. *The Universe* was a weekly Catholic newspaper, which came out on Sundays. It had been founded in 1860 and in the 1940s it was distributed from the publishers' premises in Manchester.
19. Department of External Affairs memorandum on new proposals regarding restrictions on travel permit issues to workers [9 May 1944], p.4 (written by J.P. Walshe, secretary of the department) quoted in Delaney, *Demography, State and Society*, p.134 and in L. Earner-Byrne, 'The Boat to England: An Analysis of the Official Reactions to the Emigration of Single Expectant Irishwomen to Britain, 1022–1972', *Irish Economic and Social History*, XXX (Dublin, 2003), pp.52–70.
20. Ibid.
21. Mr T. Henderson speaking in the Northern Ireland parliament debate on the king's speech, 26 February 1941. Reported in *The Irish Press*, 27 February 1941, p.5.
22. Acocks Green was named after the Acocks family who built a large house in the area in the eighteenth century. Originally a village, it was connected by rail to Birmingham in the nineteenth century and was gradually subsumed into the city suburbs. O. Mason (ed.), *Bartholomew Gazetteer of Britain* (Edinburgh: Bartholomew & Son, 1977), p.2.
23. Earner-Byrne, 'The Boat to England: An Analysis of the Official Reactions to the Emigration of Single Expectant Irishwomen to Britain, 1022-1972', p.65.
24. Portstewart is a town on the northern coast of Co. Derry, close to the border with Co. Antrim.
25. The Womens' Volunteer Service ran canteens for the troops as part of their war work.
26. Cookham was actually comprised of three villages; the main one was Cookham and within a mile on either side on the London road were Cookham Rise and Cookham Dean. Cookham is a riverside resort on the River Thames, three/four kilometres north of Maidenhead. Mason, *Bartholomew Gazetteer of Britain*, p.61.
27. *Wartime Social Survey: an investigation of the attitudes of women, the General Public and ATS Personnel to the Auxiliary Territorial Service* (New Series, Number 5, October 1941), p.9 and Mass-Observation, *People in Production* (London, John Murray, 1942), p.152 quoted in P. Summerfield and N. Crockett, '"You Weren't Taught that with the Welding": lessons in sexuality in the Second World War', *Women's History Review*, 1, 3 (1992), pp.435–54, (p.439).
28. Maidenhead was the most industrialized town in the area of Berkshire nearest to Cookham. In Edwardian times it was considered to be a favourite spot for the 'fun-loving younger generation', although the old town had been encircled by modern development by the time the Second World War started. Llewellin and Saunders, *AA Book of British Towns*, p.277.
29. M. Davis, *Comrade or Brother? The History of the British Labour Movement 1789–1951* (London: Pluto Press, 1993), p.186.
30. N. Fishman, *The British Communist Party and the Trade Unions, 1933–45* (Aldershot: Scolar Press, 1995); Davis, *Comrade or Brother?*, pp.187–8.

31. Sonya O. Rose, *Which People's War? National Identity and Citizenship in Wartime Britain 1939–1945* (Oxford: Oxford University Press, 2003), p.110.
32. Amy Johnson (1903–41) was a pioneer aviator, born in Hull, in north east England. She was the first woman to fly solo from England to Australia in 1930 and to Japan via Siberia in 1931. She also set a record for the first female solo flight to Cape Town in 1932. She became a pilot in the Air Transport Auxiliary during the Second World War and was working in that capacity when she was killed in 1941. D. Crystal (ed.), *The Cambridge Biographical Encyclopaedia* (Cambridge: Cambridge University Press, Second Edn, 1998), p.498.
33. Delaney, *Demography, State and Society*, p.135.
34. Nancy was referring to the danger of torpedo attack by German U-boats. Although significant numbers of British merchant vessels were sunk in British coastal waters in the early stages of the war (from September 1939 to March 1941), by 1943 the U-boat fleet had moved its operations into the North Sea and the Atlantic waters south of Ireland, rather than being anywhere near the Irish Sea. The U-boats again operated in British coastal waters in the final months of the war, but by that time the number of Allied naval vessels so outnumbered the German fleet that the average life of a U-boat and its crew had shrunk to three months. J. Keegan, *The Second World War* (London: Hutchinson, 1989), pp.105–23, 'The Battle of the Atlantic'.
35. Parbold is in south Lancashire. Until the middle of the nineteenth century it was only a village, but with the coming of the railway it began to develop as a dormitory town of Liverpool. Mason, *Bartholomew Gazetteer of Britain*, p.188.
36. Dr Gawne was the Chief Medical Officer for Lancashire County Council.
37. This meant working as a temporary nurse for a nursing agency. Olive could have found herself nursing just one patient or being moved around on a regular basis, neither being a prospect that appealed to her, not least because agencies at that time demanded very long working hours from their employees.
38. This was the Queen Victoria hospital in East Grinstead, in Sussex.
39. The *Nursing Times* was published in London and was distributed throughout the United Kingdom and Ireland. Prior to 1941 it was known as the *Nursing Mirror and Midwives Journal*.
40. Sir Archibald McIndoe (1900–60) was born in Dunedin, New Zealand. He was appointed by the Emergency Medical Service in September 1939 to set up the burns unit in the Queen Victoria hospital. He was renowned for the innovative methods of plastic surgery that were developed in the unit, particularly in the aftermath of the Battle of Britain. Crystal, *Cambridge Biographical Encyclopaedia*, p.601.
41. Former patients of Sir Archibald McIndoe set up the Guinea Pigs' club. Qualification for acceptance depended on being a member of an aircrew and having at least one operation in the hospital. Scientists, doctors and surgeons from the burns unit were honorary members and benefactors to the fundraising activities of the Guinea Pigs were known as Friends of the Club. Sir Archibald was elected honorary president for life. Crystal, *Cambridge Biographical Encyclopaedia*, p.601. See also the website for The Queen Victoria Hospital NHS Trust at www.qvh.nhs.uk.
42. Citizens of Éire had to go to Northern Ireland or to mainland Britain if they wanted to join the armed forces. M. Hill, *Women in Ireland. A Century of Change* (Belfast: The Blackstaff Press, 2003), p.117.
43. Delaney, *Demography, State and Society*, p.136.
44. Appendix 4(8) is based on information tabulated by Fee, *The Effects of World War II on Dublin's low income families*, p.65.

45. Rose, *Which People's War?*, pp.74–5.
46. *Belfast Telegraph*, 24 March 1942, p.3.
47. L. Ryan, 'Sexualising Emigration: Discourses of Irish Female Emigration in the 1930s', *Women's Studies International Forum*, 25, 1 (2002), pp.51–65.
48. Ibid., p.52.
49. Earner-Byrne, 'The Boat to England: An Analysis of the Official Reactions to the Emigration of Single Expectant Irishwomen to Britain, 1922–1972', p.62.
50. Ibid., p.64.
51. Grantham is a town on the border of Lincolnshire and Leicestershire. It is famous for being the place where Sir Isaac Newton went to school. Coaching inns played a vital role in its development, because of its position on the main roads connecting several major towns. Llewellin and Saunders, *AA Book of British Towns*, p.164.
52. Sheridan (ed.), *Wartime Women*, p.164.
53. Ibid., p.170.
54. The Boots pharmacies were a chain of chemists' shops throughout Britain.
55. Slough was at that time the commercial centre of Berkshire. In the 1930s, 850 new factories were established and the town was thriving industrially throughout the war. Llewellin and Saunders, *AA Book of British Towns*, p.366.
56. Mass-Observation Archives, Day Nurseries Box 1 [245].
57. Lord Rushcliffe was nominated to head the committee by the British Hospitals Association, in consultation with the King Edward's Hospital Fund for London and the Nuffield Trust. *Nursing Mirror and Midwives' Journal*, LXXIV, 1917 (December 1920), p.163.
58. As well as Lord Rushcliffe, the committee had representatives from the County Councils Association; the Association of Municipal Corporations; London County Council; the Urban District Councils Association; the Rural District Councils Association; the Queen's Institute of District Nursing; the Royal College of Nursing; the Trades Union Congress; the National Association of Local Government Officers; the Royal British Nurse's Association; the British College of Nurses and the Association of Hospital Matrons.
59. This was only the case during the 1940s when there was a shortage of nurses. The rules for registration of nurses were changed in the early 1950s to include a mandatory period of study and by the mid 1960s a candidate would have to complete a two-year course of study and pass an examination in order to qualify for conversion from an SEN (State Enrolled Nurse) to an SRN (State Registered Nurse).
60. Boston is in Lincolnshire. Pioneers from the town emigrated from it during the seventeenth century to found Boston, Massachusetts. Llewellin and Saunders, *AA Book of British Towns*, p.50. The Pilgrim hospital where Frances worked has been amalgamated with the Grantham hospital where she did her training in the United Lincolnshire Hospitals Trust.
61. Poliomyelitis was still being called infantile paralysis in the 1940s, because it was thought only to affect children. It is extremely infectious.
62. Impetigo and scabies are highly contagious skin diseases, often associated with malnourishment.
63. Bed-wetting.
64. Calder, *The People's War. Britain 1939–1945*, pp.223–4.
65. Kingston-upon-Thames, situated on the left bank of the River Thames, was the site for coronation of the Saxon kings. Petersham is also located on the River Thames, on the right bank. Both towns are located in the borough of Richmond, which is a

dormitory suburb of London. Mason, *Bartholomew Gazetteer of Britain*, pp.135 and 193.
66. The Chrysler factory had been in Kew since 1925, turning out cars named after nearby districts, such as the Wimbledon, the Kingston, the Mortlake and the Croydon. The factory was turned into a manufacturer of aircraft components and military trucks in 1939. In 1944, in the incident to which Meta referred, it was actually a landmine that was dropped on the factory, killing seven men. History of Chrysler website http://media.chrysler.co.uk.
67. Rose, *Which People's War? National Identity and Citizenship in Wartime Britain 1939–1945*, pp.79–80.
68. S. Hylton, *Their Darkest Hour. The Hidden History of the Home Front 1939–1945* (Stroud: Sutton Publishing, 2001), pp.142–4.
69. The first Lyons Corner House was opened in London in 1909. They were huge restaurants on four/five levels, employing hundreds of staff. They were known for their long opening hours, which were as much as twenty-four hours in London.
70. Delaney, *Demography, State and Society*, p.126.
71. Lang, *Keep Smiling Through. Women in the Second World War*; Hartmann, *The Home Front and Beyond. American Women in the 1940s*; Anderson, *Wartime Women: Sex Roles, Family Relations and the Status of Women during World War II*.
72. International Labour Organisation, *The War and Women's Employment. The Experience of the United Kingdom and the United States* (Montreal: ILO, 1946).

CHAPTER FIVE

1. Richard Von Weizäcker, President of the Federal Republic of Germany, speaking in May 1985 on the fortieth anniversary of the German surrender, quoted in C. and E. Townsend, *War Wives. A Second World War Anthology* (London: Grafton Books, 1989), p.xi.
2. Richard Doherty has written several books about Irish participants in the Allied war effort, both inside the armed forces and in civilian terms. He included extracts from interviews and correspondence with women who served in the Allied forces in Britain and throughout the world, in professional and voluntary capacities in the following books: *Irish Men and Women in the Second World War* (Dublin: Four Courts Press, 1999) and *Irish Volunteers in the Second World War* (Dublin: Four Courts Press, 2002). In Romie Lambkin's *My time in the war: An Irishwoman's Diary* (Dublin: Wolfhound Press, 1992) she describes her experiences in the Auxiliary Territorial Services.
3. D. Collett Wadge, *Women in Uniform* (London: Sampson Low, 1946), p.5.
4. The Adelaide hospital was founded in Dublin in 1839 and its nursing school was established in 1859. In the hospital's annual report for that year, it was noted that 'they hoped soon to be in a position to effect one of the main objects of this hospital: a training system for Protestant Nurses'. D. Mitchell, *A 'Peculiar' Place. The Adelaide Hospital, Dublin. Its Times, Places and Personalities 1839 to 1989* (Dublin: Blackwater Press, 1989), p.86.
5. Southern Irish women had to go to Belfast if they wanted to enlist in the armed services. The ATS had started recruiting even before the war commenced and Irish women could join the WAAFs from late in 1939. The only women's service that did not encourage recruitment from Éire was the Women's Royal Naval Service, known

as the Wrens, but Irish women who wanted to enlist could do so in England using the addresses of friends and family there. Doherty, *Irish Men and Women in the Second World War*, pp.259–61.
6. As a Protestant institution, it might be suggested that Adelaide staff were more likely to be sympathetic to the Allied cause and to join the armed forces, but Richard Doherty's work shows that religious affiliation had little or nothing to do with the decision to enlist. He also dismisses the notion (particularly prevalent in unionist circles in Northern Ireland) that southern Irish recruits to the Allied forces were motivated primarily by financial reasons. Doherty points out that this claim does not hold up when the very low levels of soldiers' pay is taken into account (2/- per day for a private soldier). Doherty, *Irish Men and Women in the Second World War*, pp.12–14.
7. Collett Wadge, *Women in Uniform*, p.6.
8. A. Kershen, 'The 1905 Aliens Act', *History Today*, 55, 3 (March 2005), pp.13–19.
9. Tedworth House is a Palladian mansion in Tidworth South, Hampshire which was used as a military hospital during the Second World War. It is still in use as the Officers' mess for the Tidworth, Netheravon and Bulford garrison of the British army. Tidworth North, which is the northern part of the town, is in Wiltshire and the Tidworth barracks is situated midway between Tidworth North and Tidworth South. O. Mason (ed.), *Bartholomew Gazetteer of Britain* (Edinburgh: Bartholomew & Son, 1977), p.213.
10. P. Summerfield and D. Peniston-Bird, 'Women in the Firing Line: the Home Guard and the Defence of Gender Boundaries in Britain in the Second World War', *Women's History Review*, 9, 2 (2000), pp.231–55.
11. Collett Wadge, *Women in Uniform*, p.7.
12. Friedrich Wilhelm Froebel devised the Froebel system of kindergarten education in the nineteenth century.
13. The Auxiliary Territorial Service.
14. Ballymena is a town in Co. Antrim. It was granted a charter of borough status in December 1937.
15. The Women's Auxiliary Air Force was formed on 28 June 1939 from Royal Air Force companies of the Auxiliary Territorial Service. It was decided to create a separate organization because of the recognition that there was considerable difference in the type of work undertaken by women working for the RAF and those working for the army. Collett Wadge, *Women in Uniform*, p.172.
16. The national broadcasting station, Radio Éireann, was controlled and operated by the state in accordance with the censorship directives enabled by the Emergency Powers Act of 1939. However, nothing was done to prevent people using their radio sets to listen to both Allied and Axis propaganda. This was partly on the grounds of safety because radio was an effective means of communicating with the people in times of special emergency and partly because the government was less concerned with preventing reception than it was with maintaining the state's neutrality. D. Ó Drisceóil, *Censorship in Ireland 1939–1945. Neutrality, Politics and Society* (Cork: Cork University Press, 1995), p.14.
17. Women had to give their consent in writing before being allowed to handle lethal weapons, unlike men. G. DeGroot, 'Whose Finger on the Trigger? Mixed Anti-Aircraft Batteries and the Female Combat Taboo', *War in History*, 4 (1997), pp.434–53.
18. Collett Wadge, *Women in Uniform*, p.172.
19. Melksham is a small town in Wiltshire.

20. The Whitworth Whitley was a twin-engined monoplane bomber. It was entered into service with the RAF in March 1937 and was used until 1946. The Whitley was one of the first heavy night bombers of the RAF, and the first RAF aircraft with a stressed-skin fuselage. R. Sturtivant and M. Burrow, *Fleet Air Arm Aircraft 1939 to 1945* (London: Air Britain (Historians) Ltd., 1995).
21. Group Captain John 'Cat's Eyes' Cunningham CBE, DSO and two Bars, DFC and Bar, (27 July 1917–21 July 2002), was an officer in the Royal Air Force during the Second World War and a test pilot, both before and after the war. By the end of the Blitz in May 1941 he had become the most famous night fighter pilot, successfully claiming fourteen night raiders using AI (Airborne Interception – the aircraft version of what became later know as radar.) His nickname of 'Cat's Eyes' came from British propaganda explanations in order to cover up the use of AI. It was claimed a special group of British pilots ate carrots for many years to develop superior night vision. U. McGovern (ed.), *Chambers' Biographical Dictionary* (London: Chambers Harrap Publishers, 2002, 7th edn), p.383.
22. G. DeGroot, 'I Love the Scent of Cordite in Your Hair: Gender Dynamics in Mixed Anti-Aircraft Batteries during the Second World War', *History*, 82 (1997), pp.73–92.
23. Ibid., p.88. Female gunners were paid only two-thirds of the wages received by their male colleagues.
24. The British Raj (known from 1911 as the Indian empire) was the period during which most of the Indian subcontinent, or present-day India, Pakistan, Bangladesh and Myanmar, were under the colonial authority of the British empire. The Raj ended with the partition of India in 1947.
25. There were difficulties in recruiting sufficient numbers for the auxiliary services and in December 1941 the British government used the National Service Act (No.2) to conscript all childless widows and single women between the ages of 20 and 30. This was later expanded to include all women between the ages of 19 and 43 but, in practice, it was mainly women between 19 and 24 who were actually conscripted, and like Pat, they were given a choice of occupation. R. Pope, *War and Society in Britain, 1899–1948* (London: Longman, 1991), p.42.
26. Quoted in Collett Wadge, *Women in Uniform*, p.114.
27. Women in the ATS wore a khaki uniform. Penny Summerfield found that the ATS uniform was seen both as defeminizing women, turning them into 'sexual sluts' or it could make them masculine and uninterested in heterosexual relationships. P. Summerfield and N. Crockett, '"You Weren't Taught that with the Welding": Lessons in Sexuality in the Second World War', *Women's History Review*, 1, 3 (1992), pp.435–54.
28. *Wartime Social Survey: An Investigation of the Attitudes of Women, the General Public and ATS Personnel to the Auxiliary Territorial Service* (New Series, Number 5, October 1941), p.47, quoted in Summerfield and Crockett, '"You Weren't Taught that with the Welding"', p.437.
29. A. Calder, *The People's War. Britain 1939–1945*. (London: Pimlico, [1969] reprinted 1993), p.54.
30. Jacob's factory in Bishop Street was a Dublin institution – they were the second biggest employer in the city, next to the Guinness brewery, and their employees were mostly women. Thom's Commercial Directory of 1944 lists the company as 'W. & R. Jacob & Co. (Ltd.), Biscuit Manufacturers'. The company offices were situated in 28 to 30 Bishop Street while the factory and the stores covered a large block stretching from Peter's Street to New Row and Whitefriar Street.

31. S. Rose, *Which People's War? National Identity and Citizenship in Wartime Britain 1939–1945* (Oxford: Oxford University Press, 2003), pp.33–4.
32. The Farnborough RAF station is in Hampshire. It was first used in the closing days of the First World War and is still in operation as a base for the RAF.
33. Under a regulation called 'Paragraph 11' a woman could be discharged for being pregnant and would be unable to re-enlist.
34. T. Stone, 'Creating a (Gendered?) Military Identity: the Women's Auxiliary Air Force in Great Britain in the Second World War', *Women's History Review*, 8, 4 (1999), pp.605–24.
35. E. Taylor, *Women Who Went to War* (London: Grafton Books, 1989), pp.330–2.
36. Trincomalee is a port city on the northeast coast of Sri Lanka. *Philip's Concise World Atlas* (London: Reed International Books Limited, 1995, 4th edn,), p.60.
37. Batavia is an island in Indonesia. It was the centre of a large trade network in the seventeenth century and was the main administrative and military centre of the Dutch foothold in Indonesia until the Second World War. The capital is Jakarta, which is also the capital of Indonesia.
38. Sumatra is in Indonesia and is the sixth largest island in the world. It was the subject of dispute between The Netherlands and Britain from the first colonization in the seventeenth century. In the nineteenth century it was effectively handed over to The Netherlands but a growing nationalist movement throughout the first half of the twentieth century was able to establish independence when the Japanese were expelled at the end of the Second World War.
39. A tonga is a form of transport – a light cart pulled by a horse.
40. Srinagar is the summer capital of Kashmir. It is famous for its beautiful lakes.
41. Comilla is a district in present day Bangladesh (part of India until the partition of India in 1947), near the border with Myanmar (Burma in the Second World War). The hospital where Hilda worked was at the end of the famous Burma Road that links China and Myanmar. It was used by the British army to transport arms to the Chinese before Japan declared war on Britain in 1942. It was closed by the Japanese between April 1942 and January 1945.
42. Bisterne is in Hampshire. It is a small town on the road south to Christchurch Bay.
43. The Burma Star medal has a red centre with orange and dark blue edges. The red represents the Commonwealth forces and the orange, the sun. The stars were awarded for one day or more of operational service during the Burma campaign between 11 December 1941 and 2 September 1945. Burma Star Association website: http://www.burmastar.org.uk/.
44. Every QAIMNS sister who had one or two years of service was required to take a turn lecturing to the male nursing orderlies. The lectures were given systematically at the same time at every station so that if an orderly was moved his lectures would carry on at the next station at the point he had reached at the previous posting. Collett Wadge, *Women in Uniform*, p.7.
45. D. Sheridan, 'Ambivalent Memories: Women and the 1939–45 War in Britain', *Oral History*, 18, 1 (Spring 1990), pp.32–9.
46. The De Havilland Mosquito was a twin-engined aircraft of plywood monocoque construction, designed originally as a fast, unarmed light bomber. The Mosquito served with distinction as fighter-bomber, reconnaissance aircraft and night-fighter. E. Bishop, *Mosquito: The Wooden Wonder* (Shrewsbury: Airlife Publishing, Ballantine Books, 1995.)
47. The RAF Central Band was based in Uxbridge but WAAF voluntary marching bands were formed in nearly every RAF station in Britain and overseas throughout the war

years. The WAAF Central Band was formed from members of the voluntary marching bands. B.R. Williams, *They Shall Have Music. The story of the WAAF Voluntary Marching Bands from 1939* (Surbiton: Brigwill, 1995).
48. General Dwight David 'Ike' Eisenhower was Supreme Commander of the Allied Forces in Europe from December 1943. He was elected 34th President of the United States of America in 1953 and served two terms.
49. B.E. Escott, *The WAAF* (Buckinghamshire: Shire Publications, 2003), p.38.

CHAPTER SIX

1. Books such as A. Calder, *The People's War. Britain 1939–45* (London: Pimlico, 1992) and S. Hartmann, *The Home Front and Beyond. American Women in the 1940s* (Boston, MA: Twayne Publishers, 1982) are particularly useful in this regard. Other works not quoted directly are included in the bibliography.
2. William Beveridge produced a *Report on Social Insurance and Allied Services* in 1942 following lengthy discussion and consideration of social policy in Britain. The recommendations in the report were intended to form the basis of legislation for the post-war welfare state.
3. M.E. Daly, *The Buffer State. The Historical Roots of the Department of the Environment* (Dublin: Institute of Public Administration, 1997), pp.275–6.
4. *Northern Ireland Census Report, 1951.*
5. Dorothy Bates, Mass Observation Diary 5245, 16 March 1941.
6. This was Moya Woodside's emphasis.
7. Moya Woodside, MO 5462, 23 August 1941.
8. The Gaelic Athletic Association was founded in 1884 by Michael Cusack. As well as overseeing such games as Gaelic football, hurling, camogie and handball, it supports activities that are intended to foster Gaelic culture and the Irish language.
9. The Young Women's Christian Association hall where Alice attended services is now run as a hostel, on Lisburn Road, close to Queen's University.
10. Mountjoy ward was part of the Dublin No. 2 electoral borough, which also included the Ballybough, Clontarf, Drumcondra, North Dock and Raheny wards. The city councillors for this borough included such notable figures as Kathleen Clarke and Alfie Byrne (who both became Lord Mayor) and Jim Larkin. *Thom's Directory 1940*, p.1,089.
11. Department of Industry and Commerce, *Register of Population, 1941.* (Dublin, Government Stationery Office, 1944), pp.90–1.
12. It was also called Sean McDermott Street then and comprised mainly of tenement buildings, although there were a few businesses on the street, including a horse dealer's premises, the St Mary Magdalen asylum and the headquarters of the Carpenters' and Joiners' Trade Society (*Thom's Directory 1939*, p.1,411).
13. R. McManus, *Dublin, 1910–1940: Shaping the City and Suburbs* (Dublin: Four Courts Press, 2002).
14. Ibid.
15. This road ran from Drumcondra Road, one of the main arteries of the north city, down to Ballybough. There was a mixture of houses and businesses, with the houses ranging from small to medium, indicated by the rateable valuation which ranged from £6 10s to £26. *Thom's Directory 1940*, pp.1,384–5.
16. The houses in Marino were leased for ninety-nine years in the rental purchase scheme.

17. This is a major artery on the north side of the city, leading from Amiens Street to Annesley Bridge.
18. In *Thom's Directory*, Dowth Avenue is described as having sixty houses, with rateable valuations of £9 to £10.10s. There were shops at the end of the road that included a pharmacy, a pork butcher, a bakery, a victualler and a drapery store. *Thom's Directory 1937*, p.1,243.
19. Sean T. O'Kelly was TD for Dublin North West during the 1930s. He was also an Alderman on Dublin City Council and was the Minister for Local Government and Public Health from 1932 to 1939, the period during which the houses were built in Cabra.
20. This was defined by the corporation as the means to feed and clothe a family on the most frugal level. In 'Tuberculosis: A Social Survey', Dr Kidney referred to a discussion with Professor T.W.T. Dillon during which the latter said that the minimum income necessary for the purchase of necessities in 1943 would be at least 18/- per week per adult and 9/- per week per child. Professor Dillon referred to the 'health standard' of income in an article entitled 'The Social Services in Eire', *Studies*, XXXIV (September 1945), pp.325–36. This would provide for adequate nutrition but just above starvation level, with a proportionate allowance for rent and other expenses. He suggested that this level was set following an international inquiry and was the standard of living of 'Shanghai coolies'. He thought that the income required to sustain this level at 1945 prices would be 21/- weekly for an adult and higher, at 23/- per week, for an adolescent in order to maintain healthy growth and development. Children under 15 were assessed at needing an average of 10/- per week and 5/- weekly for children less than 5 years of age.
21. D. Ferriter, *Lovers of Liberty? Local Government in 20th Century Ireland* (Dublin: National Archives of Ireland, 2001).
22. Report of the Unemployment Assistance Board for Northern Ireland for the year ended 31 December 1938, Ministry of Labour, HMSO, 1939, p.7.
23. Great Western Square is off the North Circular Road, a major road circling the north side of Dublin city, from the North Strand at one end ending at the Phoenix Park at the other.
24. Grafton Street is a shopping street on the south side of Dublin, linking St Stephens Green and College Green. It is about four miles from there to Cabra, a working-class area on the north side of the city.
25. This was Nelson's Pillar, a Dublin landmark in O'Connell Street, the main street of the city, until it was demolished by a bomb in 1966.
26. Doyle's Corner is at the junction of North Circular Road and Phibsborough Road. There is an old public house called 'John Doyle's' on the corner. *Thom's Directory for the year 1935*, p.897.
27. Woodside, MO 5462, 16 September 1940.
28. Ibid., 31 January 1941.
29. Bates, MO 5245, 6 May 1941.
30. Maud Gonne was born in England but her father was of Irish descent. She was very active in republican activities in Ireland and France and she also supported the Afrikaners in the Boer War. She was one of the founder members of Inghinidhe na hÉireann (Daughters of Erin), with whom she worked to alleviate poverty in Ireland. She married John MacBride in 1903. He was executed in 1916 for his part in the Easter Rising and in 1918 Maud Gonne MacBride was interned in Holloway Jail together with other women leaders of the Irish Republican movement. She was opposed to the Treaty that ended the War of Independence and founded the Women's

Prisoners Defence League and was imprisoned without charge by the Irish Free State government during the Civil War, where she went on hunger strike. She died in 1953 and is buried in the republican plot in Glasnevin cemetery in Dublin. K. & C. Ó Céirín, *Women of Ireland. A Biographic Dictionary* (Co. Galway: Tír Eolas, 1996), pp.86–8.
31. Cumann na mBan was founded in 1914 as an auxiliary of the Irish Volunteers. Under its constitution, the primary aim of the organization was to 'advance the cause of Irish liberty' and 'teach its members first aid, drill, signalling, and rifle practice in order to aid the men of Ireland'. When the Irish Volunteers split in 1914 over the question of recruitment for the British army, Cumann na mBan elected to support the minority who refused to enlist. They fought alongside their male comrades in 1916 and the War of Independence and the majority of Cumann na mBan members were anti-Treaty in 1922.
32. Woodside, MO 5462, 1 February 1941.
33. Ibid., 3 May 1941.
34. Chichester Street runs from Donegall Square North to Oxford Street. It is named after Arthur Chichester, the progenitor of the Donegall dynasty, after whom Belfast's central square and streets are named. M. Patten, *Central Belfast. An Historical Gazeteer* (Belfast: Western Architectural Heritage Society, 1993), p.61.
35. B. Barton, *The Blitz. Belfast in the War Years* (Belfast: Blackstaff Press, 1989, reprinted in 1990), p.100.
36. Maguire and Paterson's also had a large factory in Dublin, at Church Street in the north inner city. Like the factory in Belfast, it was in the centre of a densely inhabited residential area but the local authorities took no precautions in either city to secure the safety of the people who lived near such potentially dangerous plants.
37. Donegall Road runs from Shaftesbury Road to the Falls Road, linking to Sandy Row along the way.
38. Barton, *The Blitz*, pp.61–2.
39. Ibid., p.62.
40. Woodside, MO 5462, 25 March 1940.
41. The Albert Bridge was first built in 1831 and was known as the 'Halfpenny Bridge' because of the toll charged. The bridge that Alice was crossing was erected in 1890 after two arches of the original bridge had collapsed. Patten, *Central Belfast. An Historical Gazeteer*, p.4.
42. Cromac Square runs off Cromac Street, which links Victoria Street to the Ormeau Road in Belfast's Markets area. Patten, *Central Belfast*, p.91.
43. D. Smyth, *Days of Unity in the Docklands of Sailortown, 1907–1969* (Belfast: Portlight Press Project, 1992), p.22.
44. Woodside, MO 5462, 20 April 1941.
45. Quoted in S. Hylton, *Their Darkest Hour. The Hidden History of the Home Front 1939–1945* (Stroud: Sutton Publishing, 2001), p.46.
46. C.E.B. Brett, *Housing a Divided Community* (Dublin: Queen's University of Belfast, Institute of Public Administration in association with the Institute of Irish Studies, 1986), p.26.
47. *Census of Population 1946* (Vol.IV, Part II Social Amenities), pp.112, 188 and 208.
48. 'Of Interest to Women' column, *Irish Times*, 7 March 1941.
49. P. Hamilton, *Up the Shankill* (Belfast: Blackstaff Press, 1979), p.16.
50. The British government decided to cut Irish fuel imports early in 1941.
51. Most turf was collected from small plots belonging to families and was cut manually and then dried out during the summer. Because of the uncertain climate in Irish

summers, turf could often be quite damp or even wet in the winter and did not give off much heat. There had been some efforts even before the Emergency to devise methods that would give more reliable fuel, but these were not coordinated by the government.

52. The Phoenix Park comprised 1,760 acres of woodland which had been designated as a public park in the reign of Charles II. *Thom's Directory for the year 1940*, p.1,079.
53. Emergency Powers (Control of Prices) Order No.106 of 1941.
54. G. Fee, 'The Effects of World War II on Dublin's Low-Income Families 1939–1945' (Unpublished PhD thesis, University College Dublin, 1996), p.145.
55. J. Blake, *Northern Ireland in the Second World War* (HMSO, 1956), pp.91–3.
56. Woodside, MO 5462, 23 October 1940.
57. The 'glimmer man' was not an official title but it became widely used in both Northern Ireland and Éire and the impact of the job on the public imagination in Dublin is evidenced by the number of public houses in the city that are called 'The Glimmer Man'.
58. W.R. Jacob & Co. Ltd. was a large biscuit manufacturer based at 28 Bishop Street, Dublin. The company was controlled by the Jacob family, although J.P. Fox was the managing director during the Emergency, with W.F. Bewley as company secretary. *Thom's Directory 1941*, p.1,104.
59. Clare's father was a barman and presumably he had secured the champagne bottle through his job, as her parents were strictly teetotal.
60. Report in *Pictorial Weekly*, 9 January 1943, p.2.
61. Woodside did not name the hotel or its location but the main Belfast newspapers carried regular advertisements for the Rosapena Hotel in Co. Donegal which seems to fit her description. It was situated on seven hundred acres of land on the north west coast of Donegal and the tariff was advertised as 18/6 per day.
62. Woodside, MO 5462, 3 September 1940.
63. Letter from G.H. Parr, Divisional Food Officer, Belfast to W.D. Scott, Ministry of Commerce, Belfast, 5 October 1939. PRONI, Northern Ireland Ministry of Commerce Files, Com/61/92.
64. Ibid.
65. Prices of Goods Act 1939.
66. *Irish Trade Journal and Statistical Bulletin*, XV, 1 (Dublin: Government Stationery Office, March 1940), p.14.
67. *Irish Trade Journal and Statistical Bulletin*, XXI,1 (March 1946), p.36.
68. Woodside, MO 5462, 13 March 1940.
69. This particular column appeared in the *Irish News* on a daily basis and it included items on making and mending clothes, recipes and household hints. The other main Belfast newspaper, the *NewsLetter*, carried a column called 'Mainly for Women', which covered gossip from 'Mayfair' and the British Court.
70. *Model Housekeeping*, July 1943, p.386.
71. Soldiers got three times the civilian ration of butter.
72. Letter from Mollie Lee, owner of Lee's Temperance Hotel, Coleraine to Lord Craigavon, October 1939. PRONI COM/61/182.
73. Ministry of Health, 'On the State of the Public Health during six years of War'. Report of the Chief Medical Officer of the Ministry of Health, 1939–45. HMSO, 1946.
74. Woodside, MO 5462, 29 November 1940.

CHAPTER SEVEN

1. B. Inglis, *A History of Medicine* (London: Weidenfeld and Nicholson, 1965), p.171.
2. Response to Mass-Observation directive on health by Dr R.H. Trinnick, MO 2837, February 1942. Mass-Observation Archive, University of Sussex.
3. Some medical personnel suggested that maternal ignorance was a major cause of the high infant mortality rates in the region. In discussions on post-war health policy in Northern Ireland undertaken by officials of the Ministry of Health in 1945, it was proposed to have mothercraft instruction in girls' schools and to intensify the work of child welfare clinics.
4. Rickets is a disease which mainly affects children. The characteristic feature is a disturbance of bone growth, associated with a deficiency in calcium absorption.
5. Dr F.M.B. Allen, *Report of the 1946 Annual Meeting of the Royal Maternity Hospital*. Public Records Office of Northern Ireland (PRONI), File HLG1/2.
6. *Department of Local Government and Public Health Report 1939–1940*, p.41.
7. J. Deeny and E. Murdock, 'Infant Mortality in the City of Belfast', *Journal of the Social and Statistical Society of Ireland*, Vol. XVII, 1943–44, (1943–44), pp.221–40.
8. Memorandum from the J.V. Rank bakery to the Taoiseach, dated 29 April 1941, entitled 'White flour v. brown'. National Archives, SA S12064.
9. *National Nutrition Survey, Part I. Methods of Dietary Survey and Results from Dublin Investigation* (Dublin: Government Stationery Office, 1946), p.50.
10. Woodside, MO 5462, 18 March 1940.
11. T.W.T. Dillon, 'Tuberculosis: A Social Problem', *Studies*, XXXIV (June 1943), pp.163–74.
12. G. Jones, *'Captain of all these men of death'. The History of Tuberculosis in Nineteenth and Twentieth Century Ireland* (Amsterdam: Wellcome Trust Centre for the History of Medicine, 2001).
13. J.E. Counihan and T.W.T. Dillon, 'Irish Tuberculosis Death Rates: A Statistical Study of their Reliability with some Socio-economic Correlations', *Journal of the Social and Statistical Society of Ireland*, Vol. XVII, 1943–44, (1943–44), pp.169–88.
14. Ibid., p.188.
15. R. Barrington, *Health, Medicine and Politics in Ireland 1900–1970* (Dublin: Institute of Public Administration, 1987), pp.161–2.
16. Dr James Deeny was a general practitioner in Lurgan, Co. Down when he applied for the position of Chief Medical Officer in the Department of Local Government and Public Health in Éire. He had an impressive record of research and publications on socio-medical problems, including a study on 'Poverty as a Cause of Ill-health' which he presented to the *Journal of the Social and Statistical Society of Ireland (JSSISI)* in May 1940, in which he studied the health of a group of low income women in Lurgan. *JSSISI*, Vol. XVI, 1939–40, (1940), pp.75–89.
17. T. Inglis, *Moral Monopoly: the Catholic Church in Modern Irish Society* (Dublin: Gill and MacMillan, 1987). See also J.H. Whyte, *Church and State in Modern Ireland, 1923–1979* (Dublin: Gill and MacMillan, 1980).
18. Diphtheria is a highly contagious infection, which causes severe respiratory problems and a swelling of the throat which can cause the patient to asphyxiate. A vaccine was developed in the United States in the 1950s but until that development, it was very widespread.
19. Scarlet fever is a disease caused by an infection of the throat with streptococcal bacteria. It is highly infectious and in years prior to the wide availability of antibiotics, was a very serious childhood illness.

20. The full name of the hospital was the House of Recovery and Fever Hospital in Cork Street and it was founded in 1801. It had 276 beds for the relief of patients suffering from fevers and other infectious diseases. *Thom's Directory for 1942*, p.827.
21. Annual Report of the Department of Local Government and Public Health 1939–41.
22. Sir Patrick Dun's hospital is in Grand Canal Street in Dublin. It was one of the hospitals approved by the Minister for Local Government and Health to treat tuberculosis cases that required surgery. The hospital provided a screening service for tuberculosis and presumably had quarantine facilities available to deal with the possibility of contagion.
23. The Hardwicke hospital was one of the House of Industry hospitals in North Brunswick Street. The others were the Richmond surgical hospital and the Whitworth medical hospital.
24. Altogether 57,616 Dublin children were vaccinated in the year 1943–4 and at the end of the year the greatest decrease in incidence and mortality nationwide was in the city. Cork Street fever hospital treated 438 of the city's cases and none of the thirty-nine patients who subsequently died had been immunized. G. Fee, 'The Effect of World War II on Dublin's Low-Income Families' (Unpublished PhD thesis, University College Dublin, 1996), p.177.
25. R. Blaney, *Belfast. 100 Years of Public Health* (Belfast: Belfast City Council and Eastern Health and Social Services Board, 1988).
26. Scabies is an itchy condition of the skin caused by a tiny mite which may be passed easily by close contact and commonly starts at the wrist. The itching is due to an allergic reaction to the tiny mites, and is associated with a rash of red, raised spots. The itch is worse at night, and may often affect more than one family member.
27. Woodside, MO 5462, 4 October 1940.
28. The Iveagh Baths is a public bath-house with a swimming pool, on Bride Street in Dublin.
29. Barrington, *Health, Medicine and Politics in Ireland*, p.139.
30. Castleblayney is a town in Co. Monaghan, which was very small during the war years. According to the 1936 census it had a population of 1,725.
31. James Hinton's examination of the role played by upper- and upper-middle-class women characterized the WVS as hierarchical and autocratic in its structure, mainly due to the influence of its founder, Lady Reading. He found that the leadership of the post-war organization gradually gave way to younger and professional social workers. J. Hinton, *Women, Social Leadership, and the Second World War. Continuities of Class* (Oxford: Oxford University Press, 2002).
32. Report of the Senior Maternity and Child Welfare Officer to the Ministry of Health, March 1946.
33. Report by Dr Thomson, Medical Superintendent Officer of Health, submitted to the Maternity and Child Welfare Committee of Belfast City Council, 24 January 1945. The Ministry of Health officials persuaded the city administrators to adopt Dr Thomson's recommendations, apart from the proposal to pay a retaining fee, which they refused to countenance. PRONI, File HLG1/1/2 Maternity and Child Welfare. General Policy.
34. Chapter 5, 'Some Aspects of Pregnancy and Childbirth', in C. Clear, *Women of the House. Women's Household Work in Ireland 1922–1961* (Dublin: Irish Academic Press, 2000), pp.95–125.
35. C. Ó Gráda, *A Rocky Road. The Irish Economy since the 1920s* (Manchester: Manchester University Press, 1997), p.207.

36. *Department of Local Government and Public Health Report 1944–45* (Dublin: Government Stationery Office, 1946), p.38.
37. Woodside, MO 5462, 8 March 1940.
38. Ibid., 4 November 1941.
39. S. Lyon, 'Some Observations on Births in Dublin in the years 1941 and 1942', JSSISI, 6th Session, Vol. XVII (1942–43), pp.144–68.
40. Woodside, MO 5462, 29 November 1940.
41. Woodside was honorary secretary of the Belfast branch of the Society for Constructive Birth Control from 1937 until she left Belfast in 1941.
42. A catalogue of publications relating to sexual health and behaviour showed that the following titles were available in Belfast: *Marriage and Birth Control* by Brenda Barwon; *Sexual Knowledge for the Young Woman* by Hayden Brown; *Radiant Motherhood* by Marie Stopes; *Enduring Passion* by Marie Stopes and *Married Love*, also by Marie Stopes.
43. G. Jones, 'Marie Stopes in Ireland: The Mother's Clinic in Belfast', *Social History of Medicine*, 5, 2 (August 1992), pp.255–78.
44. K. Fisher, 'Uncertain Aims and Tacit Negotiations: Birth Control Practices in Britain, 1925–1950', *Population and Development Review*, 26, 2 (February 2000), pp.295–317; K. Fisher, '"She was quite satisfied with the arrangements I made": Gender and Birth Control in Britain 1920–1950', *Past & Present*, 169 (November 2000), pp.161–93; S. Szreter, *Fertility, Class and Gender in Britain, 1860–1940* (Cambridge: Cambridge University Press, 1996); L.A. Hall, G. Hekrna and F. Eder (eds), *Sexual Cultures in Europe: Vol. II Studies in Sexuality* (Manchester: Manchester University Press, 1999).
45. Fisher, '"She was quite satisfied with the arrangements I made"'.
46. Woodside, MO 5462, 22 October 1940.
47. Minutes of the executive committee of the Belfast Society for Providing Nurses for the Sick Poor 1937–1946. PRONI, File D1630/6.
48. M.P. Kelly, *Home Away from Home. The Yanks in Ireland* (Belfast: Appletree Press, 1994), pp.39–40.
49. Syphilis is a highly contagious venereal disease that progresses from infection of the genitals via the skin and mucous membranes to the bone, muscles and brain, frequently resulting in insanity.
50. Gonorrhoea is also very infectious but the consequences are not as severe as those of syphilis, although, if untreated, it can lead to infertility. It is diagnosed after the appearance of an inflammatory discharge from the urethra or vagina.
51. A. Calder, *The People's War* (London: Pimlico Press, 1997), p.313.
52. Quoted in S. Hylton, *Their Darkest Hour, The Hidden Story of the Home Front 1939–1945* (Stroud: Sutton Publishing, 2000), p.155.
53. This was an American film, lasting one and a half hours, which had been used as part of a VD information campaign in Britain.
54. PRONI, Belfast. File No.HLG1/2/2, Venereal Disease, Publicity and Propaganda.
55. Ó Gráda, *A Rocky Road. The Irish Economy since the 1920s*, p.208.
56. L. Earner-Byrne, '"In Respect of Motherhood": Maternity Policy and Provision in Dublin city, 1922–1956' (Unpublished PhD thesis, University College Dublin, 2001).

CHAPTER EIGHT

1. Letter from J. Walsh, Ulster Bank Buildings, 3 Lower O'Connell Street, Dublin to Eamon De Valera, 15 May 1937. Department of the Taoiseach, File S 9880, Position of women under the Constitution (Dublin: National Archives).
2. B. Barton, *The Blitz. Belfast in the War Years* (Belfast: Blackstaff, 1989) and *Northern Ireland in the Second World War* (Belfast: Ulster Historical Foundation, 1995).
3. This view is consistent with the results of research in other countries, such as H. Bradley, *Men's Work, Women's Work. A Sociological History of the Sexual Division of Labour in Employment* (Cambridge: Polity Press, 1989) and Elizabeth Roberts' books.
4. P. Coleman, *Ageing and Reminiscence Processes. Social and Clinical Implications* (London: Wiley, 1986); J. Bornat (ed.), *Reminiscence Reviewed: Achievements, Evaluations, Perspectives* (Oxford: Oxford University Press, 1993); D. Middleton and D. Edwards, *Collective Remembering* (London: Sage, 1990).
5. A. Thomson, *Anzac Memories. Living with the Legend* (Oxford: Oxford University Press, 1994), p.8.
6. Recent useful examples of research in Ireland are: L. Connolly, *The Irish Women's Movement. From Revolution to Devolution* (Dublin: The Lilliput Press, 2003); D. Keogh, F. O'Shea and C. Quinlan (eds), *Ireland in the 1950s. The Lost Decade* (Cork: Mercier Press, 2004).

APPENDIX 2

1. T. Harrison and C. Madge, *First Year's Work* (London: Lindsay Drummond, 1938).
2. Ibid., p.66.
3. A. Calder and D. Sheridan, *Speak for Yourself. A Mass-Observation Anthology 1937–1949* (Oxford: Oxford University Press, 1985).
4. T. Harrisson and C. Madge, *Britain by Mass-Observation* (London: Hutchinson, 1986; first published in 1939).
5. Ibid., pp.226–7.

Appendix 1

(1) SHORT BIOGRAPHICAL NOTES

ALICE grew up in Belfast with her sister and brother and their widowed mother. During the Second World War, Alice worked in the Ormeau Bakery in Belfast. She started as a chocolate maker and she was promoted to supervisor of her department after several years. She was in her late 80s when the interview took place in 1999 at Alice's retirement home in Saintfield, Co. Down.

BETTY was born in Dublin and has lived there all her life. She was the eldest daughter of six children and during the war years she was mainly engaged in helping her mother to care for her younger brothers and sisters, although she was still in primary school. Betty participated in the interview with her mother, Catherine, in 1996, when she was in her early 70s.

CATHERINE was born in Dolphin's Barn in Dublin and she worked in Dollards printers from when she was 13. She left when she married and subsequently had six children. Her husband was a cooper in Guinness's and he died from a duodenal ulcer in 1943. Catherine then went to work as a cleaner in the Guinness brewery. The interview was conducted jointly with her daughter Betty in 1996, at which time Catherine was in her 90s.

CLARE was 11 when the war began in 1939. She lived in both the Drumcondra and Phibsborough districts of Dublin during the war years, with her parents and her two sisters and three brothers. She has very clear memories of the domestic impact of the Emergency and of the various methods used by her mother to overcome the stringencies imposed by rationing. The interview took place in 2002.

COLETTE was born in Dublin and grew up with her brother on the south side of the city. Colette spent practically all her working life in Guinness's brewery, which she remembers with great fondness and admiration. She entered Guinness's as a lady clerk in 1941 and she had been retired for some years when she was interviewed in 1997.

DAISY worked in the Blackstaff mill after she left school at 14 but when she was in her 20s she left to go and live with an aunt who needed a housekeeper and for whom Daisy worked for board and keep rather than pay. The interview was conducted jointly with her sister Ivy in 1996.

EMILY lived on or near the Falls Road in Belfast all her life. She worked as a clerk in the NAAFI during the war and remembered that pay for that work was considerably greater than any comparable work she had done in the pre-war period. She was interviewed in 1996.

ETHEL was born in Dublin and when she was 21 she went to Belfast to enrol in the Women's Auxiliary Air Force. She qualified as an electrician and spent the war years repairing aircraft. When the war ended she was moved to the WAAF band as a drummer and she travelled around Europe in this capacity until she left the WAAF in the late 1940s to return to Ireland. She was interviewed in 2005. Sadly, Ethel died in July 2006.

FLORA went to work as a counter girl in Woolworths in Belfast 1937 and worked for the company for forty-three years, eventually retiring as a supervisor. Her memory is very clear about pay and conditions throughout the years she worked in Woolworths. She was interviewed in her home in Belfast in 1996.

FRANCES was sent to work at a convent boarding school in Birmingham when she was only 15 years old in 1941. She worked as a cleaner and launderer in the convent until she was 16 when she was sent to a family in Lincolnshire to work as a maid. She enrolled for training as a nurse in Boston hospital in Lincolnshire and worked there until 1947. The interview was conducted in Frances' home in London in 2003.

HILDA was born in Dublin, where she trained as a nurse. After completing her training, she joined the Queen Alexandra's Imperial Military Nursing Service (QAIMNS) and she spent the war nursing in India and Burma (now Myanmar). She was demobbed to England before her return to Ireland at the end of the war. The interview with Hilda took place in her home in Ballymore Eustace, Co. Kildare in 2005.

IVY went to work in the Blackstaff mill in Belfast when she was 14 years old and she continued there until her marriage some years later. She never went back to work in the mill after the birth of her first child because the work was too hard. She was interviewed with her sister Daisy in Ivy's home in Belfast in 1996.

JEAN lived in Belfast, although she was born in Scotland, coming to Northern Ireland with her parents when she was a young woman. She helped her husband run a small grocery store during the war years. She had one daughter and she was very informative about the Belfast Blitz. The interview was a joint one with her friend Susan and was conducted in Susan's home in Belfast in 1996.

JOSIE was a schoolgirl in Dublin when the war started and although she left school in the course of the Emergency, due to the shortage of work she remained at home helping her mother. She was interviewed jointly with her sister Letty, in Josie's daughter's home in Dublin, in 2002.

KATHLEEN was brought up in Portstewart but she spent most of her adult life in the south of England, after moving there during the war to be with her husband, who was a member of the British army. She worked in a factory making aircraft altimeters during the war. She moved back to Portstewart after her husband's death and she was interviewed in her home there in 2003.

LETTIE was born in Dublin and went to work in a sewing factory when she left school at 14. When work became scarce during the Emergency, she was laid off, and in 1942 she applied for a place in a munitions factory in England, where she worked for three years until the war ended. Her interview took place with her sister Josie in 2002.

MARY was born in Newcastle-upon-Tyne in early 1939 but she was brought as a small baby to Coney Island in Co. Down, where her parents (who were both schoolteachers) had been used to spending their summers. When the war started, Mary's mother remained with her family in Lisburn with her two young children and they moved to Coney Island with Mary's aunt early in the war. The family repeatedly told stories of the war years, some of which Mary repeated in her interview.

MAUREEN was born in Belfast, on the Falls Road, from which she only moved after her retirement. She worked in a sewing factory after leaving school at the age of 14 and continued in this job throughout the war years. She was interviewed in 1999 in her home in Castlewellan, Co. Down, where she moved after her retirement.

META was born and brought up in Coleraine but after completing school she could not get work locally so she went to Liverpool to help her older sister with her young baby. While there, she trained to become a nurse. During the war she spent some years running an evacuation centre for children. Her husband was in the Royal Engineers and when he was moved to Richmond, just outside London, Meta followed him and took up work in the accident and emergency department of Richmond hospital. She moved to Surrey after her husband's death and she was interviewed there in 2003.

MINNIE was 11 when the war began. Her father was in the Irish army throughout the Emergency and rarely at home in Dublin, so that the main responsibility for the family of five brothers and Minnie fell on her mother. Minnie's sister had died at a young age and she was always conscious of being the only girl in the family. Her interview took place in her home in Dublin in 2002.

NANCY went to Birmingham during the war to study nursing because it would have been too expensive to do her training in Dublin, where she lived. Although her mother would have preferred her to go to a Catholic hospital she was offered a place in the Birmingham public hospital at Sellyoak and she undertook her training during the war years. She retired to Dublin after many years travelling the world for the World Health Organisation and she was interviewed in 2003.

NORA came from Mountmellick in Co. Laois originally and she moved to Dublin in 1941 to work as an executive officer in the Department of Supplies. She progressed steadily through the civil service during her working lifetime and retired at a very senior level. She still lives in Dublin and the interview with her was conducted in her home in 2002.

OLIVE came to Dublin when she was 18 to become a student nurse and she qualified in 1943. She went to England at the end of the war to work with burns victims, mainly pilots from the RAF. She returned to Dublin in 1948 to get married. She was interviewed in her home in Dublin in 1996.

PAT was born in Liverpool to Irish parents who brought their children to live with the mother's family in Carlow when the war began and Pat was still at school. Their father stayed in England where he was an air raid warden. When Pat turned 18, she returned to England and signed up for training in the Auxiliary Territorial Service (ATS) in Liverpool. She was assigned to be an office worker supporting the armed forces at the Royal Air Force (RAF) base in Farnborough until she was demobbed in 1946. She was interviewed in her home in Ashbourne, Co. Meath in 2002.

SALLY was born in Dublin, where she trained to be a Froebel teacher. She was persuaded by a friend to enlist in the armed forces in Northern Ireland and she worked as a cook in the Women's Auxiliary Service at a barracks in Belfast and later in Ballymena. She was interviewed in her Dublin home in 2000. Sadly, she died there in 2005.

SHEILA was at school in Dublin during the war years. Her mother worked as a cleaner in Guinness's brewery after Sheila's father suffered a stroke in 1938, leaving him unfit for work. Sheila's mother employed a variety of strategies to make the most of her income and to deal with the wartime conditions. Sheila was interviewed in Kilmuckridge, Co. Wexford in 1998, where she and her husband have lived since their retirement.

SUSAN was born in Co. Wexford but went to boarding school in Belfast because her grandmother lived there and there was no Methodist secondary school in her local area. She taught music for several years and then went to London University to train as a medical social worker, or almoner. She worked in the Rotunda hospital with extremely poor patients from Dublin's inner city until she moved to Belfast in 1944 to work in the Royal Victoria hospital, where she was also dealing with very deprived patients, as well as British and American troops stationed in Northern Ireland. She was interviewed jointly with her friend Jean in 1996.

(2) MASS-OBSERVATION DIARISTS

MOYA WOODSIDE was born in 1908. She was married to a doctor and she did regular work for the Belfast Welfare Relief Committee. She was also active in the Belfast branch of the Society for Constructive Birth Control and the Northern Ireland Labour Party. As a 'woman of the house' her life was adversely affected by the various emergency measures adopted for the wartime conditions in Belfast. Her diary, which she wrote on an almost daily basis between early 1940 and the end of 1941, offers fascinating insights into the impact of the Second World War on the people of the city, including her account of the Belfast blitz. The diary ended when Woodside went to England to study psychiatric social work.

DOROTHY BATES worked as a tax inspector during the war and she lived in Purley in Sussex. She was the single mother of twins and many of her observations are devoted to the difficulty of coping with the wartime conditions. She responded to Mass-Observation directives rather than being a regular diarist, probably because of the pressures on her time. In 1941 she was posted to Belfast for five months and she wrote several reports during that time.

R.H. TRINICK was a general practitioner in Belfast. He responded to Mass-Observation directives about specific subjects.

Appendix 2

The Mass-Observation Organization

Mass-Observation was founded in 1937 by Tom Harrisson (a self-taught anthropologist and sociologist), Charles Madge (a poet who later left Mass-Observation to become a professor of sociology) and Humphrey Jennings (a documentary photographer). The work began with 'day surveys', the original purpose of which was 'to collect a mass of data without any selective principle, as a preliminary to detailed studies of carefully chosen topics'.[1] Between January 1938 and the outbreak of war in 1939, they concentrated on recording activities on special holidays, such as Easter, and the collation of responses to directives on specific topics. In September 1939, they resumed the collection of diaries from the panel of volunteers.

> Mass-Observation has always assumed that its untrained Observers would be *subjective* cameras, each with his or her own distortion. They tell us not what society is like but what it looks like to them.[2]

By the late summer of 1939 Mass-Observation was well known throughout Great Britain although it was the following year before observers were recruited in Northern Ireland. Initially, the male panel members outnumbered females by two to one, but by the latter half of the war, this ratio had been reversed. Most of the panellists described themselves as middle or upper class, with fewer than one in six judging themselves to be working class.[3] Mass-Observation at its peak had recruited less than 2,000 observers and some of these reported very irregularly. Although diarists and directive respondents remained amateur, Mass-Observation tendered for contracts to secure its financial existence and in early 1940 was secretly commissioned to supply reports on national morale to the Ministry of Information, in particular on civilian reactions to being bombed.

Harrisson and Madge outlined the determining philosophy of the founders of Mass-Observation[4] as follows:

Basic in Britain is the right to say what you think or at the least think what you think and express it privately through the secret ballot. This right of each adult is essential and total in democracy. It is also essential and total in science. On democracy plus science our industrial civilisation is now inescapably founded. And while we can in the future reject a good deal of the democracy, the material circumstances and consequences of science are inescapable ... It is, of course, a job of science, which has caused so much of this chaos, to illuminate and analyse our own relations, forgetting all about ideals and abstractions, describing and arranging only ascertained facts ... To be of any use, of course, this sort of social science has got to go on all the time, with an immediate and constantly changing programme, coping daily with working problems.[5]

Appendix 3

Occupied Population aged 14 years and over (excluding persons out of work) – Northern Ireland 1926–51

Industrial Group	1926 Males	1926 Females	1951 Males	1951 Females	1926–51 Percentage Increase/decrease	
Agricultural occupations	1,290	38	476	38	−63	No change
Chemical processes	425	63	672	225	+58	+257
Clerks, draughtsmen (not civil service), accountants; typists	6,075	5,483	5,237	6,920	−14	+26
Commercial, finance and insurance	14,753	6,281	2,117	920	−86	−85
Entertainment and sport*	844	227	5,491	8,765	+551	+3,761
Foods, drinks and tobacco	4,243	1,692	7,472	3,941	+76	+133
Leather/skin workers	209	62	74	97	−65	+56
Makers of textile goods/clothes	3,467	16,247	1,796	10,132	−48	−38
Makers of watches, clocks etc.	219	4	349	166	+59	+4,050
Metal (not precious metals)	19,699	32	254	7	−99	−78
Other undefined workers; distributive trades*	8,638	600	17,168	9,915	+99	+1553
Others working with unspecified materials	163	23	580	225	+256	+878
Paper, printers, books	1,907	1,596	1,954	1,505	+2	−6
Personal service (including catering)	3,511	13,321	Not defined	Not defined		
Public administration and defence (not typists)	4,963	482	7,754	2,545	+56	+428
Textile workers	7,369	25,663	9,003	22,544	+22	−12
Transport and communication	15,014	413	14,565	1,219	−3	+195
Wood workers and furniture	7,498	182	1,681	259	−78	+42

*These groups were re-categorized between 1926 and 1951.

Source: Census of Population of Northern Ireland, 1926 and 1951.

Appendix 4

Rates of wages set by Northern Ireland Trade Boards from 1939–45, showing earliest and latest changes in the period in weekly time rates for female and male adults

Trade Board	August 1940			September 1942		
	Female	Male	% Male : Female Rate	Female	Male	% Male : Female Rate
Aerated Waters (NIA 10–20)	26/5¼	43/9½	1.62:1	35/3	48/11½	1.38:1
	November 1940			August 1944		
Baking trade (NIBk. 8–32)	47/0	80/0	1.70:1	50/6	87/0	1.72:1
	May 1940			January 1945		
Boot and shoe repairing (NIBS 28–45)	43/6	66/0	1.52:1	52/3	81/0	1.55:1
	March 1940			February 1945		
Dress-making/women's clothing (NIWD 32–47)	34/0	51/0	1.50:1	37/2½	60/8½	1.63:1
	December 1941			September 1943		
General waste materials (NIWR 12–20)	31/4	53/10¼	1.72:1	39/2	60/8½	1.55:1
	May 1940*			No change before 1946		
Hat, cap and millinery trade (NIHM 15–16)	30/4¼	53/10¼	1.77:1	–	–	–
	December 1941**			No change before 1946		
Linen & cotton handkerchief (NIHHG 62–74)	30/4¼	47/6	1.56:1	–	–	–
	December 1941			January 1945		
Laundry trade (NIL 10–24)	35/3	58/9	1.68:1	46/01/4	72/5½	1.57:1
	May 1940			April 1944		
Paper box trade (NIB 17–33)	29/6	45/0	1.53:1	38/6	60/0	1.56:1
	April 1940			March 1945		
Rope, twine and net trade (NIR 30–44)	29/0	44/0	1.52:1	50/0	70/0	1.40:1
	March 1941			October 1944		
Shirt-making trade (NIS 20–30)	37/0	66/0	1.78:1	42/0	80/0	1.90:1
	March 1941			November 1944		
Sugar, confectionery, food Preserving (NIF 11–21)	30/0	49/0	1.63:1	41/0	64/0	1.56:1

* These rates were the average wage for adult general workers. Female knife cutters or blockers who had three years experience or more could earn up to 43/1 per week, whereas male workers did not do this skilled work. In this case, the difference between the female rate and the male rate was 20%.

** This rate was last changed in February 1938 when female workers were paid 24/5 $^{3}/_{4}$ for a 47-hour week and male workers were paid 41/1 $^{1}/_{2}$ for the same hours. The percentage excess in the male rate was 68%.

Source: Northern Ireland Ministry of Labour, Orders under the Trade Boards Acts.

Appendix 5

Rates of wages in relation to Emergency Powers Order 260 – Weekly time rates for male and female adults 1939–45

Trade Board	1 September 1939			7 May 1941 Standstill Order				28 April 1944 Present rate			
	Female	Male	Percentage male excess	Female	Male	Percentage male excess		Female	Male	Percentage male excess	
Aerated Waters	29/4½	50/11	73.33	29/4½	50/11	73.33		37/2½*	58/9*	57.89	
Boot and shoe repairing	40/6	65/-	60.49	40/6	65/-	60.49		46/7	74/9	60.47	
Brush and broom other than twigs and birch	31/-	66/-	112.90	40/-	84/-	110.00		#	#	–	
Button-making	22/6	No rates	–	27/6	61/6	123.64		32/6	66/6	104.62	
General waste materials	22/6	46/-	104.44	22/6	46/-	104.44		30/-	54/-	80.00	
Handkerchiefs and household piece goods	25/8	–	–	28/5	–	–		32/1	–	–	
Packing	29/4	50/-	70.45	29/4	50/-	70.45		33/-	53/8	62.63	
Paper box making	34/8¼	54/4½	56.76	34/8¼	54/4½	56.76		37/6	57/2¼	52.50	
Shirt-making	26/-	54/6	109.62	29/4	64/2	118.75		33/-	71/2	115.66	
Sugar confectionery	30/-	54/-	80.00	30/-	56/-	86.67		36/6¾*	67/6*	84.62	
Tailoring	34/10	68/3	95.93	34/10	68/3	95.93		44/-	82/3	86.93	
Tobacco	32/6	50/6	55.38	35/-	55/6	58.57		40/-	63/6	58.75	
Twigs and birch	32/-	68/-	112.50	40/-	82/-	105.00		#	#	–	
Women's clothing and millinery	31/2	55/-	76.47	37/3¼	60/6	62.33		40/6½	71/6	76.36	

* For 12 months only
# Increase since Standstill Order by way of Bonus Order
Source: Department of Labour, File TIA 321, Trade Board.

Appendix 6

Éire: Cost of Living Index 1938–1945.
Base is July 1914 = 100

(I) FOOD

Year	February	May	August	November
1938	159	156	159	163
1939	160	157	158	178
1940	177	180	182	194
1941	196	197	201	212
1942	209	208	223	250
1943	243	237	249	261
1944	263	256	263	264
1945	263	259	261	271

(II) CLOTHING

Year	February	May	August	November
1938	226	226	226	225
1939	225	225	225	246
1940	270	289	295	299
1941	305	308	311	317
1942	326	340	348	372
1943	393	421	427	439
1944	443	444	445	438
1945	438	438	437	431

(III) FUEL AND LIGHT

Year	February	May	August	November
1938	183	179	179	184
1939	184	180	180	207
1940	217	236	243	244
1941	263	275	304	314
1942	318	319	322	325
1943	331	335	332	338
1944	336	337	338	335
1945	333	332	330	327

(IV) ALL ITEMS

Year	February	May	August	November
1938	173	171	173	176
1939	174	172	173	192
1940	197	204	206	214
1941	218	220	229	237
1942	237	240	250	273
1943	273	275	284	294
1944	296	292	296	296
1945	295	292	293	298

Source: Irish Trade Journal and Statistical Bulletin, XXI, 1 (March 1946), p.37.

Appendix 7

Travel permits issued for employment in Britain, classified by sex 1940–46

Year	Dublin Males	Dublin Females	Total Dublin	Éire Males	Éire Females	Total Éire
1940	6,094	1,564	7,658	17,080	8,884	25,964
As % of Total	**79.58**	**20.42**	**100.00**	**65.78**	**34.22**	**100.00**
1941	10,576	1,068	11,644	31,860	3,272	35,132
As % of Total	**90.83**	**9.17**	**100.00**	**90.69**	**9.31**	**100.00**
1942	10,525	4,201	14,726	37,263	14,448	51,711
As % of Total	**71.47**	**28.53**	**100.00**	**72.06**	**27.94**	**100.00**
1943	6,111	4,344	10,455	29,321	19,003	48,324
As % of Total	**58.45**	**41.55**	**100.00**	**60.68**	**39.32**	**100.00**
1944	2,013	1,011	3,024	7,723	5,890	13,613
As % of Total	**66.57**	**34.43**	**100.00**	**56.73**	**43.27**	**100.00**
1945	2,305	1,373	3,678	13,185	6,094	19,279
As % of Total	**62.67**	**37.33**	**100.00**	**68.39**	**31.61**	**100.00**
1946	1,246	2,352	3,598	10,829	19,205	30,034
As % of Total	**34.63**	**65.37**	**100.00**	**36.06**	**63.94**	**100.00**

Source: Ireland Statistical Abstract 1947–48, p.21.

Appendix 8

A comparison between the wage rates and cost of living in Éire and Britain 1939–45

Britain	Wage Rates Sept. 1939 = 100	Official Cost of Living Index Sept. 1939 = 100	Weekly Earnings Oct. 1938 = 100
1939	104	104	–
1940	113–14	121	130
1941	122	128	142
1942	131–2	129	160
1943	136–7	129	176
1944	143–4	130	181.5
1945	150–1	133.5	180.5

Éire	Wage Rates 1 January 1939 = 100	Official Cost of Living Index September 1939 = 100
1940	100.6	118
1941	105.4	130
1942	106.9	144
1943	109.8	162
1944	118.1	170
1945	121.6	169

Source: Department of Industry and Commerce, *Some Statistics of Wages and Hours of Work in 1946 with Comparative Figures for Certain Previous Years* (Dublin: Government Stationery Office, November 1946) and *Report of Ministry of Labour 1939–46*, pp.304–5 quoted in Gerard Fee, *The Effects of World War II on Dublin's Low Income Families* (Unpublished PhD Thesis, University College Dublin, 1996), p.65.

Appendix 9

Total population and total number of houses (by wards) in Belfast County Borough 1937–51

Wards	Total Population 1937	Total Population 1951	Total Number of Houses 1937	Total Number of Houses 1951	Intercensal change (+/-) in population Number	Intercensal change (+/-) in population Percentage	Intercensal change (+/-) in No. Houses Number	Intercensal change (+/-) in No. Houses Percentage
Belfast Co. Borough	438,086	443,671	106,535	110,619	5,585	+1.3	4,084	+3.8
Clifton	46,584	51,538	12,185	12,731	4,954	+10.6	546	+4.5
Court	17,698	16,970	3,948	3,638	728	-4.1	310	-7.9
Cromac	23,896	22,810	5,877	6,081	1,086	-4.5	204	+3.5
Dock	17,473	14,702	3,629	3,140	2,771	-15.9	489	-13.5
Duncairn	34,882	36,259	8,802	9,469	1,377	+3.9	667	+7.6
Falls	31,746	33,213	6,666	7,052	1,467	+4.6	386	+5.8
Ormeau	45,390	45,040	11,959	12,473	350	-0.8	514	+4.3
Pottinger	45,637	46,024	11,584	12,189	387	+0.8	625	+5.4
St. Anne's	30,357	30,832	6,744	6,686	475	+1.6	58	-0.9
St. George's	15,770	14,847	3,472	3,391	923	-5.9	81	-2.3
Shankill	33,298	31,566	8,453	8,476	1,732	-5.2	23	+0.3
Smithfield	10,840	10,539	2,316	2,186	301	-2.8	130	-5.6
Victoria	33,724	37,042	8,433	9,548	3,318	+9.8	1,115	+13.2
Windsor	27,014	26,977	6,561	7,054	37	-0.1	493	+7.5
Woodvale	23,777	25,312	5,926	6,505	1,535	+6.5	579	+9.8

Source: Northern Ireland Census of Population 1937 and 1951.

Appendix 10

Total population and religious affiliation (by ward) in Belfast County Borough, 1937 and 1951

Wards	1937 Roman Catholic population (as % of Total)	1937 Presbyterian population (as % of Total)	1937 Church of Ireland population (as % of Total)	1937 All others (as % of Total population)	1951 Roman Catholic population (as % of Total)	1951 Presbyterian population (as % of Total)	1951 Church of Ireland population (as % of Total)	1951 All others (as % of Total population)
Belfast Co. Borough	104,372 (23.83)	137,939 (31.49)	140,310 (32.03)	44,465 (12.65)	115,029 (28.11)	134,831 (32.95)	131,855 (32.23)	27,422 (6.70)
Clifton	13,989 (30.03)	14,368 (30.84)	11,952 (25.66)	6,275 (26.55)	17,465 (36.27)	14,822 (30.79)	12,531 (26.02)	3,332 (6.92)
Court	4,343 (24.54)	4,752 (26.85)	7,403 (41.83)	1,201 (6.78)	5,045 (4.57)	4,141 (34.74)	6,775 (56.83)	460 (3.86)
Cromac	5,135 (21.49)	7,804 (32.66)	7,613 (31.86)	3,344 (13.99)	5,460 (26.01)	6,886 (32.80)	7,105 (33.85)	1,541 (7.34)
Dock	7,841 (44.87)	3,811 (21.81)	4,306 (24.64)	1,515 (8.68)	7,376 (54.20)	2,877 (21.14)	2,917 (21.44)	438 (3.22)
Duncairn	3,610 (10.35)	15,343 (43.99)	10,832 (31.05)	5,097 (14.61)	4,744 (14.70)	14,787 (45.82)	10,308 (31.94)	2,435 (7.54)
Falls	29,056 (91.53)	977 (3.08)	1,269 (4.00)	444 (1.39)	30,849 (93.86)	730 (2.22)	1,053 (3.20)	235 (0.72)
Ormeau	3,830 (8.44)	18,470 (40.69)	14,638 (32.25)	8,452 (18.62)	4,390 (10.83)	18,471 (45.47)	12,704 (31.34)	4,972 (12.27)
Pottinger	6,278 (13.76)	16,543 (36.25)	15,664 (34.32)	7,152 (15.67)	6,744 (15.95)	16,714 (39.54)	14,689 (34.75)	4,126 (9.75)
St. Anne's	11,311 (37.26)	6,424 (21.16)	9,708 (31.98)	2,914 (9.60)	12,541 (44.21)	6,425 (22.65)	8,307 (29.29)	1,093 (3.85)
St. George's	673 (4.27)	4,593 (29.12)	8,596 (54.51)	1,908 (12.10)	661 (5.03)	4,381 (33.31)	7,390 (56.19)	719 (5.47)
Shankill	1,677 (5.04)	12,919 (38.80)	13,478 (40.48)	5,224 (15.68)	2,011 (7.11)	11,730 (41.46)	12,378 (43.75)	2,173 (7.68)
Smithfield	9,865 (91.01)	148 (1.37)	734 (6.77)	93 (0.85)	9,613 (91.40)	136 (1.29)	710 (6.75)	58 (0.55)
Victoria	1,596 (4.73)	12,989 (38.52)	14,292 (42.38)	4,847 (14.37)	1,947 (5.72)	13,792 (40.52)	15,613 (45.87)	2,683 (7.88)
Windsor	4,091 (15.14)	9,500 (35.17)	9,535 (35.30)	3,888 (14.39)	4,181 (16.93)	9,588 (38.83)	8,972 (36.34)	1,951 (7.90)
Woodvale	1,077 (4.53)	9,298 (39.11)	10,290 (43.28)	3,112 (13.08)	2,002 (8.71)	9,348 (40.66)	10,433 (45.38)	1,206 (5.25)

Source: Northern Ireland Census of Population 1937 and 1951.

Appendix 11

Persons in Private Families in the Dublin County Borough classified according to size of dwelling occupied – 1941

Wards or District Electoral Divisions	Total Population	Total Persons in Private Families	1 Room	2 Rooms	3 Rooms	4 Rooms	5 Rooms	6 Rooms	7 Rooms
Dublin	468,103	424,988	80,997	67,279	76,204	65,223	50,293	32,970	52,022
*			19.06	15.83	17.93	15.35	11.83	7.76	12.24
Arran Quay	33,241	27,715	4,931	4,441	6,162	6,276	2,090	2,169	1,646
*			17.79	16.02	22.23	22.64	7.54	7.83	5.94
Ballybough	11,535	10,849	2,208	2,145	2,363	2,050	921	887	275
*			20.35	19.77	21.78	18.90	8.49	8.18	2.53
Cabra	19,119	18,078	185	388	6,993	5,645	1,453	1,330	2,084
*			1.02	2.15	38.68	31.23	8.04	7.36	11.53
Clontarf East	7,051	6,756	66	284	633	501	701	1,803	2,768
*			0.98	4.20	9.37	7.42	10.38	26.69	40.97
Clontarf West	19,103	18,369	267	681	807	3,601	9,465	1,605	1,943
*			1.45	3.71	4.39	19.60	51.53	8.74	10.58
Drumcondra	21,142	19,017	292	743	3,099	2,806	5,152	3,430	3,495
*			1.54	3.91	16.30	14.76	27.09	18.04	18.38
Glasnevin	9,348	8,409	178	384	428	1,067	1,799	1,582	2,971
*			2.12	4.57	5.09	12.69	21.39	18.81	35.33
Inns' Quay	22,805	19,992	6,633	3,774	4,152	2,677	1,512	777	467
*			33.18	18.88	20.77	13.39	7.56	3.89	2.34
Mountjoy	15,363	14,666	8,339	3,638	1,007	866	312	377	127
*			56.86	24.81	6.87	5.90	2.13	2.57	0.87
North City	6,401	5,725	2,442	1,771	535	477	177	202	121
*			42.66	30.93	9.34	8.33	3.09	3.53	2.11
North Dock	29,839	28,147	7,819	4,651	6,720	5,082	2,404	832	639
*			27.78	16.52	23.87	18.06	8.54	2.96	2.27
Phoenix Park	750	258	3	6	31	83	46	37	52
*			1.16	2.33	12.02	32.17	17.83	14.34	20.16
Raheny	3,078	3,039	26	60	414	762	1,271	215	291
*			0.86	1.97	13.62	25.07	41.82	7.07	9.58
Rotunda	18,085	15,818	7,669	4,567	1,499	862	294	406	521
*			48.48	28.87	9.48	5.45	1.86	2.57	3.29
Chapelizod	619	613	29	147	76	222	37	43	59
*			4.73	23.98	12.40	36.22	6.04	7.01	9.62
Crumlin	2,967	2,934	12	32	545	262	734	1,301	48
*			0.41	1.09	18.58	8.93	25.02	44.34	1.64
Fitzwilliam	13,865	11,252	3,001	2,545	1,614	1,929	446	477	1,240
*			26.67	22.62	14.34	17.14	3.96	4.24	11.02

APPENDIX 11

Wards or District Electoral Divisions	Total Population	Total Persons in Private Families	1 Room	2 Rooms	3 Rooms	4 Rooms	5 Rooms	6 Rooms	7 Rooms
Mansion House	10,410	9,119	4,065	2,344	1,191	658	304	131	426
*			**44.58**	**25.70**	**13.06**	**7.22**	**3.33**	**1.44**	**4.67**
Merchants' Quay	25,126	24,009	5,768	5,072	3,791	3,223	3,929	1,137	1,089
*			**24.02**	**21.13**	**15.79**	**13.42**	**16.36**	**4.74**	**4.54**
New Kilmainham	16,806	16,484	785	2,081	3,966	4,351	3,626	1,041	634
*			**4.76**	**12.62**	**24.06**	**26.40**	**22.00**	**6.32**	**3.85**
Pembroke East	16,703	15,713	1,037	2,003	3,335	1,815	1,229	1,365	4,929
*			**6.60**	**12.75**	**21.22**	**11.55**	**7.82**	**8.69**	**31.37**
Pembroke West	19,975	17,983	1,137	2,224	3,109	4,180	1,332	1,403	4,598
*			**6.32**	**12.37**	**17.29**	**23.24**	**7.41**	**7.80**	**25.57**
Rathfarnham	4,449	3,977	25	261	418	901	190	900	1,282
*			**0.63**	**6.56**	**10.51**	**22.66**	**4.78**	**22.63**	**32.24**
Rathmines/Rathgar E.	22,074	20,187	1,591	2,744	2,531	2,091	1,954	2,818	6,458
*			**7.88**	**13.59**	**12.54**	**10.36**	**9.68**	**13.96**	**31.99**
Rathmines/Rathgar W.	23,555	21,211	1,207	1,867	2,727	1,929	2,849	2,540	8,092
*			**5.69**	**8.80**	**12.86**	**9.09**	**13.43**	**11.97**	**38.15**
Royal Exchange	4,693	4,102	1,930	1,039	484	276	121	127	125
*			**47.05**	**25.33**	**11.80**	**6.73**	**2.95**	**3.10**	**3.05**
Simmonscourt	550	541	-	4	62	60	9	27	379
*			-	**0.74**	**11.46**	**11.09**	**1.66**	**4.99**	**70.06**
South City	2,860	2,455	701	686	547	276	95	59	91
*			**28.55**	**27.94**	**22.28**	**11.24**	**4.93**	**5.17**	**5.09**
South Dock	15,571	13,721	4,317	3,873	2,661	1,514	428	370	558
*			**31.46**	**28.23**	**19.39**	**11.03**	**3.12**	**2.70**	**4.07**
Terenure	14,273	14,086	134	358	6,488	2,788	510	1,055	2,753
*			**0.95**	**2.54**	**46.06**	**19.79**	**3.62**	**7.49**	**19.54**
Trinity	9,595	8,347	3,468	2,361	961	810	176	223	348
*			**41.55**	**28.29**	**11.51**	**9.70**	**2.11**	**2.67**	**4.17**
Usher's Quay	26,884	22,875	5,287	4,990	3,731	3,530	3,375	1,310	652
*			**23.11**	**21.81**	**16.31**	**15.43**	**14.75**	**5.73**	**2.85**
Wood Quay	20,468	18,541	5,445	5,115	3,124	1,653	1,352	991	861
*			**29.37**	**27.59**	**16.85**	**8.92**	**7.29**	**5.34**	**4.64**

* Figures in bold represent percentage of persons in private families per category of dwelling.

Source: Register of Population, 1941 (Dublin: Department of Industry and Commerce, Stationery Office, 1944), pp.90–1.

Appendix 12

Average prices of essential foodstuffs (based on returns from 120 towns, large and small, in Ireland) between 1938 and 1945

Date	1. Eggs (Per dozen)	2. Butter (creamery) (Per 1lb.)	3. Cheese (Per 1lb.)	4. Fresh Milk (per quart)	5. Bread (per 2lb. loaf)	6. Potatoes (Per 14 lbs.)	7. Tea* (Per 1 lb.)	8. Sugar (per 1lb.)	Total cost of items 1-8f	Percentage fluctuation from previous measurement
Nov. 1938	2/4¼	1/5¾	¼	0/5¼	0/5	0/9¾	2/8	0/3¼	9/9¼	—
Feb. 1939	1/5½	1/6½	¼	0/5½	0/5	1/1¼	2/8	0/3¼	9/3	−5.63%
Nov. 1939	2/8½	1/6½	1/4¼	0/5½	0/5¼	0/10½	2/8¼	0/4½	10/3¼	+11.04%
Feb. 1940	1/10	1/6½	1/4¼	0/5½	0/5½	0/11	2/8½	0/4¾	9/6	−7.51%
Nov. 1940	3/2	1/7½	1/4½	0/6	0/5¾	1/2½	2/8	0/4¾	11/3	+18.42%
Feb. 1941	2/2¾	1/7¾	1/4¾	0/6	0/5¾	1/2½	2/9¾	0/4¾	10/8	−5.19%
Nov. 1941	3/3¾	1/7½	1/4¾	0/6	0/5¾	1/0¼	3/3	0/4¾	11/11¾	+12.30%
Feb. 1942	2/9¼	1/7½	1/4¾	0/6¼	0/5¾	1/1¼	3/3	0/4¾	11/11¾	0.00%
Nov. 1942	3/10¼	2/0½	1/6¾	0/6¾	0/6¼	1/5	3/11½	0/4¾	11/4½	−5.04%
Feb. 1943	2/9	2/1	1/7	0/6¾	0/6½	1/5¾	3/11¾	0/5	13/4	+17.22%
Nov. 1943	3/9	2/0	1/7½	0/7½	0/6½	1/8½	3/11¾	0/5	14/8¾	+10.47%
Feb. 1944	2/10	2/4	1/8¼	0/7½	0/6¾	1/9	3/11¾	0/6	14/3¼	−3.11%
Nov. 1944	3/6¾	2/4	1/9	0/7½	0/6¾	1/6¼	3/11¾	0/6	14/10	+3.94%
Feb. 1945	3/2	2/4	1/9	0/7½	0/6¾	1/9½	3/11¾	0/6	14/8½	−0.84%
Nov. 1945	4/1	2/4	1/9	0/7½	0/6¾	1/9	4/0	0/6	15/7¼	+6.09%

Source: *Irish Trade Journal and Statistical Bulletin*, Vols. XIV–XXI (1939–45).

Appendix 13

Model Housekeeping – Recipes for July (1943)

Day	Breakfast	Dinner	Tea or Supper
Monday	Cereal. Raspberries (Stewed). Cream. Bread and Butter. Tea. Coffee.	Stewed Breast of Lamb. Spinach. Steam Potatoes. Fruit Jelly. Coffee.	Welsh Rarebit. Oatmeal Biscuits. Butter. Tea. Coffee. Milk.
Tuesday	Porridge or Cereal. Fruit. Poached Eggs. Bread and Butter. Marmalade. Tea. Coffee.	Boiled Tongue. Greens. New Potatoes. Loganberry Meringue. Coffee. Biscuits.	Bread and Butter. Cold Tongue. Lettuce and Tomato Salad. Tea. Coffee. Milk.
Wednesday	Cereal. Oranges. Fried Rashers. Poached Eggs. Bread and Butter. Marmalade. Tea and Coffee.	Beef Galantine Salad. Sauté Potatoes. Chocolate Junket. Stewed Fruit. Coffee.	Cold Tongue Croquettes. Bread and Butter. Baked Custard. Tea. Coffee. Milk.
Thursday	Cereal. Stewed Fruit. Brown Scones. Bread and Butter. Grilled Sausages. Tea. Coffee.	Oxtail Brawn. Beetroot Salad. Potatoes. Strawberry Flan.	Sausage Rolls. Bread and Butter. Tea. Coffee.
Friday	Porridge and Milk. Fresh Fruit. Boiled Eggs and Toast. Bread and Butter. Marmalade. Tea. Coffee.	Spinach Soup. Moulded Salmon. Potatoes. Irish Salad. Caramel Custard. Fruit. Coffee.	Stuffed Eggs. Bread and Butter. Tea. Coffee. Milk.
Saturday	Fruit. Cereal. Grilled Rashers. Tomatoes. Bread and Butter. Marmalade. Tea. Coffee.	Potato Soup. Stuffed Steak. Onions and Sauce. Mashed Potatoes. Raspberry Tart. Coffee.	Tongue Croquettes. Tea. Coffee.
Sunday	Fruit. Grilled Rashers. Poached Eggs. Toast. Butter. Marmalade. Tea. Coffee.	Tomato Soup. Stuffed and Roast Shoulder of Mutton. Cauliflower Sauce. Strawberry Shortcake. Coffee.	Creamed Salmon on Toast. Fresh Fruit. Tea. Coffee. Milk.

Source: *Model Housekeeping* (July 1943), p.386.

Select Bibliography

Primary sources, including contemporary commentaries, are cited in the endnotes to each chapter.
The following is a selection of secondary sources:

Akenson, D.H., *Education and Enmity: The Control of Schooling in Northern Ireland 1920–50* (Newton Abbot: Queen's University of Belfast, Institute of Irish Studies Publications, David and Charles, 1973).
Anderson, K., *Wartime Women: Sex Roles, Family Relations and the Status of Women during World War II* (Connecticut: Greenwood Press, 1981).
Baddely, A., *The Psychology of Memory* (New York: Harper and Row, 1976).
Barrington, R., *Health, Medicine and Politics in Ireland 1900–1970* (Dublin: Institute of Public Administration, 1987).
Barton, B., *The Blitz. Belfast in the War Years* (Belfast: Blackstaff, 1989).
Barton, B., *Northern Ireland in the Second World War* (Belfast: Ulster Historical Foundation, 1995).
Beaumont, C., 'Women, Citizenship and Catholicism in the Irish Free State, 1922–1948', *Women's History Review*, 6, 4 (1997), pp.563–85.
Bew, P., P. Gibbon and H. Patterson, *The State in Northern Ireland, 1921–72. Political Forces and Social Classes* (Manchester: Manchester University Press, 1979).
Blake, J.W., *Northern Ireland in the Second World War* (Belfast: HMSO, 1956).
Bleakley, D., *Sadie Patterson. Irish Peacemaker* (Belfast: Blackstaff Press, 1980).
Bornat, J. (ed.), *Reminiscence Reviewed: Achievements, Evaluations, Perspectives* (Oxford: Oxford University Press, 1993).
Bourke, J., *Husbandry to Housewifery: Women, Economic Change and Housework in Ireland 1890–1914* (Oxford: Oxford University Press, 1993).
Boyd, A., *The Rise of the Irish Trade Unions* (Dublin: Anvil Books, 2nd Edn, 1985).

Bradley, A. and M.G. Valiulis (eds), *Gender and Sexuality in Modern Ireland* (Amherst, MA: University of Massachusetts Press, 1998).
Bradley, H., *Men's Work, Women's Work. A Sociological History of the Sexual Division of Labour in Employment* (Cambridge: Polity Press, 1989).
Braybon, G. and P. Summerfield, *Out of the Cage. Women's Experience in two World Wars* (London: Pandora, 1987).
Brett, C.E.B., *Housing a Divided Community* (Dublin: Institute of Public Administration, in association with the Institute of Irish Studies, Queen's University of Belfast, 1986).
Brown, M., *Evacuees. Evacuation in Wartime Britain 1938–1945* (Stroud: Sutton Publishing Limited, 2000).
Brown, T., *Ireland. A Social and Cultural History, 1923–1985* (London: Fontana Press, 1985).
Buckland, P., *The Factory of Grievances. Devolved Government in Northern Ireland 1921–1939* (Dublin: Gill and Macmillan, 1979).
Calder, A., *The People's War. Britain 1939–45* (London: Pimlico, 1993).
Clear, C., *Women of the House. Women's Household Work in Ireland 1922–1961* (Dublin: Irish Academic Press, 2000).
Coleman, P., *Ageing and Reminiscence Processes* (London: Wiley, 1986).
Cosgrove, A. (ed.), *Marriage in Ireland* (Dublin: College Press, 1985).
Cott, N., *The Grounding of Modern Feminism* (New Haven, CT: Yale University Press, 1987).
Cousins, M., 'The Introduction of Children's Allowances in Ireland, 1939–1944', *Irish Economic and Social History*, XXVI (1999), pp.35–53.
Cullen, M. (ed.), *Girls Don't Do Honours. Irish Women in Education in the 19th and 20th Centuries* (Dublin: Women's Education Bureau, 1982).
Cullen Owens, R., *Louie Bennett* (Cork: Cork University Press, 2001).
Daly, M.E., *Women and Work in Ireland* (Dublin: Economic and Social History Society of Ireland, 1997).
DeGroot, G., 'Whose Finger on the Trigger? Mixed Anti-Aircraft Batteries and the Female Combat Taboo', *War in History*, 4 (1997), pp.434–53.
Delaney, E., *Demography, State and Society. Irish Migration to Britain, 1921–1971* (Liverpool: Liverpool University Press, 2000).
Doherty, J., *Post 381. The Memoirs of a Belfast Air Raid Warden* (Belfast: Friar's Bush Press, 1989).
Doherty, R., *Irish Men and Women in the Second World War* (Dublin: Four Courts Press, 1999).

Duby, G. and M. Perrot (eds), *A History of Women in the West. Vol. IV Emerging Feminism from Revolution to World War* (Cambridge, MA: Belknap Press, Harvard University Press, 1993).

Earner-Byrne, L., 'The Boat to England: An Analysis of the Official Reactions to the Emigration of Single Expectant Irishwomen to Britain, 1922–1972', *Irish Economic and Social History*, XXX (Dublin: 2003), pp.52–70.

Elders, M., E. Kiely, M. Leane and C. O'Driscoll, 'A Union in those days was Husband and Wife: Women's Narratives on Trade Unions in Munster, 1939–60', *Saothar* 27 (Dublin: Irish Labour History Society, 2002), pp.121–30.

Ferriter, D., *'Lovers of Liberty' Local Government in 20th Century Ireland* (Dublin: National Archives of Ireland, 2001).

Ferriter, D., *The Transformation of Ireland 1900–2000* (London: Profile Books, 2004).

Fisher, K., 'Uncertain Aims and Tacit Negotiations: Birth Control Practices in Britain, 1925–1950', *Population and Development Review*, 26, 2 (February 2000), pp.295–317.

Fisher, K., '"She was quite satisfied with the arrangements I made": Gender and Birth Control in Britain 1920–1950', *Past & Present*, 169 (November 2000), pp.161–93.

Fisk, R., *In Time of War. Ireland, Ulster and the Price of Neutrality 1939–45* (London: Paladin, 1987).

Fitzpatrick, D., 'Divorce and Separation in Modern Irish History', *Past and Present*, 114 (1987), pp.172–96.

Fitzpatrick, D., *The Two Irelands 1912–1939* (Oxford: Oxford University Press, 1998).

Girvin, B. and G. Roberts (eds), *Ireland and the Second World War. Politics, Society and Remembrance* (Dublin: Four Courts Press, 2000).

Hartmann, S.M., *The Home Front and Beyond. American Women in the 1940s* (Boston, MA: Twayne Publishers, 1982).

Hennessey, T., *A History of Northern Ireland 1920–1996* (Dublin: Gill and Macmillan, 1997).

Hensey, B., *The Health Services of Ireland* (Dublin: Institute of Publication Administration, 1959).

Hepburn, A.C., *Employment and Religion in Belfast, 1901–1971* (Belfast: Fair Employment Agency for Northern Ireland, 1982).

Hepburn, A.C., *A Past Apart. Studies in the History of Catholic Belfast 1850–1950* (Belfast: Ulster Historical Foundation, 1996).

Hill, M., *Women in Ireland. A Century of Change* (Belfast: The Blackstaff Press, 2003).

Hinton, J., *Women, Social Leadership and the Second World War. Continuities of Class* (Oxford: Oxford University Press, 2002).
Honey, M., *Creating Rosie the Riveter. Class, Gender and Propaganda during World War II* (Amherst, MA: University of Massachusetts Press, 1984).
Hylton, S., *Their Darkest Hour. The Hidden Story of the Home Front 1939–1945* (Stroud: Sutton Publishing, 2001).
Inglis, T., *Moral Monopoly: The Catholic Church in Modern Irish Society* (Dublin: Gill and Macmillan, 1987).
Isles, K.S. and N. Cuthbert, *An Economic Survey of Northern Ireland. Government of Northern Ireland* (Belfast: HMSO, 1957).
Jones, G., *'Captain of all these men of death' The History of Tuberculosis in Nineteenth and Twentieth Century Ireland* (Amsterdam: The Wellcome Trust Centre for the History of Medicine, 2001).
Jones, M., *These Obstreperous Lassies. A History of the Irish Women Workers' Union* (Dublin: Gill and Macmillan, 1988).
Keegan, J., *The Second World War* (London: Hutchinson, 1989).
Kelly, M.P., *Home Away from Home. The Yanks in Ireland* (Belfast: Appletree Press, 1994).
Kennedy, L. and P. Ollerenshaw (eds), *An Economic History of Ulster 1820–1939* (Manchester: Manchester University Press, 1985).
Keogh, D. and M. O'Driscoll (eds), *Ireland in World War Two. Neutrality and Survival* (Cork: Mercier Press, 2004).
Kossoudji, S. and L. Dresser, 'Working Class Rosies: Women Industrial Workers during World War II', *The Journal of Economic History*, 52, 2 (June 1992), pp.431–46.
Lambert, S., *Irish Women in Lancashire. 1922–1960: Their Story* (Lancaster: University of Lancaster, Centre for North-West Regional Studies, 2001).
Lang, C., *Keep Smiling Through. Women in the Second World War* (Cambridge: Cambridge University Press, 1989).
Lawrence, R.J., *The Government of Northern Ireland. Public Finance and Public Services 1921–1964* (Oxford: Clarendon Press, 1965).
Lennon, M., M. McAdam and J. O'Brien (eds), *Across the Water. Irish Women's Lives in Britain* (London: Virago, 1988).
Lewis, J. (ed.), *Labour and Love: Women's experience of Home and Family 1850–1940* (Oxford: Oxford University Press, 1986).
MacCurtain, M. and D. Ó Corráin (eds), *Women in Irish Society. The Historical Dimension* (London: Arlen House, 1978).
MacDonald, S., P. Holden and S. Ardener (eds), *Images of Women in Peace and War. Cross-Cultural and Historical Perspectives* (Basingstoke: Macmillan, 1992).

MacKeown, P. (ed.), *Women's Voices, An Oral History of Northern Irish Women's Health 1900–1990* (Dublin: National Union of Public Employees (NUPE), Attic Press, 1992).

McManus, R., *Dublin, 1910–1940: Shaping the City and Suburbs* (Dublin: Four Courts Press, 2002).

Marwick, A., *Britain in the Century of Total War. War, Peace and Social Change 1900–1967* (Harmondsworth: Penguin, 1970).

Marwick, A., *War and Social Change in the Twentieth Century* (London: Macmillan, 1974).

Marwick, A., *Total War and Social Change* (London: Macmillan, 1988).

Messenger, B., *Picking up the Linen Threads. Life in Ulster's Mills. A Study in Industrial Folklore* (Belfast: Blackstaff Press, (1975) 1988).

Mitchell, B.R., *European Historical Statistics 1750–1970* (London: Macmillan, 1975).

Mitchell, B.R., *British Historical Statistics* (Cambridge: Cambridge University Press, 1988).

Muldowney, M., 'A World of its own': Recollections of Women Workers in Guinness's Brewery in the 1940s', *Saothar*, 23 (Dublin: Irish Labour History Society, 1998), pp.103–17.

Muldowney, M., 'Just the way things were'. Recollections of Women Workers in Dublin and Belfast 1939–45', *UCD History Review*, 13 (Dublin: UCD History Society, 2002), pp.12–21.

Muldowney, M., 'Women Workers in Belfast and Dublin during the Second World War', in A. Hayes and D. Urquhart (eds), *Irish Women's History* (Dublin: Irish Academic Press, 2004), pp.168–86.

Muldowney, M., '"New Opportunities for Irish Women". Employment in Britain during the Second World War', *University of Sussex Journal of Contemporary History*, 10 (2006), pp.1–18.

Muldowney, M., 'Woman in Wartime. The Mass-Observation Diary of Moya Woodside', in Clare O'Halloran (ed.), *Public and Private Voices: Irish Women's Personal Writings in Historical Perspective* (Dublin: Irish Academic Press, Women's History Association of Ireland, Spring 2007 forthcoming).

Murphy, J.A., *Ireland in the 20th Century* (Dublin: Gill and Macmillan, 1975).

Nicholson, M. (ed.), *What did you do in the war, Mummy? Women in World War II* (London: Chatto and Windus, 1995).

Noakes, L., *War and the British. Gender, Memory and National Identity* (London: Tauris, 1998).

Nowlan, K. and T.D. Williams (eds), *Ireland in the War Years and After, 1939–51* (Dublin: Gill and Macmillan, 1969).

Ó Drisceoil, D., *Censorship in Ireland, 1939–1945. Neutrality, Politics and Society* (Cork: Cork University Press, 1996).
Ó Gráda, C., *Ireland. A New Economic History 1780–1939* (Oxford: Clarendon Press, 1994).
Ó Gráda, C., *A Rocky Road. The Irish Economy since the 1920s* (Manchester: Manchester University Press, 1997).
Ó hÓgartaigh, M., 'Nurses and Midwives in Ireland in the Early Twentieth Century', in B. Whelan (ed.), *Women and Paid Work in Ireland 1500–1930* (Dublin: Four Courts Press, 2000), pp.133–47.
O'Connell, T.J., *History of the Irish National Teachers' Organisation 1868–1968* (Dublin: INTO, 1968).
O'Connor, E., *A Labour History of Ireland 1824–1960* (Dublin: Gill and Macmillan, 1992).
O'Dowd, M. and S. Wichert (eds), *Chattel, Servant or Citizen. Women's Status in Church, State and Society* (Belfast: Queen's University, Institute of Irish Studies, Historical Studies XIX, 1995).
O'Halpin, E., *Defending Ireland. The Irish State and Its Enemies since 1922* (Oxford: Oxford University Press, 1999).
O'Leary, E., 'The Irish National Teachers' Organisations and the Marriage Bar for Women National Teachers, 1933–1958', *Saothar*, 12 (Dublin: Irish Labour History Society, 1987), pp.47–52.
Offen, K., R. Pierson and J. Rendall (eds), *Writing Women's History. International Perspectives* (Basingstoke: Macmillan, 1991).
Roach Pierson, R. and N. Chaudhuri (eds), *Nation, Empire, Colony: Historicizing Gender and Race* (Bloomington: Indiana University Press, 1998).
Roberts, E., *A Woman's Place. An Oral History of Working-Class Women, 1890–1940* (Oxford: Blackwell, 1984).
Roberts, E., *Women and Families. An Oral History 1940–1970* (London: Blackwell, 1995).
Rose, S.O., *Which People's War? National Identity and Citizenship in Wartime Britain 1939–1945* (Oxford: Oxford University Press, 2003).
Rupp, L., *Mobilizing Women for War: German and American Propaganda 1939–45* (Princeton, NJ: Princeton University Press, 1978).
Ryan, L., 'Sexualising Emigration: Discourses of Irish Female Emigration in the 1930s', *Women's Studies International Forum*, 25, 1 (2002), pp.51–65.
Schweitzer, M.M., 'World War II and Female Labor Force Participation Rates, *The Journal of Economic History*, 40, 1 (March 1980), pp.89–95.
Sheridan, D. (ed.), *Wartime Women. A Mass-Observation Anthology 1937–45* (London: Phoenix Press, 1990).

Sheridan, D., 'Ambivalent Memories: Women and the 1939–45 War in Britain', *Oral History*, 18, 1 (Spring 1990), pp.32–40.

Sheridan, D. and A. Calder (eds), *Speak for Yourself. A Mass Observation Anthology 1937–1949* (London: Penguin, 1984).

Smith, H., 'The Effect of the War on the Status of Women', in H. Smith (ed.), *War and Social Change: British Society in the Second World War* (Manchester: Manchester University Press, 1986) pp. 208–29.

Smith, H., *Britain in the Second World War* (Manchester: Manchester University Press, 1996).

Spring-Rice, M., *Working-class Wives: Their Health and Conditions* (1939; re-issued London: Virago, 1981).

Summerfield, P., *Women Workers in the Second World War. Production and Patriarchy in Conflict* (London: Croon Helm, 1984).

Summerfield, P., 'Women and War in the Twentieth Century', in J. Purvis (ed.), *Women's History. Britain, 1850–1945* (London: University College London Press, 1995), pp.307–32.

Summerfield, P., '"My Dress for an Army Uniform": Gender Instabilities in the Two World Wars'. An Inaugural Lecture delivered at the University of Lancaster, 30 April 1997.

Summerfield, P., *Reconstructing Women's Wartime Lives. Discourse and Subjectivity in Oral Histories of the Second World War* (Manchester: Manchester University Press, 1998).

Summerfield, P. and N. Crockett, 'You Weren't Taught that with the Welding': Lessons in Sexuality in the Second World War', *Women's History Review*, 1, 3 (1992), pp.435–54.

Summerfield, P. and C. Penniston-Bird, 'Women in the Firing Line: the Home Guard and the Defence of Gender Boundaries in Britain in the Second World War', *Women's History Review*, 9, 2 (2000), pp.231–55.

Szreter, S., *Fertility, Class and Gender in Britain, 1860–1940* (Cambridge: Cambridge University Press, 1996)

Thébaud, F. (Ed.), *A History of Women. Toward a Cultural Identity in the Twentieth Century* (Cambridge, MA: The Belknap Press of Harvard University Press, 1994).

Tilly, L. and J. Scott (eds). *Women, Work and Family* (Boston, Rinehart and Winston, 1978).

Townsend, C. and E. (eds) *War Wives. A Second World War Anthology* (London: Grafton Books, 1989).

Travers, P., '"There was nothing for me there": Irish Female Emigration, 1922–1981', in P. O'Sullivan (ed.), *The Irish World Wide, Volume 4: Irish Women and Irish Migration* (London: Leicester University Press, 1995), pp.146–67.

Tweedy, H., *A Link in the Chain. The Story of the Irish Housewives Association, 1942–1992* (Dublin: Attic Press, 1992).

Valiulis, M. and M. O'Dowd, *Women and Irish History. Essays in Honour of Margaret MacCurtain* (Dublin: Wolfhound Press, 1997).

Vaughan, W.E. and A.J. Fitzpatrick (eds), *Irish Historical Statistics. Population 1821–1971* (Dublin: Royal Irish Academy, 1978).

Walby, S., *Theorizing Patriarchy* (Oxford: Blackwell, 1990).

Ward, M., *Putting Women into Irish History* (Dublin: Attic Press, 1991).

Ward-Perkins, S. (ed.), *Select Guide to Trade Union Records in Dublin. With details of unions operating in Ireland to 1970* (Dublin: Irish Manuscripts Commission, 1996).

Whyte, J.H., *Church and State in Modern Ireland. 1923–1979* (Dublin: Gill and Macmillan, 1980).

Wolf, J.B., 'Withholding their Due. The Dispute between Ireland and Great Britain over Unemployed Insurance Payments to Conditionally Landed Irish Wartime Volunteer Workers', *Saothar*, 21 (Dublin: Irish Labour History Society, 1996), pp.39–46.

Index

Abbey Theatre 127
Acocks Green 78, 82
Adelaide Hospital 98
Administration of Justice (Emergency Provisions) (Northern Ireland) Act 1939 36
Aerial warfare 20
Air Raid Precautions (Northern Ireland) Act 1938 27
Air raid precautions 22, 24, 27, 39, 41, 43, 98, 101, 104, 118, 126, 157
Albert Bridge 130
Alexandra Hospital, Singapore 111
Aliens Act 1905 98
Amalgamated Transport and General Workers' Union 54
American soldiers 82, 162
Anderson shelters 129, 146
Anti-aircraft batteries 103
Anti-profiteering 150
Approved ports 37
Ardglass 140
Army Nursing Service 98, 115
Auxiliary Territorial Service (ATS) 47, 100, 103, 105, 107, 109, 110, 116

Bairds Engineering 45
Baking Trade 50–52, 185, 212
Ballymena 100
Bangor Castle 101
Batavia 111
Bates, Dorothy 121, 126–127
Battle of Britain 80

Belfast Blitz 39–41, 119, 120, 121, 129, 131–132, 133, 150, 170
Belfast News Letter 164
Belfast Telegraph 83
Bennett, Louie 53, 185
Beveridge Report 8, 119, 150, 165, 166, 178, 196
Bevin, Ernest 77
Bicycles 125–126
Birmingham 39, 74, 78, 87
Birth control 12, 160–161, 165–166, 172
Bisterne 115
Black Mountain 130, 131
Blackout 24, 38, 42, 65, 75, 126, 128, 130, 139, 145, 169
Blackpool 79
Blake, John 72, 169
Bonus orders 26
Boston Hospital, Lincolnshire 71, 90, 191, 205
Britain ix, x, 76, 80, 84, 90, 128, 160, 167, 168
  1905 Aliens Act 98
  Armed forces 107
  Army hospital 99
  Attitudes to women 119
  Beveridge Report 119, 178
  Birth Control 160–161
  Birth rate 159
  Censorship 29
  Civil Defence 21–22, 163–164
  Coal imports from 138
  Conscription 18, 36
  Effect of war on women 2, 44

Employment of women 10, 13, 16, 44–46, 169
Evacuation 133
Food rationing 32–34
IRA bombing campaign 26
Mass-Observation Organisation 4, 15
Ministry of Information 18
Motor Fuel Rationing Order 1939 128
Part-time work 14, 64
Perception of 25
Research 169
Strikes 37
Subjects 98
Total war 150
Trade Union registration 55
Travel to 4, 37–38, 145
War Ministries 145
War work 70–72
Wartime Social Survey 15
Women's role 167–168
B-Specials 24
Bunreacht na hÉireann (see Constitution)
Burma 104, 111

Cabra 43, 124, 125, 197, 220
Calder, Angus 159
Castleblayney 156
Catholic 173, 187, 189, 200, 207, 219
  Birth control 160
  Clergy 83–84
  Ethos 7, 122
  Hospital 78
  Housing areas 120–121
  Minority in Northern Ireland 9, 24
  National Anti-Tuberculosis League 151
  Newspapers 74
  Sectarianism 108, 121, 140
  Social control 122
  Social teaching 5, 7, 8, 173
  Social Welfare Bureau 76
  Special position 178

Censorship 28–30, 58, 101, 130, 161
Census of Population of Ireland (Eire) 48, 168
Census of Population of Northern Ireland 120, 124
Ceylon (see Sri Lanka)
Cherry Orchard 153
Chichester Street 128
Childbirth 12, 150, 158, 159, 172, 201
Childcare 13, 18–19, 64, 87, 91–92
Children's Allowance 7, 173
Civil defence 20, 22–25, 27, 39–40, 41, 43, 130
Civil Defence Act (Northern Ireland) 1939 27, 128
Civil Nursing Reserve 79
Civil Service in Éire 48–49, 60, 61, 62
Class 1, 4, 65, 70, 79, 107, 114, 176, 177, 178, 180, 202
Coal (see also Fires and Fireplaces) 32, 34, 60, 129, 136, 137, 138, 183
Comilla 113
Commission on Vocational Organisation 53
Conditions of Employment Act 1936 (Éire) 36, 48
Conditions of Employment Act 1939 (United Kingdom) 36
Coney Island 134
Conscription 18, 26, 36–37, 44, 72, 84, 96, 99, 105, 168, 169
Constitution 26, 53
Contraception (see Birth Control)
Cookham 76
Cork Street Fever Hospital 95, 152, 153
Cost of living 67, 81, 141, 145, 169
Craig, James 24,
Cromac Square 130
Cumann na mBan 128
Cunningham, 'Cat's Eyes' 103, 118
Cushendun 28

D-Day 93
De Valera, Eamon 25, 167
Deeny, James 148, 151
Defence Regulation 33B 163–164
Department of External Affairs 72, 74
Department of Local Government and Public Health 146, 149, 158
Department of Social Welfare (Éire) 71
Department of Supplies 32, 65, 139
Diphtheria 151, 153
Dispensary doctors 156
Divisional Food Officer for Northern Ireland 32
Doherty, James 41
Doherty, Richard
Domestic role of women 10, 12, 20, 43, 46, 70, 145, 167, 172, 173
Domestic service 12, 47, 81,
Donegall Road 129, 130
Dowth Avenue 124
Drimnagh 134
Dublin Corporation Rental Purchase Scheme 123–124
Dublin Gas Company 139
Durban 104

Eisenhower, Dwight 118
Electrician work 102
Emergency Powers (Control of Lights) Order 1939 42
Emergency Powers (Defence) Act 1939 27
Emergency Powers Act 1939 26
Emigration 70, 72, 83,
Employment 10–11, 26, 33, 36, 44, 46, 72, 80
Engineering work 15, 45, 68,
Equal Pay 17, 50–52, 68, 77, 96, 168
Essential Work (General Provisions) Act 1941 77
Evacuation 22, 27, 91, 132–133, 148, 152
Ewart and Company 54

Factories (Hours of Employment of Women and Young Persons) Northern Ireland Order 1942 64
Falls Road 119, 120, 121, 122, 128, 136
Family Allowances 8, 34,
Farnborough 108
Ferriter, Diarmaid 2, 177, 188, 197
Fianna Fáil 7, 8, 165, 184
Fires and fireplaces 136–137
First World War 25, 77, 95, 98, 168, 172
Fisher, Kate 161
Food 169, 182, 183, 185, 199, 211, 215, 222
   Offices 30, 32, 33, 141
   Price controls 32, 33, 43, 140, 141, 144, 149
   Control Committees 32
   Ministry of Food 32, 33, 140, 141, 143, 145
   Standards 34, 81, 84, 85, 100, 132, 136, 140, 166
   Preparation 139, 143
   Storage 139
   Food Control Committees 32
   Scarcity 16, 33, 61, 86, 141, 143, 144, 150
   Rationing 20, 26, 31–35, 85, 138, 144–149, 160, 169

Gaelic Athletic Association (GAA) 122
Gas masks 22–23, 25, 41,
Gender 1, 4, 5, 7, 11–15, 18–19, 52, 61, 96, 97, 102–103, 109, 171, 174
German bombs on Éire 42–43
Glimmer men 138–139
Gonorrhoea 163
Government of Ireland Act 1920 26, 145
Grafton Street 125, 197
Grantham 84, 92

Guinea Pigs Club 80
Guinness's Brewery 48–49, 57–58, 63, 67, 134, 156
Gwynne-Vaughan, Dame Helen 105

Handywomen 12, 159
Haybox cookers 139
Holidays 140–141
Home Defence 148
Home Front 2, 3, 14–15, 17–18, 77, 108, 119–145, 167, 169, 172, 180, 192
Home Guard 23–24
Honeyborne 102, 108
Housework 12, 60, 76, 134, 136, 150, 159
Housing 39, 119–120, 123, 133, 148
Housing Trust 133

Impetigo 148
Income 7, 11, 12, 14, 43, 48, 58, 66, 79, 85, 119, 124, 133, 141, 144, 145, 148, 149, 168, 169, 171, 188, 191, 197, 199, 200, 201, 208, 217
India 104
Industrial disputes (see Strikes)
Infant death 148
International Labour Organisation 11
IRA 26, 29, 37,
Irish Housewives Association 32, 183
Irish Independent 83
Irish National Teachers' Organisation 53–54
Irish News 164
Irish Women Workers' Union 32, 53, 185, 186
Iveagh Baths 73, 155

Jacob's Biscuits Factory 107, 139
Johnson, Amy 77–78
Jones, Greta 160

Kashmir 104, 112

Laundry 46, 64, 81, 134–136, 138, 153, 155, 184, 212
Life expectancy 165
Life review 172
Live Register 25, 47
Liverpool 75, 78, 91, 95, 104, 105
Local Defence Forces 43
Local Defence Volunteers 24
Lyons Corner House 93

MacBride, Maud Gonne 128, 197
MacEoin, Uinseann 29
Mackies 45
Maguire and Paterson's Match Factory 129, 198
Maidenhead 77, 87, 95, 189
Manchester 75
Marie Stopes Family Planning Clinics 160–161
Marino 123
Marlborough 110
Marriage bar 49, 53, 61, 79
Marriage rates 62
Mass-Observation Organisation viii, 4, 15, 33, 35, 65, 73, 76, 85, 121, 146, 165, 171, 174, 200, 203, 208, 209
Maternal mortality 158
Maternity services 157, 161–162, 165, 172
McIndoe, Archibold, 80
McQuaid, John Charles 151
Measles 156
Medical social work 61, 163
Melsham 102
Middle class 1, 12, 123, 129, 132, 149, 157, 201, 209
Middle East 104, 117
Midwifery 12, 79, 95, 158
Ministry of Commerce (Stormont) 45
Ministry of Food (Stormont) 145
Ministry of Food (Westminster) 140–141

Ministry of Health (Westminster) 87, 110, 162, 164, 165
Ministry of Information (Westminster) 18, 72
Ministry of Labour (Stormont) 45–46
Ministry of Labour (Westminster) 13, 37, 76, 80, 81, 85
Ministry of Local Government (Stormont) 146, 164
Ministry of War (Westminster) 54
Model Housekeeping 143
Money management 58–60, 82, 125
Mosquito aircraft 116–117
Motor Fuel Rationing Order 1939 128
Mountjoy Ward 123
Munitions work 45, 73, 85, 95
Murdock, Eric 148

NAAFI 45, 47, 128
National Anti-Tuberculosis League 151
National Council of Women (NCW) 164
National Health Service (NHS) 165
National Nutrition Survey 1946 149
National Registration Act 1939 33
National Service Act 1939 72
Neutrality 2, 25, 28, 62, 80, 150, 170, 182, 184, 193
North Strand 42–43, 124
Northern Whig 164
Nursing 49, 61, 78–80, 87–90, 91, 97
Nutrition 31, 148–150, 166, 173, 197, 200

Ó Gráda, Cormac 158
O'Connell Street 126, 127
O'Kelly, Sean T. 124
Offences against the State Act 1939 26
Office of Civilian Defence 25
Official Secrets Acts 1939 30
Oral history 2, 4, 6, 161, 168

Ormeau Bakery 50, 56, 62–63, 66, 67–68, 156
Overtime 56–57

Part-time work 14, 64
Pension schemes 62
Phibsborough 125, 126
Phoenix Park 137
Pilots 77–78
Pneumonia 156
Polio epidemic 90
Portstewart 76
Poverty 121, 123, 124, 132, 137, 144, 148–149, 150, 165
Pregnant women 34, 84, 109, 110, 144
Prices of Goods Act 1939 33
Protestant 24, 84, 108, 121–122, 140, 151, 160, 173, 181, 192, 193
Puerperal sepsis 158
Purley 121

Quarantine 152
Queen Alexandra's Imperial Military Nursing Service (QAIMNS) 98–99, 115
Queen Victoria Hospital 95

Raj, The 104
Rathfarnham 126
Rationing in Britain 84–86
Rationing in Éire 26, 31, 32, 43, 137, 145, 149, 150, 165, 169
Rationing in Northern Ireland 32, 33–36, 38, 43, 138, 144, 148, 150, 165
Rawalpindi 104, 111
Recruitment to Allied war effort 9, 46, 80, 85, 94, 96, 99, 101
Religion 53, 120–122, 173, 189, 193, 219
Rent 124–125, 133
Richmond Road 123
Rickets 148, 149

Rome 150
Rose, Sonya 14, 93, 108
Rotunda Hospital 61, 149, 157–158, 163
Royal Air Force (RAF) 94, 102, 108, 109–110, 118
Royal Engineers 91
Royal Tournament 117–118
Royal Victoria Hospital 61, 162, 163
Rushcliffe Committee on the Pay of Nurses (for England and Wales) 89
Ryan, Louise 83

Sanitation 133–134, 136
Sawdust cookers 139
Scabies 148, 153–155
Scarlet fever 151–152
Sean McDermott Street 123
Secretarial work 48, 108
Sectarianism 34, 119, 121–122, 170
Selly Oak Hospital 78, 87
Servicemen's allowance 8–9, 86
Sexual morality 82–84, 92–93, 107
Sexually transmitted diseases (see Venereal Disease)
Shanley, John 151
Sheridan, Dorothy 116
Shirt-making Trade 52
Shop workers 64–65
Shropshire 94
Singapore 111
Sir Patrick Dun's Hospital 152
Skills dilution 15, 47, 77, 172
Slough 87
Slum clearance 39, 119, 123, 133
Social Enemy No. 1 164
Social policy 13, 149
Social welfare 7, 49
Society for the Nursing of the Sick Poor 161–162
South Africa 104
Spitfire aircraft 117
Sri Lanka 111

Srinagar 112
St. James's Gate Fanciers and Industrial Association 67
St. John's Brigade 149
Standing Joint Committee of Working Women's Organisations 87
Strikes 36–37, 54, 77
Submarine warfare 25, 78, 93, 105
Sumatra 111, 114
Summerfield, Penny 13
Syphilis 163

Teaching 49, 60, 100
Tedworth House 98, 100
Thatcher, Margaret 89
Thompson's Bakery 50
Tidworth 98, 104
Times Pictorial Weekly, The 53
Town Children through Country Eyes 132
Trade Board regulations (Éire) 52, 66
Trade Board regulations (Northern Ireland) 51–52
Trade Union Act 1941 36
Trade union membership 47, 55–56
Training for women workers 46, 61, 78–80, 87–89, 100, 101–102, 105–107
Travel permits 37–38, 71, 73, 93–94
Treachery Act 1940 31
Treason Act 1939 26
Treaty ports 25
Trincomalee 111
Trinnick, Dr. R.H. 146, 166
Tuberculosis (TB) 132, 150–151, 165
Turf 38, 136, 137–138, 155, 198, 199
Turf Development Board 137

Unemployment Assistance 7, 125
Unemployment Benefit 39, 73
Unemployment in Éire 44, 47
Unemployment in Northern Ireland 44, 48

Unemployment Insurance (Emergency Powers) Order 1940 44
United States 15–17, 24–25, 96, 167
Universe, The 82
Urban design and planning 20–21
Uxbridge 102, 103

Venereal disease 93, 113, 162–165, 166

WAAF Central Band 117–118
Wages Standstill Act 1941 36, 43, 52, 66, 169
Wartime conditions 20–22, 38, 168
Wartime Social Survey 15, 76, 107
Washing clothes (see Laundry)
Whitley aircraft 102
Widows' and Orphans' Pension Schemes 7, 48
Women's Auxiliary Air Force (WAAF) 101, 103, 107, 109–110, 117, 118
Women's citizenship 5, 14
Women's Consultative Committee 13
Women's employment 2–5, 7, 9–11, 12–13, 15–16, 18, 25, 43–46
Women's Institute 34, 132
Women's Labour Advisory Council 34
Women's Royal Air Force 118
Women's Voluntary Service (WVS) 22, 24, 76, 156
Women's War Effort Association 46
Woodside, Moya viii, 4, 132, 133, 141, 171, 172, 174, 177, 181, 182, 183, 184, 186, 187, 196, 197, 198, 199

Air raid protection 27
Belfast Blitz 131
Belfast Blitz 39–41
Biographical details 208
Birth control 160–161
Birth rates 159
Censorship 28–30, 58
Civil Defence 130
Discrimination against Catholics 24
Dublin 126–127
Health 146, 150, 153–154
Local Defence Volunteers 24
Public Transport 128, 140
Rationing 65, 142–143
Rising Prices 33, 138, 144
Sectarianism 121
Unemployment 44
Wartime conditions 38
Women – political organisation
Women's Volunteer Service (WVS) 157
Women's work 47
Woolworth 60
Working class 4–5, 119, 123–125, 178, 179, 186, 209
  Birth control 160
  Definition 1, 176
  Families 11, 123, 185
  Health 150
  Housing 39, 129, 134, 136
  Income 10, 124, 141, 179
  Tenancy 125
  Voters 8
  Wives and mothers 11, 157

York Street, Belfast 41, 83
YWCA 122